ILLICIT TRAFFICKING

A Reference Handbook

Other Titles in ABC-CLIO's
**CONTEMPORARY
WORLD ISSUES**
Series

Antisemitism, Jerome A. Chanes
Civil Liberties in America, Samuel Walker
Counterterrorism, Graeme C. S. Steven and Rohan Gunaratna
Cybercrime, Bernadette H. Schell and Clemens Martin
Defendant Rights, Hamid R. Kusha
Drug Use, Richard Isralowitz
Global Aids Crisis, Richard G. Marlink and Alison G. Kotin
Healthcare Reform in America, Jennie Jacobs Kronenfeld and
    Michael R. Kronenfeld
Media and American Courts, S. L. Alexander
Nation-Building, Cynthia A. Watson
Profiling and Criminal Justice in America, Jeffrey B. Bumgarner
USA Patriot Act, Howard Ball
Voting in America, Robert E. DiClerico
World Poverty, Geoffrey Gilbert

Books in the Contemporary World Issues series address vital issues in today's society such as genetic engineering, pollution, and biodiversity. Written by professional writers, scholars, and nonacademic experts, these books are authoritative, clearly written, up-to-date, and objective. They provide a good starting point for research by high school and college students, scholars, and general readers as well as by legislators, businesspeople, activists, and others.

Each book, carefully organized and easy to use, contains an overview of the subject, a detailed chronology, biographical sketches, facts and data and/or documents and other primary-source material, a directory of organizations and agencies, annotated lists of print and nonprint resources, and an index.

Readers of books in the Contemporary World Issues series will find the information they need in order to have a better understanding of the social, political, environmental, and economic issues facing the world today.

Library of Congress Cataloging-in-Publication Data
Kelly, Robert J.
    Illicit trafficking : a reference handbook / Robert J. Kelly, Jess Maghan, Joseph D. Serio.
        p. cm.—(ABC-CLIO's contemporary world issues series)
    Includes bibliographical references and index.
    ISBN 1-57607-915-5 (hardback : alk. paper)
    ISBN 1-57607-916-3 (ebook)
1. Transnational crime. 2. Smuggling. 3. Illegal arms transfers. 4. Drug traffic. 5. Money laundering.   I. Maghan, Jess, 1936– II. Serio, Joseph, 1964– III. Title. IV. Series: Contemporary world issues.

HV6252.K45 2005
364.1'35—dc22   2005013790

09   08   07   06   05   10   9   8   7   6   5   4   3   2   1

This book is also available on the World Wide Web as an eBook.
Visit abc-clio.com for details.

ABC-CLIO, Inc.
130 Cremona Drive, P.O. Box 1911
Santa Barbara, California 93116-1911

This book is printed on acid-free paper.
Manufactured in the United States of America

ILLICIT TRAFFICKING

A Reference Handbook

Robert J. Kelly
Jess Maghan
Joseph D. Serio

**CONTEMPORARY
WORLD ISSUES**

A B C ☰ C L I O

Santa Barbara, California • Denver, Colorado • Oxford, England

Contents

Preface

On September 11, 2001, at approximately 8:46 A.M., a hijacked Boeing 767, United Airlines Flight 11, exploded into the North Tower of the World Trade Center. At 8:58 A.M., United Flight 175 was diverted from its course to Los Angeles and directed to New York City; at 9:03 A.M. it exploded into the South Tower of the World Trade Center. By 10:30 A.M. lower Manhattan was submerged in ash and debris. Earlier, at 9:38 A.M., as the great towers of the World Trade Center tottered on the brink of collapse, yet another jumbo jet, American Airlines Flight 77, hijacked from Dulles International Airport in Washington, D.C., slammed into the northwest side of the Pentagon. All the passengers (fifty-eight), two pilots, and four flight attendants were killed, including 199 Pentagon employees dead or missing. The stark awareness of a terrorist attack became total reality as a fourth plane, United Flight 93, was diverted from its objective of crashing the United States Capitol or the White House (National Commission on Terrorist Attacks Upon the United States 2003) by the heroism of passenger Todd Beamer and his fellow passengers in a fierce resistance to their hijackers, causing United Flight 93 to veer off-course and crash in an empty field near Shanksville, Pennsylvania, twenty minutes flying time from Washington, D.C.

The United States, a nation grievously shocked by the terrorist attacks of 9/11—as the calamitous event has become known—immediately focused on Afghanistan and destroying its radical Islamist Taliban regime, which had harbored the al-Qaeda leadership. The nationalities of the 9/11 hijackers were varied: twelve Saudis, one Egyptian, one United Arab Emirate, one Lebanese, and four of unknown nationalities. The ensuing hunt for the elusive prime perpetrator of this terrorist attack, Osama bin Laden, and his extremist al-Qaeda terrorist network continues aggressively.

The struggle against terror has profoundly transformed the world in many ways, especially in terms of power alignments, international and diplomatic relationships, and treaty arrangements. The effects of these newly fashioned political strategies, agreements, and confrontations on illicit trafficking and transnational crime remain to be seen. Afghanistan and regions of northern Pakistan had been deeply immersed in the production and distribution of opium, the basic building block of heroin. Will the intervention in Afghanistan and the assertion of military authority in Pakistan against the power and influence of radical fundamentalist and jihad terrorists change the equation of illicit drug and arms trafficking in Southwest Asia and across Western Europe and the United States?

On September 11, 2001, war was declared against the United States not by another nation but rather a nonstate criminal organization, a terrorist group dedicated to the destruction of American influence in the Muslim world. The war against terrorism is global and strikingly unconventional; it is a struggle in which the safety and security of the American homeland is at stake. The war against terror is rapidly evolving into a total war with a complexity of ancillary intrigues, corruption, and illicit trafficking.

It took only nineteen individual terrorists on September 11, 2001, to perpetrate this massive attack on New York City and Washington, D.C.; one could speculate that it would take far fewer fanatics, each with a suitcase containing a nuclear weapon, to cripple the nation (and the world). To say that it is highly improbable is to beg the question of just how *probable* was it that four hijacked airplanes could be turned into kamikaze-guided missiles killing thousands of innocent civilians and disrupting the economy of the most powerful nation in the world?

Will transnational crime accelerate in the new terrorist war environment? Or will it diminish and transform itself into a new and sophisticated network of illicit trafficking in order to survive the exigency of stepped-up surveillance, police action, and security measures? A positive outcome of the antiterrorism campaign is the concomitant enhancement of anticrime controls and constricting of illicit trafficking. On the other hand, the effect of this "new face of war," where governments are unhinged, toppled, and threatened, may weaken capacities to enforce the law and contain trafficking. What will unfold depends on complex factors. The structure(s) of illicit trafficking, operative cases, and potential areas of growth or decline constitute the scope in this book.

Illicit trafficking refers to behavior that facilitates the illegal entry of persons or prohibited products into a territory. Such behavior, typically involving transactions that violate laws and statutes, is deemed criminal. Trafficking organizations are made up of not only rigid, hierarchical, corporate-type Cosa Nostra crime families, but also small, flexible criminal groups specifically structured to carry out its tasks, such as a "Snakehead" (Chinese alien smuggling group), which may include agent/recruiters in the home country, document and transport specialists, host-country handlers who arrange housing, and job placements. In contrast, a weapons-trafficking organization is likely to be more technically sophisticated requiring experts in freight management documents packaging and weapons assessment. A drug-trafficking group may vary widely depending on the levels of its operational parameters and its horizontal and vertical organizational integration.

The challenges posed by illicit trafficking are formidable. Nations and international organizations have made some progress, however, in developing methods and procedures to combat the individuals and criminal enterprises engaged in these activities. This volume offers a picture of these efforts. It is organized to provide information on the kinds of trafficking that have emerged in terms of illegal markets and their operations, and how governments, organizations, and interest groups have developed various initiatives to control and contain trafficking.

This book seeks to explain the rise and increase in illicit trafficking, its operations and markets, and the various ways in which trafficking is organized. It also provides reference to and offers analyses of specific criminal trafficking activities such as the smuggling in women and children, and the markets in light weapons and nuclear materials. The book also examines the political, juridical, and law enforcement responses to these crimes, with attention to the approach of Interpol, the United Nations' Office of Crime Prevention and Drug Control, and various national strategies such as those developed by the Federal Bureau of Investigation (FBI) and the U.S. Department of Justice and the growing number of nongovernmental organizations (NGOs).

The book also examines the requirements for a more coordinated and comprehensive antitrafficking strategy worldwide. A key component is the *United Nations Convention Against Transnational Organized Crime*. While describing the progress made by the international community, the book also highlights difficulties that must be confronted concerning the enduring challenges in the future.

Illicit trafficking problems derive from numerous sources: they are in part the unintended consequences of decades of sustained and deliberate Western policies aimed at opening economic/business markets, encouraging open, democratic societies, and spreading sophisticated modern technologies in commerce, trade, economics, and high finance. The very success of such endeavors created the infrastructure that makes trafficking possible and profitable.

As will be seen, trafficking problems are difficult to solve and to control for several reasons. First, they are crimes that cross borders, their nature precludes unilateral solutions. Second, illicit trafficking requires the cooperation of a greater number of agencies and official institutional processes. Third, they often occur within the economic and social spheres of states where corruption thrives and autocracy rules.

Chapter 1 presents a historical outline, focusing on the conditions that promote these problems. The circumstances and settings that give rise to illicit trafficking are explored.

Chapter 2 examines illicit trafficking as a contemporary phenomenon. It looks at the root causes of the most prominent types of trafficking. Two key questions round out the discussion: What are the best methods of coping with the problem, and what proposals and recommendations for controlling and containing the problem have been implemented? The chapter concludes with a consideration of the effects of this criminal activity on local communities and government institutions.

Chapter 3 presents a chronology of key events since 1945, which marks the end of World War II and the beginning of the Cold War. The issues suggested here concern how the political and economic relationships involved in trafficking have extended into the twenty-first century.

Chapter 4 offers a succinct montage of the major criminals involved in trafficking, including profiles of their respective criminal careers in illicit trafficking.

Chapter 5 focuses on four types of trafficking: trafficking in human beings, narcotics, small arms and light weapons, and nuclear materials. Using the web site addresses provided, the reader may access vast numbers of documents of all types.

Chapter 6 provides information about intergovernmental organizations (IGOs) and NGOs that advocate and lobby government over trafficking issues and monitor state and international initiatives to control illicit trafficking. Many IGOs fall under the umbrella of the United Nations system; other bodies have come into existence as a result of treaty commitments and through the sponsorship of regional organizations.

Chapter 7 lists books, articles, films, and other media products along with official reports from international and national organizations regarding illicit trafficking. The bibliographic review also includes Internet and web sites that offer more informational links across a broad spectrum of source materials.

Chapter 8 offers an analysis and overview of the new-generation illicit crime patterns, including new integrative mechanisms that cross public/private sector boundaries as witnessed in the tsunami catastrophe of December 2004 in Asia. By systematizing interagency and public/private sector contacts, it is proposed that trafficking problems may be more effectively deterred.

Our special thanks to Mildred Vasan who stimulated interest in the project and to Alicia Merritt of ABC-CLIO whose determination and enthusiasm carried the project forward. The keen assistance of Criminal Justice student research associates, Brett Finn and Amanda Farrell, in cataloging current professional resources in the Illicit Trafficking field greatly enriched the content and scope of this book.

Reference

National Commission on Terrorist Attacks upon the United States. 2003. *The 9/11 Commission Report.* Authorized Edition. New York: W. W. Norton.

1

Illicit Trafficking: A Brief History

What is globalization? What are its impacts on nations and peoples worldwide? With the end of the Cold War, profound economic and political changes liberated masses of people and at the same time created new conditions and prospects for crime. Modern illicit trafficking is an outcome of a general socioeconomic phenomenon known as *globalization*, which may be roughly defined as the emergence of a variety of systems or activities of economic and commercial production, trade, and services that are worldwide rather than national or regional in scope and that are generally not controllable by nation-states alone.

The basic processes of globalization involve mergers of industrial companies and business, investment of capital in foreign countries, purchase of existing assets, and construction of new production facilities. As a result of major improvements in communication technology and engineering and scientific developments in the basic industrial production of goods and services, these processes have accelerated massively during the past twenty-five years. The growth of transnational economic activity marked by the steady dispersal of production elements (where, for example, the parts of an American automobile are manufactured in thirty countries and then assembled in the United States) has nearly obliterated the traditional understanding of trade and commerce.

The multinational corporations (MNCs) are, collectively, the brains and muscle of this new system. The political and social impacts of this revolution are only now being felt across the world economies. Globalization has had tidal effects on national economies, transportation, and the information industry. It has also changed the way people around the world see themselves, identify their interests, and stake out their futures. As noted, the process has been fueled primarily by technological innovations that continually reshape the world. It is also supported by an ideology, a set of ideas and beliefs that have been labeled *market fundamentalism*. This ideology states primarily that economic markets are supreme and that the common interest is best served by allowing markets to develop unconstrained and unfettered by social/political interventions that otherwise would seek to control them and inhibit their capacity to generate wealth.

In everyday life globalization often translates into significant changes in jobs, income, benefits, educational needs, family structure, lifestyle, and the like. Globalization has altered the occupational system and job security, and it has created radically new forms of work. However, other consequences of globalization include new and heightened forms of crime, violence, and social and ethnic xenophobia, which have worked to disrupt and sometimes entirely erode traditional patterns of family and community.

With the unfolding of this process, new categories of winners and losers have emerged. New ideologies, political movements, and criminal organizations have arisen to address the psychological and economic needs of those who have been dislocated by the global economic revolution. Our focus in this volume is on the criminal activity that is developing as a response to globalization.

What Is Illicit Trafficking?

Illicit trafficking is not a new form of crime that emerged with the end of the Cold War; it is as old as human civilization itself. However, the challenge illicit trafficking has posed with the collapse of the Soviet Empire in 1991, coupled with the spectacular technological advances in information and computer science today, has been both dramatic and unexpected and has transformed world markets. Cybertechnologies in manufacturing and commercial trade have swept across the world, revolutionized business activities, and accelerated the uprooting of political systems such as the communist bloc within the Warsaw Pact. At the same time, as we have said, these computer and information technology developments in world commerce and trade have also created new criminal opportunities. Modern criminals are exploiting the globalization of trade and finance and the machinery of economic technology that drives it. New technological and economic developments have helped produce new mechanisms for trafficking contraband, conducting illicit trade, laundering money, and engaging in large-scale economic crimes (Soros 1998; Salzman 2001).

Traditional organized crime groups have also greatly benefited from these developments. More importantly, the sheer pace of globalization and technological advancements has enabled modern criminal organizations to penetrate legitimate business that once appeared to be immune to criminal abuse and exploration (Kelly 2001). These trends are jeopardizing vital U.S. interests, threatening Americans' very business and financial institutions.

There are good reasons for defining organized crime clearly and comprehensively, since so much illicit trafficking involves organized criminal groups of varying size, structure, sophistication, and operational perimeters. From the law enforcement standpoint, an authoritative definition enables government to effectively measure the extent of such crime and to determine how resources may be allocated in attacking it. If it cannot be defined, it cannot be measured, and if it cannot be measured it is difficult to assess the effectiveness of anticrime control efforts. The problem encountered in defining organized crime stems not from the word "crime" but from the word "organized." Beyond the sensational examples of the Cosa Nostra, no standard consensus has been reached as to when a criminal group is "organized" or how well organized it may be. Moreover, because organized crime has become so interwoven into American politics and economic life, not everyone agrees about the seriousness of particular manifestations of it. A variety of activities that are defined officially as organized crime—extortion, sports betting, loan sharking, labor racketeering, for example—are not universally viewed as equally criminal or socially harmful. Credible threats of violence and the capacity to enforce these threats, coupled with the ability to neutralize law enforcement, are among the defining features of organized criminal groups that distinguish them from ordinary street gangs and criminal entrepreneurs.

What Are the Roles of Organized Crime and Transnational Crime in Illicit Trafficking?

Organized crime may be defined as continuing criminal conspiracy that derives profits from illegal activities and goods that the public demands. The existence and structure of criminal groups are sustained through the use of violence, corruption of police and public officials, intimidation, credible threats, and control of particular illicit markets in drugs, gambling, loan sharking, and extortion. One of the most dangerous developments in organized crime at the end of the twentieth century was the trend toward the formation and consolidation of transnational organized crime groups. These groups collaborate and cooperate in ways that facilitate the delivery of illicit goods and services on a vast international scale (Mueller 2001).

The transnational style of many modern crime organizations does not appear to have resulted from a conscious master plan concocted by some arch criminals. Rather, it emanates from the organizational flexibility of some group to respond to nuances within the complex economic environment. Many crime syndicates are suited for the cyber age: namely, they have informal organizations, and they are sensitive to changes in their surroundings, alert to opportunities and threats from law enforcement or from competing criminal organizations. Law enforcement (first-responder) agencies are also rooted in local conditions and therefore are not able to aggressively attend to local corruption and sophisticated illegal markets. In addition, regional political and economic organizations such as the European Union (EU), which promote the free flow of people and goods, simultaneously weaken national borders, thereby creating a serious dilemma. The very factors that promote economic prosperity contribute to the growth of transnational organized crime and illicit trafficking. Free trade, the movement of capital production capacities, and skilled labor, the availability of cheap labor along with wholesale and retail markets for consumer goods, also facilitate illicit trade and transnational organized crime. Russian, Polish, Italian, British, Chinese, Mexican, and Corsican syndicates, among numerous others, have responded to the new emergent reality. It is not the Mafia and Triads (secret societies of a criminal character, which flourish among overseas Chinese) that have created these opportunities; rather, it is the nation-states and MNCs that support unconstrained trade conditions, which are then exploited for criminal gain. In this regard, ethnic communities can be understood as potential resources for transnational criminal enterprises (Kelly and Cook 1998). They provide recruitment opportunities, as well as cover and support for criminal operations, and they serve as a pool of criminal activists prepared to engage in trafficking activities.

Many immigrants in economically depressed ghettos are often tempted to participate in criminal enterprises. Unfortunately, even casual participation in criminal gang activities can sometimes yield greater rewards than can be obtained through legitimate work (Kelly, Chin, and Fagan 2000).

Does Immigration Foster Illicit Trafficking?

Demographic studies indicate that migration processes driven by the push and pull factors of economic necessity will continue to affect millions of people and change the ethnic and social composition of many nations. It is estimated that between 1991 and 2025 the global workforce will increase by 1.5 billion people, of whom 1.4 billion will be in the developing world eager to find survival opportunities (Falchi 1995). The potential for increased migration by desperate people is enormous, carrying important implications for transnational criminal trafficking activities.

While most migrants are law-abiding people, among them are members of criminal organizations who bring their skill, knowledge, affiliations, and contacts with them to their new habitats. Ethnic enclaves in the United States, for example, harbor significant criminal elements (Chin and Kelly 1997). This comes as no surprise, for, historically, when criminal organizations come under pressure in their homelands from either law enforcement or internal wars, their response is to emigrate to areas with lower risks and more favorable conditions for crime. The Sicilian Diaspora of the 1960s and 1970s in places as diverse as Australia, Venezuela, and Germany is a good example. Another example is the Cuntera crime family in Venezuela, which has become a key link between Italian organized crime and cocaine supplies from Latin America (Jamieson 1995).

Greater international mobility has expanded the capacities of criminal organizations and has enabled their members to elude national criminal jurisdictions where they might be high-priority targets. The increase in business and leisure travel, as well as the acceleration in migration, is frustrating governments' ability to monitor and control ingress and egress from the national territories.

The dissolution of national barriers that occurred following the collapse of the Soviet Empire also helped intensify alien smuggling (Kelly and Rieber 2001). Moreover, changes in immigration policy, especially in the West, have led to the increasingly diversified nationality of illegal immigrants as well as a continued growth in their number. The result has been the extension and intensification of alien trafficking groups.

Air transport affords unprecedented opportunities for those seeking to enter developed nations. The technology also facilitates the commission of smuggling crimes and acts of terror as the events of 9/11, which killed approximately 3,000 people and brought down the Twin Towers, powerful symbols of American economic power, so dramatically illustrate.

The ethnic communities newly formed since 1965, together with more traditional enclaves reinvigorated with new arrivals, have created new Diasporas that provide a useful bridge for newcomers to their new culture. But they also serve more sinister purposes: the ethnic communities as an enclave, barrio, or ghetto can afford a cover for potential recruits and linkages that facilitate crime activities. Because immigrant communities are not easily penetrated by law enforcement, they often provide a built-in security against the American Cosa Nostra—specifically the Mafia in America or the "Syndicate" (which the underworld refers to as *Cosa Nostra*) and the Mafia, as constituting the global crime family originating in Sicily—but are far less effective when targeted against the criminal networks established by the Chinese and Russians. These newer groups employ a range of obscure dialects unfamiliar to law enforcement, thereby confounding attempts at electronic eavesdropping. Moreover, it is difficult to identify and recruit informers in immigrant communities because these new immigrants are reluctant to make contact, let alone cooperate with law enforcement.

What Is the Relationship of the Volume of Illicit Trafficking to Globalization?

Globalization has meant the vast growth of international trade. Lowering tariffs coupled with free trade arrangements and the gradual integration of the former Soviet bloc nations into the worldwide trading system led to huge increases in trade in the 1990s (Clark 1996). The growth in air, sea, rail, and truck traffic is projected to remain constant throughout the first decade of the twenty-first century. The favorable economic conditions also provide an environment conducive to transnational crime. The growth of global trade brings many important benefits for criminal groups. The opportunities to embed illicit goods in licit commerce are multiplying; the increased volume of trade is reducing the risks of detection and exposure of illicit goods; the random inspection of shipping containers, as well as the increased freight, translates into comparatively few containers being inspected; and, most ominously, opportunities for smuggling weapons of mass destruction (WMD) into the United States and other Western societies are increasing exponentially. In short, as we posited at the beginning of this chapter, the growth of legitimate commerce and trade worldwide has been accompanied by an expansion of illicit trade and trafficking. Like a smuggler's paradise, the global commerce system offers so many opportunities for rapid growth that law enforcement agencies cannot keep pace.

What Is the Relationship of the Growth of Global Finance to Illicit Trafficking?

The new financial infrastructure in the geopolitical environment consists of a finance system that links nation-states, huge banks, and their correspondents (affiliates and subsidiaries) with brokerage houses, stock markets, and investment and currency portfolios in a system that operates twenty-four hours a day. The finance system has many points of access and makes it possible to trade anonymously, to move money easily and rapidly, as well as to obscure the origin and ownership of money profiteering, hence blurring the distinction between "dirty" and "clean" money. The mobility of capital parallels that of the transnational criminals themselves and could not be better suited to the activities of transnational organized crime. Huge sums of money move through the mega-system of global finances and its offshore archipelagos of banks, insurance firms, and credit houses, making illicit monies enormously difficult to identify, track, and control.

The finance network means that profits from illicit trafficking can be repatriated to criminal groups and networks with little difficulty. Much of what is known as "money laundering" is not about disguising or cleaning money earned from criminal activities as it is about recirculating it from the host state to the home state of the criminal organization where it can be used with impunity. Put differently, drug money earned and then deposited in New York State banks can be wired back through a set of portfolios and company accounts to, say, Burma or Afghanistan where opium poppies are cultivated, harvested, and manufactured chemically into heroin.

How Do Worldwide Communication Technologies Affect Illicit Trafficking?

The growth of information technology and the sophisticated means of transmitting data provide greater opportunities for intellectual property and data theft. Tampering with computer data files via "hacking" has had major repercussions, disrupting air traffic control systems, impairing automated computer-controlled ware and energy supply systems, and affecting pharmaceutical and food production processes. Interference with financial transactions in banks and stock markets is a serious issue, perhaps constituting novel opportunities for extortion. For example, criminal groups could threaten computer systems in an attempt to extort payments from firms willing to pay in order to keep operating in a very competitive business environment.

What Are the Defining Characteristics of Transnational Crime Groups?

The dominant image of organized crime in the United States has been that of the Mafia clans and crime families that constitute the operational units of the American version of the Mafia, which is known as the Cosa Nostra. The Cosa Nostra in the United States is structurally different than its Italian cousin. The Cosa Nostra has a Commission, an executive body of crime bosses who oversee interfamily affairs and resolve family disputes that cannot be resolved locally. It also advises and consents to new leadership in the crime families when top positions are open or vacated by death or imprisonment of Mafiosi (Kelly 1990). The Mafia, Italy's most infamous criminal organization, and other groups, including the Neapolitan Camorra, emerged at various times in Italian history in response to foreign and indigenous political oppression and economic exploitation. The Mafia, in particular, survived and strengthened its grip over segments of the peasantry in the rural areas and over the working-class poor in the impoverished urban ghettos by acting as protectors of the poor and their interests while ruthlessly exploiting and terrorizing them at home and abroad in the Italian immigrant enclaves (Kelly 2002).

Over time, the culture of mutual protection embedded in a shadowy, informal system of power degenerated into a parasitic system of extortion. Selling protection as a commodity in an environment filled with criminogenic assets spread easily and widely. Control over illicit markets hastened the degeneracy of the Mafia into a purely criminal enterprise. Drugs especially, and the struggles they engendered, left carnage in the streets, and ultimately the Mafia as an organization of gratuitous violence was left in tatters.

The breakup of the Mafia in America began with an aggressive law enforcement campaign in the mid-1970s and culminated with the "Commission" and the "Pizza Connection" prosecutions (See Chapter 3, year 1987, Pizza Connection), which put the major Mafia bosses behind bars for life. In Italy, the anti-Mafia campaign gathered momentum after the brutal murders of the courageous magistrates Giovanni Falcone and Paolo Borsellino in 1992. The crackdown led to the arrest of Toto Riina, the Corleonesi boss. *Peniti* (informers) became numerous, especially when confessions meant lighter sentences. But cynicism has reappeared as it begins to dawn on the authorities that the detailed testimony of self-described turncoats might in itself be another curtain pulled over the truth. Nonetheless, there are now nearly 2,000 *peniti* under government protection (Kelly 1994). The Mafia and its sinister cousins in different lands are redefining their structures and goals. The new markets for exploitation lie in the global economies that operate across national boundaries involving trafficking in drugs, weapons, aliens, and money laundering (Arlacchi 1985). Since the 1993 arrest of Riina and his heir, Giovanni Brusca, by the year 2000 important Mafia chiefs like Bernardo Provenzano have become fugitives in hiding. It is likely that the Mafia will respond to government pressures and public education by shrinking its involvement in exposed criminal projects and by making organizational and operational adjustments, including restructuring itself into smaller compartmental-type cells with tightened security (Maloney and Kelly 2000).

Although the Mafia model of a hierarchical power structure with specialized roles and responsibilities has been challenged, it is still considered a threat in the U.S. law enforcement circles. The reality of the situation generally refers to criminal organizations that are more loosely organized. The former Soviet bloc of countries has many well-organized gangs that variously operate on their own initiative, act together in partnerships, or sometimes against one another. Consequently, organized crime in these settings is best understood as a diffuse and changing network of individuals and groups (Holyst 1998). This may be a more relevant and accurate description of contemporary organized crime in many regions of the world than the Cosa Nostra–type crime family with its hierarchical structure. Actually, family and kinship ties are often an important component of criminal affiliation networks (Lupsha 1986). The ties binding criminal organizations are also based on more extensive social mechanisms such as shared ethnicity or common experience (e.g., prisoners doing time or street gang membership) or even, in the Chinese case, on the notion of *guanxi* or reciprocal obligation that can span generations and continents (Chin, Kelly, and Fagan 1994). These bonds and collaborative mechanisms create a basis for trust and make it difficult for law enforcement to penetrate or infiltrate the criminal organizations.

Network organizations tend to be fluid, highly adaptable, and resistant to disruption. They possess resilience that other groups may lack. It is an ideal type of structure for maintaining organizational integrity; networks are characterized by redundancy, which means that linkages can be maintained through a variety of different connections. If connections are broken or infiltrated, they can be replaced so that the criminal organization can effectively reconstitute itself. In the event that the core—the leadership and power base of a crime network—is penetrated by law enforcement through undercover work or the cultivation of informants, it can still be insulated through the imposition of safeguards and cautious restrictions on access to the leadership (Williams 1999). These flexible organizations are streamlined and possess only the skills, membership, and resources that they need to sustain themselves and support their criminal projects. As such, these organizations tend to extend their influence into the legitimate sectors of the economy and government through coercion and corruption.

What Are the Relationships among Governments, Social Structure, and Organized Crime?

Government weakened by coercion and corruption is susceptible to organized crime. For example, Colombia, rife with corruption and violence, has become the corporate headquarters of the worldwide cocaine trade (Lee and Thoumi 1997). These conditions facilitated opportunities to create large criminal organizations that in effect became a "state within a state" with enough power to confront, if not compel, the subservience of a civil society's government (Fuentes and Kelly 1999). A classic example of the inherent threat a weak state creates to public order and stability by the very fact of its inability to provide safety and security would be Italy in the nineteenth century. In the power vacuums of Sicily and southern Italy, where police and security forces were virtually nonexistent or incompetent, the Mafia rose to fill the power gap. Just as the Mafia fashioned its own authority by offering protection and security to people in return for money, authority, and property (Gambetta 1993), so criminal organizations today continue to flourish where authority has been eroded and the state is weak.

A crucial factor in the rise of organized crime, drug trafficking, and other types of illicit trafficking in many Eastern European countries is the nascent stage of centralized democratic government and institutions. A weak state means a vulnerable infrastructure, ineffective law enforcement, hyperinflation and unemployment, a narrow tax base, poor transportation infrastructure, and limited communications. These trends also mean that there are no social safety nets to protect the public against crime and exploitation. The weakened state, as we have already suggested, therefore becomes an attractive environment in which to settle and operate a criminal organization. This development has been most alarming in Russia where the regulatory system operations and frameworks all but collapsed with the disintegration of the Soviet Union and the transitioning into capitalism and privatization in 1991 (Kelly, Ryan, and Schatzberg 2002). During this period, Russia produced a public culture in which "everything was for sale."

Even when a nation is able to take effective action against organized crime, a government may choose to tolerate some level of criminal activities either because it recognizes that crime is sometimes beneficial to the state (through export earnings, as in Colombia, Mexico, Pakistan, and Russia) or because important segments of its population benefit from crime (e.g., localized multiplier effects in the Colombian and Sicilian economies with all that available cash).

Organized crime groups that operate beyond the domestic frontiers can often represent themselves as humanitarians. For example, the infamous and powerful Japanese Yakuza (the Japanese Cosa Nostra) distributed food parcels and afforded other types of aid and assistance to victims of the Kobe earthquakes in 1999. And acting like a modern-day Robin Hood, Pablo Escobar, the top cocaine boss in the Medellín Colombian drug cartel, provided housing programs to eradicate the slums of Colombia's cities in late 1988 to 1989. Criminal organizations, including the American crime syndicates during Prohibition, have often portrayed themselves as positive forces in society. As Al Capone often exclaimed, he gave the public what it wanted; in his view, he was just a businessman. Capone opened soup kitchens and handed out money to desolate people living in the streets; his self-image was that of a public benefactor, not a dangerous crime boss (Kelly 2002b). Creating sympathy for criminal organizations is part of a strategy calculated to nullify law enforcement activities. As history has demonstrated, an alienated population whose needs are not met by a state that criminalizes certain goods and services in demand (e.g., alcohol, sex) is likely to provide an economic base of support for organized criminals. When, however, crime groups like the Sicilian Mafia or the Colombian drug cartels embark on violent campaigns against the state and harm the public, government and individual tolerance declines rapidly.

Corruption is another tool through which crime organizations can disarm the state. The extensive penetration of criminal corruption activities into the state immunizes criminals from law enforcement. When the corruption is deep and persistent, a virtual partnership develops between criminal organizations and government officials that embrace one another in a symbiotic relationship (Kelly 1979; 1986). Criminal groups located in a state whose government is weakened by corruption tend to possess a secure safety net in which to operate. In the corrupt state, such as Italy before the anti-Mafia reforms of the 1990s, many segments of the government may be engaged in collusive relationship, such that key government figures become partners with gangsters in a variety of criminal enterprises. Such was the case with the Mafia.

Borders and locations are important for criminal organizations because they represent different levels of risks and demarcate different markets. Crime organizations are more likely to develop in home bases where the risks are low and where they may act as sanctuaries and safe havens. From these cocoons, criminals can engage in illicit activities and enterprises with impunity. And as long as the main bases of criminal organizations remain out of reach, state actions in host states against local subsidiaries or branches of the major organization will not have a decisive anti-crime impact. The Sicilian Mafia, operating drug-trafficking rings in the United States, Venezuela, and Brazil, was not completely destroyed by the "Pizza Connection" drug cases against its groups in the United States (Alexander 1998). Russia, Nigeria, and the Central Asian republics that were part of the former Soviet Union are examples of safe havens for organized crime groups.

Do Ethnic Conflicts and State Dissolution Facilitate Illicit Trafficking?

Toward the end of the twentieth century when the Soviet Union collapsed and the Cold War that had shaped the world's politics since 1945 ended, some nations simply disintegrated into warring factions. Ironically, these tendencies toward fragmentation are part of the globalization trends that are enveloping the world. For some, the collapse of nations in Africa, Central Asia, and Central Europe represent the "retribalization" of societies that offers new opportunities and environments for criminal organizations. State crises involving ethnic conflicts offer numerous opportunities for trafficking in arms. An important feature of the war in the former

Yugoslavia in Serbia, Bosnia, Croatia, and Kosovo involved deals characterized by arms for drugs as ethnic groups figured out ways of acquiring the resources for armed struggle. Linkages between warring parties (as in Chechnya, Russia) and criminal organizations appear to be mutually beneficial (Barber 1995). In some cases, the dangerous liaison is broken, and the purely criminal organization is cut out as the nationalist/ethnic guerrilla insurgents engage in criminal activities of their own—where the terrorist fighters turn into felons (Kelly and Schatzberg 1995). Criminal endeavors provide a financial substitute that enables them to sustain their political struggle as occurred with the Bolsheviks in Czarist Russia and the Vietnamese Vietminh in the aftermath of the French colonial occupation (Kelly 1973).

Do Political Instability and Military Conflict Contribute to Criminal Activities?

Political instability and military conflict pose both problems and opportunities. Criminal organizations flourish in conditions of war and unrest, as is clear from recent evidence of large-scale opium production in war-torn Afghanistan. It is therefore difficult to avoid the conclusion that whatever posture they assume— either as guerrillas turning into criminals or as members of mafias with an alliance of crime and revolution—creates mutual resources of monies and weapons to the war machines of terror, counterterror, revolution, and counterrevolution. The links between crime and terrorist insurrections masquerading as revolutions appear to be growing stronger and also perpetrate conflicts that encourage terrorism and make peace more elusive. In addition, the perpetuation of the crime and political conflict nexus may bring about hybrid organizations that are part criminal and part terrorist. Thus, ethnic conflict such as the Bosnian war between Christians and Muslims may have dangerous ramifications for crime and terrorist activities long after the fighting subsides. First, incentives may develop that will promote criminal activity earmarked to support political struggles. Second, ethnic, social, and religious conflicts can create and then perpetuate hatreds that transcend national boundaries and the immediate locale of the conflict. The Turkish/Armenian animosities, for example, continue nearly a century after the expulsion of the Armenian masses from Eastern Anatolia and Thrace during World War I by the Turks. Soon after these Armenian clearances, hundreds of thousands of Muslim refugees, many of them Kurds, came flooding in from Russian Transcaucasia. The forced migrations and concomitant immigration continue to manifest virulent ethnic animosity. Third, criminal groups can provide cadres of specialists in violence that can be directed against governments or used by crime organizations. Fourth, as states react to the transformations of their cultures, institutions, population composition, and economic systems, some will succeed and grow, whereas others who confront opportunistic criminal groups will succumb to crime and corruption.

What Are the Trends among Transnational Crime Groups?

Safe havens, diversity of groups and products, consolidation, corruption, coopted political power, the infiltration of legitimate businesses, the formation of strategic criminal alliances, and criminal cooperation—all are trends worth watching as the global economies expand and grow beyond the boundaries of national sovereignties. The problem of safe haven countries that tolerate or welcome criminal organizations will continue and grow as long as huge amounts of criminal capital are available. Criminal sanctuaries are likely to increase among poor countries where drug money substitutes for foreign direct investments. Coupled with the spread of safe havens is the increasing diversity of criminal organizations. Not only are new groups spawned as lucrative criminal opportunities occur, but successful crime groups tend to spread out involving themselves in new enterprises. This often stimulates criminal opportunities in other ethnic groups poised to exploit whatever opportunities beckon them. When the Colombian cocaine cartels sought to export and wholesale cocaine in the United States, without becoming involved in the high-risk street distribution retail side of the business, they cultivated partnerships with the Crips and Bloods (Los Angeles street gangs) on the West Coast and the Dominicans in the Northeast of the United States (Klein, Maxson, and Cunningham 1989). The illicit traffic might also include legal products (e.g., cigarettes and legal pharmaceuticals sold more cheaply outside the United States) where the price and tax differential across borders make smuggling very attractive. Illicit traffic in goods that are prohibited but for which there is a demand (chlorofluorocarbons gases), goods for which demand greatly exceeds supply (human organs for transplant surgery), and goods that promise high levels of profit (precious objects d'art, components for nuclear weapons) are likely to promote more criminal activities. Transnational crime groups engaged in trafficking of illicit goods use couriers (so-called mules), or low-level gang members who do not fit law enforcement profiles and are likely to be out of the range of experience of domestic law enforcement. Attempting to deal with unknown criminals, organizations, and illicit goods adds considerably to the enforcement work and assessments concerning the scope of the problem of trafficking (Lee and Thoumi 2003).

Evidence suggests that in the post–Cold War environment since 1989, while crime organizations appear to be proliferating, the types of crime and crime organizations have consolidated and blurred. For instance, in Russia, organized crime and white-collar crime are increasingly indistinguishable, especially in schemes of financial fraud. In the United States, Russian criminal groups have been very successful in Medicare/Medicaid fraud in California and in running petroleum tax evasion schemes in New York and New Jersey (Handelman 1995).

Another disturbing development concerns the arrogance of crime groups that dare to move from the subordination and cooptation of political elites to the direct control of political power. The Mafia in Sicily attempted just that a decade ago: to openly control politics through violence against political leaders and government officials (Maloney and Kelly 2000). In Bolivia in the 1980s, drug traffickers actually seized government power for a short period (Lee 1998). The use of "outlaw states" such as Afghanistan under the joint influence and control of the Taliban—a fundamentalist Islamic sect that took power in 1992—and al-Qaeda—a terrorist organization involved in opium trafficking—poses significant problems. In addition to seizing political power, criminal groups are more likely to go beyond infiltration to control of legitimate business (Kelly 1999). Nearly fifty years ago in the United States, certain sectors of the economy—indeed, whole industries such as construction in New York City and skilled trade occupations (teamsters, dock workers, coal miners)—were under the control of crime families and syndicates (Block 1983; 1991). In the former Soviet Union, there are signs that the Russian mafia and other regional crime syndicates are taking control of large sectors of the economy, including the banking industry (Shelley 1995). This affords advantages to criminal groups because owning or controlling a bank means that money laundering can proceed with few obstacles and loans can be made to firms prepared to kick back or do business with mafia-endorsed business. Furthermore, through control of a pivotal financial mechanism such as a bank or credit house, strategic alliance among criminal organizations is more likely to occur. This happened in the United States when the Italian crime families formed La Cosa Nostra and also when the Sicilian Mafia coalesced around a Commission governing the numerous independent *cosche* (groups) (Servadio 1976). The efforts of law enforcement to cooperate have served as both a primary threat and an incentive for criminal organizations to cooperate. Just as alliances and mergers are more frequent in the legitimate business world, they are likely to be more common among transnational criminal organizations. Similarly, like legitimate business firms, criminal organizations will include in their division of labor specialists in money laundering, security, and transport; chemists to regulate the quality and volume of drug products; and so on. In short, as is true of legitimate businesses, criminal firms are interested in creating a hospitable operational environment, which means one in which law enforcement has been sufficiently corrupted to have its anticrime control measures neutralized. Another important element in criminal defenses are measures that rely on good counterintelligence which through infiltration of government and law enforcement agencies will reveal law enforcement's next moves.

Can Law Enforcement Operate Effectively in a Global Environment?

Illicit trafficking has benefited from the end of the Cold War and the globalization of business and travel. International crime groups—as with noncriminal entities—have unprecedented freedom of movement, making it easier for them to cross borders and to expand the range and scope of their operations. As a result, virtually every region or country in the world has seen an increase in illicit trafficking—as either a source or transit market zone for illegal contraband or products; as a venue for money laundering and illicit financial transactions; or as a base of operations for criminal organizations with global networks. Many regions and countries serve all three functions for criminal enterprises.

Besides making the security and law enforcement challenges for the United States more complex domestically, the spread of illicit trafficking activities threatens vital U.S. interests abroad. Four key questions and issues need to be addressed in order to fully grasp the forces that pose threats to American citizens and U.S. commercial, economic, and security interests. First, what are the dynamic forces regionally and in nations/states that promote illicit trafficking activities? Second, how do criminal groups take advantage of these economic and political changes that function as catalysts for crime? Third, what are the impacts of criminal activity, and the corruption related to it, on national and regional political and economic stability? Fourth and finally, what are the main criminal activities and scope of operations of major trafficking organizations in different regions and countries worldwide?

Western Europe

Like the United States, Western European states are lucrative targets and attractive operating environments for traffickers because of their wealth, communications, and transport infrastructure. Western European populations are desirable venues for drug marketing, as well as other contraband and illicit services. Moreover, the size, density, and availability of commercial and banking services in Western Europe's cities and their interconnectedness make them valuable to illicit financial transactions that include money laundering.

The market reforms enacted by the EU permit unfettered movement of goods, services, labor, and capital throughout most of Western Europe. The EU's sophisticated structure facilitating international trade attracts a huge volume of people and goods passing through airports and seaports. Traffickers and international criminals take advantage of this structure in order to move drugs, arms, illegal aliens, and other contraband to all regions of the world. Because of their sophisticated economies and financial systems, criminals also use Western European countries as a venue for money laundering and other illicit financial transactions. Indeed, even its enemies—terrorist groups and rogue states—use Western European commercial and financial centers in efforts to evade international embargoes or to acquire pro-scribed technologies and materials needed for chemical and nu-clear weapons of mass destruction. In the aftermath of September 11, most Western European governments have changed or are changing their domestic laws to conform to Financial Action Task Force on Money Laundering (FATF) anti–money laundering stan-dards. Despite these improved enforcement mechanisms, West-ern Europe remains a primary locale for money laundering. Eu-ropean states provide numerous alternative channels to place and to legitimize proceeds generated in illicit trafficking enterprise.

EU members face yet other threats from international drug traffickers and from illegal immigrants, many of who wind up employed by ethnic-based crime groups to make their liveli-hood. West European drug markets are close to rivaling those of the United States in both size and profitability. According to Eu-ropean law enforcement information, Turkish and Albanian criminal groups have dominated the wholesale distribution of Southwest Asian heroin in most of the EU countries. In addition, South American drug traffickers have been developing a grow-ing cocaine market in Western Europe since the early 1980s (Fuentes and Kelly 1999). The deep-water ports of Rotterdam and Amsterdam in the Netherlands are primary entry points for drug trafficking in northeastern Europe, as demonstrated by analysis of drug seizure data and law enforcement information (Chang 1999). In particular, cocaine seizures in Europe reported by Interpol more than tripled in the 1990s, from 14.3 metric tons in 1990 to about 44 metric tons in 1999 (National Security Coun-cil 1998). EU countries are a primary destination for illegal im-migrants, including women and children smuggled into the Continent for prostitution and pornography businesses con-trolled by organized crime.

Traditional and more modern forms of transnational organ-ized crime flourish in the poorer Mediterranean region where, compared to northern Europe, stagnant economic conditions and high unemployment rates are widespread and help to promote organized criminal activities. Many ethnic-based crime groups have also established footholds in expatriate enclaves in most EU countries (Arlacchi 2001). Cultural and linguistic ties between Spain/Portugal and South American drug traffickers have been exploited to stimulate the demand for cocaine in the profitable markets of Europe. The ethnic enclaves serve as bases for organ-ized crime where, for instance, criminal networks and cells with ties in Turkey, Iran, the Balkan countries, and North Africa have taken root. Crime groups are largely involved in contraband smuggling of drugs and arms. Turkish and Albanian crime syndicates have emerged as principal distributors of heroin cultivated in Southwest Asia targeted for Europe.

As in the United States, public opinion in many European countries ascribes high crime rates and general societal distress to foreign ethnic-organized crime groups. Also, in recent years, with addiction becoming a more serious criminal and medical problem, the Europeans have become less tolerant of drug use (Fijnaut 2001). Now, two drugs in particular, heroin and cocaine, are most often cited in drug-related crime, deaths, and HIV infection. Increasingly, EU nations are adopting a more aggressive posture toward drug trafficking. With the criminal threat having become more multifaceted since the collapse of Cold War barriers beginning in 1989, many European states have broadened and intensified their law enforcement campaigns against transnational crime that lies at the heart of illicit trafficking. For example, after the 1992 assassinations of magistrates Falcone and Borsellino, Italy targeted the Sicilian Mafia, with the result that many key Mafia bosses and soldiers were arrested and convicted (Martello 1992; Schneider and Schneider 2003). In addition, the United Kingdom and Italy are concerned about Nigerian crime groups, and Central European states such as Germany, Poland, the Czech Republic, Slovakia, and Hungary are focusing on the growing role played by ethnic Albanian and Bulgarian groups; Russian criminal groups have attracted attention not only in the United States but also in Western Europe, Israel, and the Far East (Kelly and Rieber 2001).

Greater awareness of the international crime threat has increased anticrime cooperation within Western Europe. In 1990, Europol was created as a crime-fighting initiative on the Continent. It serves as a collaborative mechanism for collecting, classifying, and sharing information with member states and groups.

Eastern and Central Europe

In 1991, driven by nationalistic fervor in many of the republics and a collapsing economy, the Soviet Union dissolved and Gorbachev resigned as president. This fall of communism and the end of tight border controls in Eastern and Central Europe led foreign criminal organizations to become involved chiefly in illicit trafficking in contraband and licit goods (Bell 2000). With the breakdown of the old order and resources redirected to fundamental political and economic problems, Russian, Italian, Colombian, Nigerian, and Chinese groups have all made inroads into these regions as well as in the Balkans and southeast Mediterranean. Several of the region's nation-states serve as transit points for heroin from Southwest Asia. Poland and Croatia may be emerging as transportation routes for South American cocaine destined for Western and Eastern Europe.

Geography is a primary factor in the growth of organized crime in Eastern and Central Europe. The region functions as a strategic crossroads between Russia and the new independent states, which are major source areas for transnational and domestic organized crime. Alcohol, tobacco, automobiles, and other high-demand consumer items that are generally unavailable or very expensive in Russia are smuggled into the region. For example, Hungary shares borders with seven countries; its relatively well-developed transportation system and road networks make it a major transit zone for all sorts of contraband smuggling. Poland and the Czech Republic also serve as crossroads for trafficking directly with Western European markets and include extensive smuggling in stolen vehicles moving from West to East. Bulgaria and Romania remain key countries on the old Balkan route between Turkey and Central Europe. The criminal entrepreneurs in these countries have expanded their rackets in the West to acquire amphetamines. Bulgaria, after China, is the world's largest source of counterfeit and pirated compact discs (CDs).

Russia, the Balkans, and the Newly Independent States

At the end of the Cold War Russia and the Newly Independent States (NIS) became fertile ground for expanding organized crime. The end of police states, the relaxation of social controls, and the opening of borders in these formerly "closed" societies have allowed both local and foreign criminal organizations unprecedented freedom to operate. Criminal networks comprised of traditional organized crime groups, skilled professionals, and corrupt politicians and officials have moved to fill vacuums created by political and economic change. Criminal groups and many public officials have become intertwined, thereby enabling criminals to aggressively cultivate business relationships with of-

ficial and private entrepreneurs who can provide "front" companies with export licenses, customs exemptions, and government
contracts. Russian organized crime was notably pervasive
throughout the former Soviet Union and served as a model in
forming more indigenous, local groups in the region. Apart from
massive drug trafficking, Russian criminal groups have penetrated the banking sector of financial institutions by periodically
providing cash infusions to troubled banks and by using extortion or sheer violent intimidation. In some cases, banks are
bought outright, and the control is used to launder illicit proceeds, to obtain financial information about potential extortion
targets, and to evade government regulators.

Some of the business enterprises suspected of association
with Russian criminal organizations are large MNCs that are engaged in the export/import trade and commodities brokerage
whose assets are sufficiently hidden in offshore banking havens
that deprive the Russian government of substantial legitimate tax
revenues (Kelly and Rieber 2003). The hard currency–earning oil
and gas sector of the Russian economy is one of the most profitable havens for organized crime. Russian organized crime has
also been extensively involved in smuggling gems and precious
metals out of the country. According to internal studies authorized by President Boris Yeltsin in 1994, 70 to 80 percent of private
businesses paid extortion to organized crime, amounting to 20
percent of their revenues, which put them in the awkward position of not being able to fulfill their tax obligations (Williams
1997).

The relative dependence of Estonia, Latvia, and Lithuania on
Russian energy supplies, coupled with the importance of Baltic
seaports for Russian transit trade, offers opportunities for crime
groups. Geographically, the Baltic States are the major commercial outlet between Russia and the West. Not surprisingly, organized crime groups take advantage of the high volume of trade
through these ports to smuggle contraband both ways. Operating
within the sizable ethnic Russian populations in the Baltic States,
crime groups have taken advantage and integrated legitimate
business enterprises into these criminal empires. Numerous front
companies are now situated in the export/import sectors that facilitate money laundering and illicit trade. In Ukraine, Moldova,
the Caucasus (Georgia, Armenia, and Azerbaijan), and Central
Asia (Kazakhstan, Uzbekistan, Kyrgyz Republic, Tajikistan, Turk-
menistan), the mountainous regions have never had adequate

law enforcement control of criminal activity. These remote areas have become alternatives to Southwest Asian/Balkan trafficking routes for drugs. Local, powerful Russian criminal organizations with international connections operate in these areas (Shelley 2003).

With close ties to a corrupt military, organized crime groups are believed to be heavily involved in illicit arms trafficking. Most of these deals involve sales of weapons and materials in Russia and the NIS. Some of the arms, however, have gone to Chechnya and to the Taliban and al-Qaeda in Afghanistan.

In the United States, Russian and Eastern European organized crime groups are now considered as significant a threat as La Cosa Nostra. With their sophistication and international connections, Russian organized crime can advantageously expand their criminal operations. American law enforcement analyses of the Russian criminal element indicate that they are better educated and more occupationally skilled than the average member of La Cosa Nostra (New York State Organized Crime Task Force and New Jersey Commission of Investigation 1996). Russian criminal organizations in the United States are involved primarily in extortion, drug trafficking, auto theft, cigarette smuggling, money laundering, trafficking in stolen art, and a wide array of schemes, including health-care fraud (Finkenauer 1994; Kenney and Finkenauer 1995).

South Asia, Southeast Asia, and China

South Asia is a primary source of heroin for the international drug trade and European markets. Drug abuse has increased dramatically in the major and transit countries that are at the crossroads of the Southwest Asia heroin trade. According to UN estimates, in Pakistan alone, the heroin addict population has grown from virtually none in 1980 to more than 2 million and perhaps as high 4 million by the turn of the century (Flynn 2000). Under predominantly Taliban rule, international terrorists and drug traffickers were able to operate with impunity in Afghanistan (Norland 2001). The Taliban gave sanctuary to renegade Saudi terrorist Osama bin Laden, allowing him to operate terrorist training camps in Afghanistan. Bin Laden, in return, used his wealth and business networks to help support the Taliban. Despite the Taliban's public condemnation of the illicit narcotics industry, virtually all of Afghanistan's opium poppy cultivation and morphine base and heroin processing were located in Taliban-controlled territory (Kelly, in press).

In Southeast Asia, drug-trafficking armies operate in Burma's remote opium-producing region. Ethnic Chinese and Thai criminal networks in Burma and Thailand play a major role as brokers, financial backers, and transporters in the heroin trade, with social and political consequences for all countries in the region (Mueller 2001). A criminal underground largely immune from law enforcement because of the corruption of powerful politicians, government officials, police, and military figures has resulted in government and institutional instability. AIDS, associated with narcotics abuse, has spread; violence and poverty have damaged societies caught up in the suffocating web of crime and trafficking.

China's role as a source of transnational criminal activity has paralleled its emergence as a global economic poser. The factors attributable to the decline of communist social policies in China have given criminal groups unprecedented flexibility. For example, the abolition of internal travel controls facilitates moving drugs, arms, and illegal aliens to coastal ports for smuggling out of the country. Corruption, particularly at the local level, has contributed to international criminal activity in China. Often what is lacking is not so much interest in proper law enforcement as modern equipment and training in sophisticated police tactics (Chin 2003). The stake that many Chinese officials have in business enterprise lends itself to profit taking priority over duty and office. Chinese arms factories, under pressure to earn hard currency and attract easy money on the black market, may be a source of weapons for Chinese arms traffickers. Similarly, in the legitimate pharmaceutical production industry, drugs may be illegally exported or diverted to the international illicit drug markets. These types of opportunities, together with Beijing's policy of inviting overseas Chinese businessmen to trade and invest in China, have allowed powerful Chinese Triads, criminal organizations operating illicit underground economies from Hong Kong and Taiwan, to establish strong footholds on the mainland. The Triads have set up numerous varied businesses in Guangdong and Fujian Provinces (Booth 1991).

By 1998, the Chinese government recognized that some of its economic policies served as an inducement rather than a deterrent to crime. For example, high tariffs and taxes and other barriers to trade made smuggling consumer goods very lucrative. Illegal imports deprive the government of customs revenue and may seriously disrupt the steady progression of start-up consumer retail business.

As one of the world's leading financial, commercial, and transportation centers, Hong Kong has long been a hub of criminal activity in East Asia. Hong Kong is one of East Asia's major sanctuaries for heroin drug profits. Hong Kong's ethnic Chinese Triads hold control over local criminal activity. Its two largest Triads, 14K and Sun Yee On, continue to "protect" many retail businesses involved in manufacturing and distributing counterfeit CDs and are engaged in buying and selling contraband CDs and other illicit goods (Chin 1991). Like Hong Kong, Taiwan has deeply entrenched organized-crime syndicates in its business and politics. Groups such as United Bamboo and the Four Seas Triads are very influential in Taiwan's local communities.

Chinese organized crime has strong roots in ethnic enclaves around the world. Local Chinese crime groups, ranging from street gangs to Tongs (version of the Chinese Triads; fraternal associations engaged in criminal activities as well as legitimate communal service) are also extensively involved in local rackets, such as gambling, loan sharking extortion, drugs, and prostitution (Kelly, Chin, and Fagan 2000). Europe and North America are major targets for Chinese criminal networks.

Japan

After the end of World War II in 1945, the Yakuza, Japan's main crime syndicate, gained power and popular appeal. The Yakuza were among the world's largest and most powerful crime confederations (Iwai 1986). They were highly structured like the traditional Italian American Cosa Nostra crime families. Yakuza have penetrated Japanese society and achieved some acceptance with society at large. Twenty years ago, according to Japan's National Police Agency, an estimated 3,000 Yakuza groups operated (Kaplan and Dubro 1986). The Yakuza were adept at international crime and set up shop in Manila's prostitution and pornography industries in the Philippines. Elements of the Yakuza also established themselves in Australia as well as in the large Japanese enclave in the Hawaiian Islands. Today, however, as has happened with the traditional La Cosa Nostra in the United States, their influence has declined.

South America and Central America: Colombia and Mexico

As the main source of cocaine for the world market, South America—especially Colombia, Peru, Bolivia, Ecuador, and Venezuela—represents the primary locus of the international drug trade (Lupsha and Cho 2001). Over the last three decades, however, transnational criminal activities linked to South America have expanded beyond the drug trade and become more multidimensional (Inciardi 1991). The continent's increased commercial and transportation links to Europe and Africa as well as the United States attracted foreign criminal organizations including the Sicilian Mafia (Blumenthal 1998). The drug trade in Colombia has helped fuel decades of corruption, violence, political strife, and terrorist insurgencies. The drug traffickers in the large cartels have bought power and influence at the highest levels of the government, judiciary, and financial institutions. Apart from drugs, Colombia is also the world leader in the production of counterfeit U.S. currency.

Although most Central American governments are strengthening their antidrug efforts, they appear to be less rigorous in dealing with the problem of alien smuggling through their countries. No major organizations or cartels control or dominate alien smuggling. Still, nearly 500,000 U.S.-bound migrants are estimated to move through Mexico, Guatemala, Honduras, Nicaragua, and Santo Domingo and are handled by several hundred independent smugglers who cooperate in loosely linked networks stretching across the region from the Gulf of Mexico to the Caribbean archipelagos.

For many years, Mexico has been a hideaway for bandits and a staging area for cross-border smuggling. Criminal activity across the U.S. Southwest border has been stimulated by a real step-up in legitimate commerce occasioned by expanded bilateral trade agreements. The substantial increase in trade between the United States and Mexico resulting from the North American Free Trade Act (NAFTA), though greatly benefiting legitimate business interests on both sides of the border, has also generated greater opportunity for traffickers smuggling in illegal immigrants, drugs, and other contraband (Rumors 2003).

Powerful Mexican drug-trafficking organizations exert considerable influence on the Mexican side of the border. More than half the cocaine smuggled into the United States comes across the southwest border with Mexico. Also, criminal groups smuggle illegal aliens and engage in product piracy, stolen vehicles/auto parts, tobacco, firearms, and alcohol. Mexico is also believed to be one of the top money-laundering countries in Latin America. Mexican drug lords reportedly repatriate much of their profits in bulk cash shipments directly from the United States and recycle these funds in money exchange houses along the border. Their power and influence have significant political and economic impact in Mexico (Lupsha 1995; Pimenal 2003).

United States

Until a decade ago, organized crime in the United States was so tenacious that it was viewed as much more than a mere outlaw way of life. Organized criminal conduct in the United States continues by performing services and providing goods for illicit activities (e.g., pornography, prostitution, and narcotics). Much of the public's fascination and ambivalence about the American underworld may be seen as a consequence of the intangible links between law-abiding and law-breaking elements. Unless someone is a direct victim of a gangster, uncompromising public hostility toward organized crime has always been muted. Moreover, businesspeople have frequently used criminal groups to break employee strikes and to participate in commercial wars over retail and wholesale markets. Gangs have been utilized by legitimate business to frustrate competition and ruin rivals. At the same time, organized crime groups have played important roles in assisting labor unions to resist employers and in putting together the multiethnic labor force. In these roles, gangsters acted as *padrones,* as labor disciplinarians, or as gatekeepers for industrialists concerned with price stability, the control of labor costs, and limiting the number of competitive firms in the industrial arena. Thus, it is naïve to suppose that businesspeople were simply preyed upon as victims. Indeed, the putative victims used the victimizers for their own ends (Kelly 2002).

For more than a century, along with the infiltration of legitimate business through extortion and their more conventional vice activities, organized criminals have enjoyed lucrative relationships with political parties and their urban "machines" (Merton 1957). Many gangsters have become "political merchants" and entrepreneurs and have played significant roles in urban politics by terrorizing and manipulating votes in local elections, by working around and through government bureaucracies, by subverting them, or by using their natural inertia to stymie reforms. As consorts of greedy and unscrupulous businesspeople and cynical politicians, organized criminals represent one element in an illicit and mutually beneficial link that reaches deeply into many social institutions. These relationships tend to blur the distinction between legitimate society and the underworld. Thus, the determination to destroy organized crime is necessarily blunted by the facts that the underworld and the upper world of American society have been dependent upon each other and have been so intertwined that isolating one from the other is almost impossible.

The successful prosecution of Italian American crime families in the 1980s and 1990s portend much about organized crime and its future. Scholarly and popular fiction writing allot much space to the Mafia because the historical record plainly demands such emphasis. Such a focus, however, distorts the contexts in which crime operates and deflects attention from gangsters of other ethnic backgrounds and social settings who are not usually thought of as part of the criminal milieu. However, prosecutors' relentless use of RICO (the Racketeer Influenced and Corrupt Organization Act) has broadened the scope of organized crime to include other ethnic criminals as well as white-collar and corporate offenders.

The idea that organized crime occurs in office suites as well as on the impoverished streets has always been a leading theme of radical criminologists (Chambliss and Block 1981). Consequently, a significant number of modern scholars focus on the conditions that breed organized criminality, the structure and organization of criminal groups, the environments in which they operate, and their ties to the larger, legitimate upper world of American society (Arlacchi 1995). Presently, organized crime in the United States is popularly understood to be a function of three major factors: conspiracy, enterprise, and ethnicity. Perhaps more than in any other area of crime in America, ethnicity matters in affecting the methods of criminal activities, in establishing positions within a crime organization, and in producing the sense of trust and loyalty necessary to unite the group. Similar ethnic background ensures, to some degree, that members share common values. For many observers, ethnicity is a delicate topic that touches on matters of political correctness, though gangsters have never felt bound by such discretion. In the 1963 government hearings where La Cosa Nostra first received public mention, informer Joseph Valachi stated: "I'm not talking about Italians, I'm talking about criminals"—a vital distinction for any discussion of organized crime activities.

American prisons are filled with gangsters of every ethnic background convicted of a wide variety of criminal offenses. Yet until fairly recently, a debate still raged about the meaning of organized crime (Cowan and Century 2002). Although this may seem odd and even trivial given the intensity of law enforcement activity and prosecutions, no one definition seems to have satisfied both practitioners and scholars. Organized crime is not restricted to the activities of the conventional and fairly well-known criminal groups such as the Mafia, La Cosa Nostra, the Triads, Colombian drug cartels, or other ethnic and racial criminal syndicates. In the savings and loan scandal of the 1980s, for example, there were criminal conspiracies between savings and loan officials, including accountants, lawyers, and real estate developers. Such criminal collusion, when compared with traditional organized crime conduct involving no-show construction jobs or protection payoffs, reveals more similarities than differences. Some examples illustrate that much organized crime is committed by otherwise legitimate and official agencies and is as harmful as the crimes of recognized criminal enterprises. Likewise in illicit trafficking, otherwise legitimate businesses and entrepreneurs may engage in illegal activities in goods and services if enforcement is slack and profits are attractive.

Over the decades, commissions, congressional investigative committees, law enforcement agencies, and the media in the United States have used the term *organized crime* to describe a formally structured nationwide conspiracy involving thousands of criminals organized to gain control over whole sectors of legal as well as illegal activities. Historically, organized crime flourished in the absence of serious opposition. In the past, local police departments and prosecutors lacked the resources and tools to mount sustained investigations and prosecution of powerful organized crime figures. Prosecutions such as those conducted by racket buster Thomas Dewey in the 1930s and 1940s in New York City were successful but failed to disrupt La Cosa Nostra's operations and power base (Dewey 1974).

Despite the important work of the Kefauver and McClellan Committees, which exposed a powerful Cosa Nostra, the FBI paid scant attention to the Mafia's existence until 1970 (U.S. Senate Special Committee to Investigate Organized Crime 1951). All that changed in 1970, when Congress passed RICO, the most important substantive anti–organized crime statute in history. Among other things, the bill defined organized crime legally and made it illegal to acquire an interest in, participate in the affairs of, or invest in the profits acquired from an enterprise through a pattern of racketeering activity.

Prior to passage of the Organized Crime Control Act of 1970, the investigation and prosecution of organized criminal groups had not been conducted in a coordinated manner. The U.S. Congress passed the RICO act with the specific intent of combating the infiltration of organized crime into legitimate businesses. Providing a wide range of criminal and civil sanctions to control organized criminal activities, RICO is employed by prosecutors to imprison heads of crime families, to exact forfeiture based on criminal earnings, and to triple the penalties associated with racketeering. Other techniques and tools such as the witness security program (witness protection and relocation), electronic surveillance, immunity from prosecution, the cultivation and recruitment of informants, and antiracketeering laws such as the Money Laundering Control Act of 1986 provide additional support and serve to challenge the status of American organized crime.

RICO made it possible in a single trial to prosecute an entire crime family or gang. Crime family members would be the defendants who participated in the affairs of the same enterprise through a pattern of criminal activity. RICO penalties appeared draconian: once the Supreme Court gave the green light to use the law against criminal enterprises, almost every significant organized crime prosecution was brought under the statute. In New York City, Rudolph Giuliani, the U.S. attorney for the Southern District of New York in the mid-1980s, brought the bosses of all the families (known as "The Commission") to trial on RICO charges and convicted them all on patterns of racketeering activity. The Commission Case is probably the most famous and important organized crime prosecution in U.S. history.

To understand the rise of organized crime, it is necessary to know something about conditions in American society that facilitated its development and evolution. Organized crime thrived in the United States long before the country became fixated on the Mafia. The outlaw gangs of the American western frontier in the nineteenth century ravaged the Native American population and preyed mercilessly on the new settlers. That early tumultuous period passed into American social history and has been sanitized in the country's romantic legends and myths of its pioneer heritage.

The modern concern with crime is associated not with bandits such as Jesse James raiding trains and stagecoaches but with the cities filling up with immigrants, many of whom were escaping from desperate conditions abroad. Nineteenth-century American history is replete with suspicions of newcomers, whose exploitation produced crime and in turn laid the foundations for xenophobic reactions and repressions. That legacy of fear of the immigrant persists even today. For some European arrivals in the nineteenth and twentieth centuries, and for some contemporary waves of immigrants from Central America and the Caribbean rim, the quick illicit money from crime often represents opportunities for rapid advancement up the first rungs of the ladder of social mobility that promised them, and still does, an escape from the squalor of slum life and poverty. Of course, the bulk of immigrants patiently endured the indignities of poverty and remained law abiding, as they do today. A small and persistent percentage of immigrants gravitated toward crime as a justifiable means of skirting the problems of assimilation and acculturation.

The history of this ethnic succession in crime describes a relationship among politics, crime, and minority social status. It first infected the Irish, who formed notorious street gangs in the large cities where they settled. By the end of World War I, the Irish virtually dominated crime and big-city politics. Eventually, the political influence they nurtured enabled them to shift into legitimate occupations in construction, trucking, public utilities, and the nascent civil services, where Irish became synonymous with police work.

The aftermath of the war also brought Prohibition, a defining moment in the American crime scene. The Volstead Act of 1920 forbade the sale and distribution of alcoholic beverages for personal consumption. From a moral standpoint the law was intended to rescue the masses, mainly workers and immigrants, from enslavement to liquor, which the legislation did to some degree. At the same time, Prohibition helped to create unprecedented criminal opportunities for ethnic gangsters who cooperated and competed with the Irish underworld. The subsequent outbreak of murder and mayhem, which was labeled the "Roaring Twenties," witnessed vicious competition and violence for control of the illegal alcohol business (Albini 1971).

La Cosa Nostra

Until the Crime Commission trials and defection of major figures in the American mob, La Cosa Nostra was the largest, most sophisticated, and most powerful crime syndicate in the history of the United States (Cressey 1969). It is unlikely in the foreseeable future that any crime organization will achieve anything approximating the influence of La Cosa Nostra in the country's economic and political life.

In different places and at different times, La Cosa Nostra or the Mafia was identified as "The Outfit," "The Combination," and "The Honored Society." The term *Cosa Nostra* is a variation on the Sicilian Mafia and Neapolitan Camorra, which some Italian immigrants brought with them as part of their cultural heritage when they immigrated to the United States in the twentieth century. La Cosa Nostra became the center, and the main source of continuity and power in the affairs of American organized crime in the mid-1930s, when the competing Italian criminal factions settled their differences in what has become known as the Castellammarese War. The bloody showdowns of gang warfare, which began in New York City, stretched all the way to Chicago and involved Al Capone's powerful syndicate as well as allies of the warring Sicilian gangsters in major cities in the Midwest and along the eastern seaboard.

When the fighting at last came to an end, the two leading antagonists in the struggle, Salvatore Maranzano and Joe (Joe the Boss) Masseria, were dead and the survivors crafted and installed, under the leadership of Charles (Lucky) Luciano, an organization that sustained the central cultural features of the Mafia. It was decreed that only those of Italian descent could be inducted as members ("Made Men") and that the individual "soldier/member" would be subordinated to and for the group and its leaders. Oaths of secrecy and modes of defense were also retained. What did change were the ways the Mafia restructured itself: the tradition of an autocratic "Boss of all Bosses" (*Capo di Tutti Capi*) was now abandoned in favor of a national commission that consisted of the leaders or representatives of the leading families across the nation (Ianni 1972). No one man dominated; decisions were reached through consensus similar to the operational style of an executive administrative apparatus in modern business organizations. Each Mafia family was autonomous on its own turf. The Commission's authority lay in its role as a forum rather than as a board of directors, and over time the Commission gave the Mafia an expansive new scope, stability, and impact across much of the nation.

Understanding the structure and operations of the Cosa Nostra requires recognizing that (1) major components of organized crime in the United States were organized in a nationwide alliance of at least twenty-four tightly knit crime families; (2) the members of these families were all Italians and Sicilians or of Italian descent; and (3) the crime families (usually named after their founders or Bosses) were organized in terms of statuses and functional roles including a "Boss" (*Don*) directing the illegal and legal activities of the members, an "Underboss" (*Sotto Capo*), section leaders (*Capos*), and soldiers at the bottom of the hierarchy. In the pyramid of power, the Bosses were protected by layers of subordinates from responsibility for the crimes committed on their orders. The Mafia families were held together by violence and secrecy known as the code of *omerta*. Over time, however, federal and local law enforcement agencies developed tools to loosen the social glue that kept the organization intact and coherent: immunity from prosecution for evidence, victim security programs to protect witnesses and their families, sophisticated electronic eavesdropping, and the power of RICO to compel evidence. All these changed, dealing the Mafia a lethal blow. Its authority and reputation in the affairs of organized crime remained intact through the 1980s (Jacobs 1999). From 1950 to 1985, it gathered vast, unpublicized power not only in strictly criminal activities but also in the allied fields of labor racketeering and urban machine politics, which deteriorated rapidly under the pressure of relentless RICO prosecutions. Even though the Cosa Nostra has been battered by intense law enforcement efforts, it would be premature to write its obituary.

Organized crime has hardly disappeared from American cities. Although the Mafia may live off its vaunted reputation, new ethnic gangs from Latin America, East Asia, and Eastern Europe have become wealthy through their control of large-scale illicit drug distribution systems (Abadinsky 1999). They are also effective extortionists in their own communities. Whether the new groups will take on Mafia-like style and capabilities is only a matter of conjecture at this point. So far, while the Colombian cocaine traffickers and the Chinese groups organized by Tongs (versions of Hong Kong Triads) have exhibited some Mafia-type entrepreneurial abilities, neither has branched out into other activities in the United States. They have not been able or have chosen not to diversify as widely as the Mafia into mainstream political and social institutions outside their own communities (United Nations 2002).

Black, Asian, Hispanic, and indigenous, multiethnic crime groups seem to be burgeoning and doing well in the United States. They represent a broader spectrum of players than was previously imagined; drugs especially have rewritten the formulas about criminal participation and strategies. The developing consensus among specialists is that organized crime is more complicated than it used to be and that the Mafia families continue to play some part in it—a decisive role in some illegal markets but merely a marginal one in others.

As the President's Commission on Organized Crime noted in 1986, the highly profitable and dangerous business of drug trafficking has attracted younger ethnic criminals, along with lower echelon members of Mafia crime families (President's Commission on Organized Crime 1986). Many of the new criminals are recent immigrants to the United States. Chinese, Vietnamese, Jamaicans, Mexicans, Russians, Colombians, Dominicans, and even Sicilians turn to crime not because the society is closed off to them but because it is so wide open. Thus, the relative freedom and anonymity possible in the United States with its diffusion of law enforcement are inviting to those wishing to "adapt" legitimacy, make as much money as possible doing whatever it takes, and hiding themselves from police scrutiny in the protective cocoons of ethnic enclaves.

One group that is exceptional to the social history sketched above is the African American. The black underworld is far from a monolithic, homogeneous structure of power wielded only by native-born black Americans. Nor is it a mere ghetto appendage of the Mafia rackets and business. Since the late 1960s, in many major U.S. cities the Jamaican Rastafarian "Posses" have operated successful drug rings alongside native blacks engaged in traditional vice activities (Schatzberg and Kelly 1997).

For African Americans and Hispanic ghetto dwellers, one of their most important problems—one that confronted white ethnic immigrants decades earlier—is how to escape poverty through socially approved means when these means are virtually closed.

This problem is resolved to some extent by crime activities. For most ghetto dwellers, the illegal provision of legal goods and services is tolerated widely because it is not seen as intrinsically evil or socially disruptive. Poverty provides its own moral climate for organized criminality in the ghetto with the exception, perhaps, of drug peddling. And even here, escape from the bondage of poverty provides emotional pressure and an acceptable, if ambivalent, context for widespread drug use. It is then the pervasive persistent poverty of the ghetto and its collective despair that is at the basis of recruitment into criminal networks.

Crack cocaine is to the ghetto gangster what illegal alcohol was to the white ethnic during the Prohibition era. Crack is the lucrative *modus vivendi* of today's ghetto drug dealer, the currency of the informal economy. Crack has helped minority criminals to generate impressive amounts of criminogenic assets such as guns, illegal capital, distribution networks, and credit with major cocaine producers. These elements have enabled cocaine gangs to develop street gangs that are much more than juvenile delinquents hanging around street corners seeking the thrills of combat with other youth gangs for control of delinquent "turf." The rise of black gangs in the mid-1980s, primarily the Crips and the Bloods of the Los Angeles ghettos, is due in large part to crack. This is another way of saying that the rise of dangerous street gangs involved in organized crime is an outcome of massive illicit trafficking of cocaine into the United States. The Crips were originally a Los Angeles phenomenon that was estimated in the 1990s at 30,000 strong, spreading eastward principally as purveyors of crack. In 1991, the U.S. Department of Justice placed the Crips and the Bloods (another southern California drug gang at 10,000 strong) in 113 cities across 32 states. Coupled with high unemployment rates among young black males, the conditions for the expansion of minority crime are ever present and ominous.

There is little reason to believe that the crime economy of the new gang will stop growing, whatever the scale of repression mounted by law enforcement, or that it will stay confined to the black ghettos. Although the epicenter remains in the ghetto, which is the zone of hardcore unemployment and utter disillusionment, the gang mystique has spread into middle-class black areas where people are close to panic or vigilantism.

The factors of size, population diversity, economic strength, modern business, transportation infrastructure, and legal protections make the United States a lucrative target for international criminals and provide an environment that supports and sustains international criminal activity originating in the United States and going beyond its borders. In its continental breadth and extensive coastlines, America offers an ideal trading crossroad for Europe, Asia, and the rest of the world—an advantage exploited by international criminals.

Both foreign and domestic crime groups mask their criminal networks and activities through the broad diversity of the U.S. population. With the world's largest and most diversified economy and a very high standard of living, the United States provides numerous opportunities for criminal ventures. Criminals also take advantage of the world's most modern telecommunications, transportation, and financial systems. In the United States, even though the law enforcement system is sophisticated, criminals can effectively hide behind individual legal protections and due process, which no other country provides. The United States is one of the world's leading sources of contraband luxury goods, firearms, and tobacco. Both domestic and foreign crime groups operating in the United States are also involved in car theft rings that illegally ship vehicles out of the country.

The tremendous volume of goods entering and leaving the United States in legitimate trade provides crime groups with unparalleled opportunities to traffic contraband through U.S. ports to overseas destinations. In addition to being a point of origin for contraband smuggled overseas, the United States is used by criminals as a transit country for goods being shipped from one country to another. In the case of Latin America drug traffickers, it is a supplier of precursor chemicals needed in the mass production of illegal drugs. Despite strict regulations and currency reporting requirements, the United States is attractive to international criminals seeking to launder money because of the complexity, strength, and stability of the American economy and financial system.

Interestingly, some U.S. crime groups have established cells and networks in foreign countries. Among the most notorious U.S. crime groups operating overseas are the outlaw elements of motorcycle gangs (Abadinsky 1997). Another powerful crime group with extensive connections abroad is the Mafia. Its Sicilian and Italian links have enabled it to reach across to Europe for drugs and new members, or into Latin America and Asia for gambling and money-laundering opportunities.

How Are Transnational Organized Crime and Illicit Trafficking Related?

As we have seen, crime has become increasingly international over the past two decades, especially in the wake of the Cold War. The post–Cold War environment witnessed the growing integration of the world's economic systems and institutions; the easing of barriers to trade, migration, and travel; and the sophistication of technologies that support global commerce and communications. All of these factors have also increased criminal opportunities across national borders for individuals and organizations worldwide. In recent years, the United States and other countries have devoted significant resources to the investigation and control of what has come to be called "transnational organized crime." At this point in time, however, reliable knowledge about the phenomenon of transnational crime—whether it is indeed a global threat to democracy and free enterprise as it is often portrayed to be—is an important issue that remains unresolved. The literature and data on transnational offenses is only beginning to emerge, and the complexities of law enforcement and political responses are only beginning to be assessed.

For the last quarter of a century, heroin and cocaine have caused great damage to many nations. Also, large-scale smuggling of illegal immigrants into the United States has become more prominent and a serious national issue in many countries. This type of crime that is unconstrained by boundaries appears to have been affected by a number of factors. In particular, the rise in the number of immigrants to the United States is unprecedented. Also, the vast improvement in communication technologies makes borders permeable. Indeed, criminal activities can be carried out in the United States without anyone stepping across a border. No doubt, these factors have played a role in the American crime picture of the past, but they have become very pronounced in the opening decade of the twenty-first century. A sufficient number of incidents have occurred to give substance to general anxieties about uncontrollable foreign crime impinging upon everyday life in America.

Transnational organized crime has attracted considerable media attention. Politically, some very visible activity is in evidence in response to the issue former President Clinton raised in two speeches before the General Assembly of the United Nations in 1995. He observed that transnational organized crime and terrorism were serious problems that threatened the integrity of all nations. He accordingly issued Presidential Decision Directive Number 42 (October 1995) authorizing government agencies to develop initiatives against such crime. In addition, at the 1995 meeting of G7 nations, control of transnational organized crime was a principal item on the agenda. Other policies emerging from these decisions at the programmatic level have included efforts to help other governments (such as Italy, Russia, and Colombia) deal with crime organizations that pose a threat to both them and the United States. During the 1990s and onward to the milestone Palermo meeting of the United Nations in 2000, the U.S. Department of Justice became interested in international crime problems, giving special attention to illicit trafficking in women, precious commodities, drugs, money laundering, and more sophisticated methods of smuggling transnationally. The U.S. government is strengthening its links through its participation in a worldwide network of criminological institutes affiliated with the United Nations. The issues now before us are to estimate the kind of knowledge needed to prevent and control this type of organized criminal conduct.

Summary

Transnational or international organized crime possesses a significance not only for the United States but for all nations. Organized crime and illicit trafficking lead to higher levels of corruption of public officials and penetration of criminals into illicit profits, compromising the integrity of the legitimate global economy. In terms of their scope of action or capabilities, criminal organizations worldwide are transforming themselves to meet the demands of survival in a new world order and to exploit the opportunities presented by a globalizing economy. The dramatic changes in the political order that have swept across the world, as well as the deteriorating economic circumstances in Africa, Latin America, and parts of Europe and Asia, have promoted conditions favorable to the growth of underground or informal economies. Among the pernicious effects, many people have been habituated into working outside the legal framework. The informal or underground economy makes access to weapons easier and generates massive flows of illegal immigrants and refugees. In addition to

the normal difficulties involved in establishing state-to-state cooperation, all of these circumstances and aftereffects work to the advantage of criminal organizations. The appearance of better-or-
ganized, international criminal groups with considerable financial
resources has created the conditions that threaten normal trade,
which in turn nourish growing illicit trafficking enterprises.

How Can States Deter and Contain Illicit Trafficking?

The international scope of the threat of global crime places a pre-
mium on bilateral and international cooperation to develop preventive strategies. If state authority continues to erode in the
wake of globalization, perhaps in a decade the international
crime threat to U.S. interests will likely be more diversified and
have an even more direct impact. The extent and magnitude of
the problem will depend on the global political, economic, and security conditions prevailing at that time. Globalization and technological innovation will change the nature of organized crime.
Although large criminal syndicates will remain powerful players
with worldwide networks, at the same time law enforcement
agencies will continue to cope with even more highly skilled
criminal entrepreneurs. The world in 2025 or 2050 may be populated with large interactive crime networks.

There are many issues relating to illicit trafficking and organized crime. The question of the structure of crime networks is one
that deserves constant oversight. What strategy or strategies
should the international community and national governments
adopt in the struggle against organized crime? What are the objectives of such a strategy? Should the initiative be eradication and destruction of organized crime—or, if that goal remains elusive,
should containment be the goal of international trafficking and
crime control? And if we accept containment as a realistic, achiev-
able objective, what sort of configurations of criminal power can
we tolerate? We believe the highlights of the United Nations
Palermo Conference in 2000 may well shed some light on these issues. The Conference marked an unprecedented step in identifying
transnational organized crime as the key infrastructure in global illicit trafficking. The UN Convention highlighted the fact that illicit
trafficking forms the dark side of globalization, spanning nations
and continents through the exploitation of today's open borders,
new technologies, and massive movement of peoples.

References

Abadinsky, Howard. 1997. *Organized Crime*. 5th ed. Chicago: Nelson-Hall.

———. 1999. *Organized Crime*. 6th ed. Chicago: Nelson-Hall.

Albini, Joseph. 1971. *Mafia: Genesis of a Legend*. New York: Appleton-Century Crofts.

Alexander, Shana. 1998. *The Pizza Connection: Lawyers, Money, Drugs, Mafia*. New York: Weidenfeld and Nicolson.

Arlacchi, Pino. 1985. *Mafia Business: The Mafia Ethic and the Spirit of Capitalism*. London: Verso.

———. 1995. "Men of Dishonor, Inside the Sicilian Mafia." *Journal of Contemporary Criminal Justice* 1 (11): 159–160.

———. 2001. "The Dynamics of Illegal Markets," In Phil Williams and Dimitri Vlassis (eds.), *Combating Transnational Crime*, pp. 5–12. London: Frank Cass.

Barber, Benjamin R. 1995. *Jihad versus McWorld*. New York: Times Books.

Bell, J. Bowyer. 2000. "Conditions Making for Success and Failure: Nonstate and Illicit Actors." *Trends in Organized Crime* 6 (1): 32–61.

Block, Alan. 1983. *Eastside/Westside: Organizing Crime in New York, 1930–1950*. New Brunswick, NJ: Transaction Books.

———. 1991. *The Business of Crime: A Documentary Study of Organized Crime in the American Economy*. Boulder, CO: Westview.

Blumenthal, Ralph. 1998. *Last Days of the Sicilians: The FBI Assault on the Pizza Connection*. New York: Time Books.

Booth, Martin. 1991. *The Triads*. New York: St. Martin's Press.

Chambliss, William, and Alan Block. 1981. *Organizing Crime*. New York: Elsevier.

Chang, Dae H. 1999. "World Ministerial Conference on Organized Transnational Crime." *International Journal of Comparative and Applied Criminal Justice* 23 (2): 141–180.

Chin, Ko-lin. 1991. *Chinese Subculture and Criminality: Non-Traditional Crime Groups in America*. Westport, CT: Greenwood Publishing.

———. 2003. *Heijin: Organized Crime, Business and Politics in Taiwan*. New York: M. E. Sharpe.

Chin, Ko-lin, and Robert J. Kelly. 1997. *Human Snakes: Illegal Chinese Immigrants in the United States*. Final Report, Grant SBR 93–11114, Law and Social Science Program, National Science Foundation, Washington, DC.

Chin, Ko-lin, Robert J. Kelly, and Jeffrey Fagan. 1994. "Chinese Organized Crime in America." In Robert J. Kelly, Ko-lin Chin, and Rufus

Schatzberg (eds.), *Handbook of Organized Crime in the United States*, pp. 213–214. Westport, CT: Greenwood Publishing.

Clark, David. 1996. *Urban World/Global City.* London: Routledge.

Cowan, Rich, and Douglas Century. 2002. *Takedown: The Fall of the Last Mafia Empire.* New York: Putnam and Sons.

Cressey, Donald R. 1969. *Theft of a Nation.* New York: Harper and Row.

Dewey, Thomas E. 1974. *Twenty against the Underworld.* Garden City, NY: Doubleday and Co.

Fagan, Jeffrey. 1989. "The Social Organization of Drug Use and Drug Dealing among Urban Gangs." *Criminology* 27 (4): 633–667.

Falchi, Nino. 1995. *International Migration Pressure.* Geneva: International Organization for Migration.

Fijnaut, Cyrille. 2001. "Transnational Organized Crime and Institutional Reform in the European Union: The Case of Judicial Cooperation." In P. Williams and D. Vlassis (eds.), *Combating Transnational Crime: Concepts, Activities and Response,* pp. 276–302. London: Frank Cass.

Finkenauer, James O. 1994. "Russian Organized Crime in America." In Robert J. Kelly et al. (eds.), *Handbook of Organized Crime in the United States,* pp. 245–268. Westport, CT: Greenwood Publishing.

Flynn, Stephen E. 2000. "The Global Drug Trade versus the Nation State: Why the Thugs Are Winning." In Maryann Cusimano (ed.), *Beyond Sovereignty: Issues for a Global Agenda,* pp. 44–66. New York: St. Martin's Press.

Fuentes, Joseph R., and Robert J. Kelly. 1999, November. "Drug Supply and Demand: The Dynamics of the American Drug Market and Some Aspects of Colombian and Mexican Drug Trafficking." *Journal of Contemporary Criminal Justice* 15 (4): 328–351.

Gambetta, Diego. 1993. *The Sicilian Mafia: The Business of Private Protection.* Cambridge, MA: Harvard University Press.

Handelman, Stephen. 1995. *Comrade Criminal: Russia's New Mafiya.* New York: St. Martin's Press.

Holyst, Bruno. 1998. "Organized Crime in Eastern Europe and Its Implications for the Security of the Western World." In S. Einstein and M. Amir (eds.), *Organized Crime: Uncertainties and Dilemma.* Chicago: Office of International Criminal Justice.

Ianni, Francis A. J. 1972. *A Family Business: Kinship and Social Control in Organized Crime.* New York: Russell Sage Foundation.

Inciardi, James. 1991. "Narcoterroism: A Perspective and Commentary." In Robert J. Kelly and Donal E. J. MacNamara (eds.), *Perspectives on Deviance: Dominance, Degradation, and Denigration,* pp. 38–104. Cincinnati, OH: Anderson Publishing Co.

Iwai, Hiroake. 1986. "Organized Crime in Japan." In Robert J. Kelly (ed.), *Organized Crime: A Global Perspective*, pp. 203–233. Totowa, NJ: Rowman and Littlefield.

Jacobs, James B. 1999. *Gotham Unbound*. New York: New York University Press.

Jamieson, Allison. 1995. "The Transnational Dimension of Italian Organized Crime." *Transnational Organized Crime* 1(2): 151–172.

Kaplan, David, and Alec Dubro. 1986. *Yakuza: Explosive Account of Japan's Criminal Underworld*. Reading, MA: Addison-Wesley.

Kelly, Robert J. 1973. "New Political Crimes and Emergence of Revolutionary Nationalist Ideologies." In R. Serge Denisoff and Charles McCaghy (eds.), *Deviance, Conflict and Criminality*, pp. 220–238. Chicago: Rand McNally Publishing Co.

———. 1979. "The Nature of Organized Crime and its Operations." In Herbert Edelhartz (ed.), *Major Issues in Organized Crime Control*. Washington, DC: National Institute of Justice: 5–51.

———. 1986, October. "The Political-Crime Nexus in the United States." In *Confronting the Security Challenge of the Political Criminal Nexus*, pp. 30–33. Georgetown University Research Colloquium.

———. 1990. "Organized Crime in the United States," In S. Einstein and M. Amir (eds.), *Organized Crime: Uncertainties and Dilemmas*, pp. 203–230. Chicago: Office of International Criminal Justice.

———. 1994, July 27. "Breaking the Seals of Silence: Anti-Mafia Uprising in Sicily." *USA Today*: 76–79.

———. 1999. *The Upperworld and the Underworld*. New York: Kluwer/ Plenum Publishing.

———. 2001. "Organized Crime in the United States," In S. Einstein and M. Amir (eds.), *Organized Crime: Uncertainties and Dilemmas*, pp. 13–28. Chicago: Office of International Criminal Justice.

———. 2002a. "Mafia." *The Encyclopedia of Organized Crime*. Westport, CT: Greenwood Publishing.

———. 2002b. "Al Capone." In *Encyclopedia of Organized Crime in the United States: From Al Capone's Chicago to the New Urban Underworld*, pp. 47–55 Westport, CT: Greenwood Publishing.

———. 2002c. "Organized Crime." In Kermit Hall (ed.), *The Oxford Companion to American Law*. New York: Oxford University Press.

———. (forthcoming). "Osama bin Laden." In *The Notorious*. Westport, CT: Greenwood Publishing.

Kelly, Robert J., Ko-lin Chin, and Jeffrey Fagan. 2000. "Lucky Money for Little Brother: The Prevalence and Seriousness of Chinese Gang Extortion." *International Journal of Comparative and Applied Criminal Justice* 24 (1): 61–90.

Kelly, Robert J., and William J. Cook, Jr. 1998. "Criminal Organizations." *Encyclopedia of Crime and Delinquency.* Vol. II, 175–178. Philadelphia: Taylor Publishers.

Kelly, Robert J., and Robert W. Rieber. 2001, July. "Twelve Years After: The Berlin Wall as Will and Idea" *Journal of Social Distress* 1 (3): 217–228.

———. 2003. *Terrorism, Organized Crime and Social Distress: The New World Order.* London: Psyche-Logo Press.

Kelly, Robert J., Patrick J. Ryan, and Rufus Schatzberg. 2002, December. "Primitive Capitalist Accumulation: Russia as a Free Enterprise." *Journal of Contemporary Justice* 11 (4): 251–275.

Kelly, Robert J., and Rufus Schatzberg. 1995. "From Pistols to Ploughshares: The IRA's Farewell to Arms." *International Journal of Comparative and Applied Criminal Justice* 19 (2): 175–177.

Kenney, Dennis, and James Finkenauer. 1995. *Organized Crime in America.* Belmont, CA: Wadsworth Publishing Co., pp. 272–282.

Klein, Malcolm, Cheryl Maxson, and Lea Cunningham. 1989. "Crack, Street Gangs and Violence." *Criminology, 29* (4): 623–650.

Lee, Rensselaer W., III. 1998. *Smuggling Armageddon.* New York: St. Martin's Press.

Lee, Rensselaer W., III, and Francisco E. Thoumi. 1997, October. "The Political Nexus in Colombia." Paper presented at the Georgetown University Research Colloquium. Washington, DC: National Strategy Information Center.

———. 2003. "Drugs and Democracy in Colombia." In Roy Godson (ed.), *Menace to Society,* pp. 71–79. New Brunswick, NJ: Transaction Books.

Lupsha, Peter. 1986. "Organized Crime in the United States." In Robert J. Kelly (ed.), *Organized Crime: A Global Perspective,* pp. 109–127. Totowa, NJ: Rowman and Littlefield.

———. 1995, Spring. "Transnational Narco-Corruption and Narco-Investment: A Focus on Mexico." *Transnational Organized Crime* 1: 84–101.

Lupsha, Peter A., and Sung-Kwon Cho. 2001. "The Future of Narco-Terrorism: Colombia, A Case Study." In S. Einstein and M. Amir (eds.), *Organized Crime: Uncertainties and Dilemmas,* pp. 423–436. Chicago: Office of International Criminal Justice.

Maloney, Wendy Hall, and Robert J. Kelly. 2000, April. "Notes on School-Based Crime Fighting: International Lessons in Moral Education." *Journal of Social Distress* 9 (2): 71–91.

Martello, Claudio. 1992. "Assessment of Anti-Mafia Legislation and

Strategies for the Future." In Ernesto Savone (ed.), *Mafia Issues: Analyses and Proposals for Combating the Mafia Today,* pp. 139–144, Vienna: United Nations-ISPAC Program.

Merton, Robert K. 1957. *Social Theory and Social Structure.* New York: Free Press.

Mueller, Gerhard O.W. 2001. "Transnational Crime: Definitions and Concepts." In P. Williams and D.Vlassis (eds.), *Combating Transnational Crime: Concepts, Activities and Response,* pp. 12–21. London: Frank Cass.

National Security Council. 1998, May. *The Global Content of International Crime.* Washington, DC: U.S. Government Printing Office.

New York State Organized Crime Task Force and New Jersey Commission of Investigation. 1996. *An Analysis of Russian-Émigré Crime in the Tri-State Region.* Rutgers, The State University of New Jersey, School of Criminal Justice, Newark, NJ.

Norland, Rob. 2001, October. "Pakistan." *Newsweek* 1: 30–33.

Pimenal, Stanley. 2003. "Mexico's Legacy of Corruption." In Roy Godson (ed.), *Menace to Society: Political-Criminal Collaboration around the World,* pp. 72–79. New Brunswick, NJ: Transaction Books.

President's Commission on Organized Crime. 1986. *Final Report: The Impact of Organized Crime Trafficking.* Washington, DC: U.S. Government Printing Office.

"Results of a Pilot Study of Forty Selected Organized Criminal Groups in Sixteen Counties." 2002, September. United Nations Office on Drugs and Crime, Vienna.

Rumors, David M. 2003. *Still the Golden Door: The Third World Comes to America.* New York: Columbia University Press.

Salzman, Michael. 2001, October. "Globalization, Culture and Anxiety: Perspectives and Predictions from Terror Management Theory." *Journal of Social Distress* 10 (4): 337–352.

Schatzberg, Rufus, and Robert J. Kelly. 1997. *African American Organized Crime: A Social History.* New Brunswick, NJ: Rutgers University Press.

Schneider, Jane C., and Peter T. Schneider. 2003. *Reversible Destiny: Mafia, Anti-Mafia, and the Struggle for Palermo.* Berkeley: University of California Press.

Servadio, Gia. 1976. *Mafioso: A History of Mafia from its Origins to the Present Day.* New York: Stein and Day.

Shelley, Louise. 1995. "Transnational Organized Crime: An Imminent Threat to the Nation-State?" *Journal of International Affairs* 48 (2): 463–489.

Shelley, Louise. 2003. "Russia and Ukraine: Transition or Tragedy." In Roy Godson (ed.), *Menace to Society: Political-Criminal Collaboration around the World.* New Brunswick, NJ: Transaction Books.

Soros, George. 1998. *The Crisis of Global Capitalism.* New York: Public Affairs.

United Nations. 2000. *World Migration Report.* Susan F. Martin (ed.). New York: International Organization for Migration.

———. 2002. United Nations Office for Drug Control and Crime Prevention (ODCCP). "The Role of the United Nations in Combating Organised Drug Crime Activities." September. Vienna: United Nations Institute for Strategic Studies.

U.S. Senate Special Committee to Investigate Organized Crime. 1951. *Interstate Commerce—Final Report.* Washington, DC: U.S. Government Printing Office.

Williams, Phil (ed.). 1997. *Russian Organized Crime: The New Threat.* London: Frank Cass .

———. 1999. "Getting Rich and Getting Even: Transnational Threats in the Twenty-First Century." In S. Einstein and M. Amir (eds.), *Organized Crime: Uncertainties and Dilemma,* pp. 19–66. Chicago: Office of International Criminal Justice.

2

Problems, Controversies, and Solutions

The prevalence of transnational organized crime at the end of the twentieth century may be as important as the end of the Cold War itself. The serious challenge that it poses has not been clearly understood, as the UN Conference in Palermo in December 2000 observed. States have been slow in coming to terms with the new features of international crime. The new global gangsters are a different breed from their predecessors: their reach extends beyond local communities, and their ambitions go beyond the borders and boundaries of their home nations. Also, the skills and orientations of modern criminals are more businesslike than the rough-and-tumble street hooligans of folklore.

Transnational Crime Survey

To determine the scope and seriousness of the problem, the United Nations and its agencies have conducted regular surveys on crime trends and the operations of national criminal justice systems (Godson and Williams 2000). The results from countries responding to survey queries concerning the presence and impact of trafficking offenses suggest the following categories in the order of their importance:

- Money Laundering
- Terrorism

- Art and Cultural Objects Theft
- Intellectual Property Theft
- Illicit Arms Trafficking
- Trafficking in Persons
- Trade in Human Body Parts
- Illicit Drug Trafficking
- Alien Smuggling
- Trafficking in Sex: Women and Child Pornography
- Nuclear Smuggling

Money-Laundering: Structure and Characteristics

Money laundering refers to banking and financial activity that seeks to make illegal funds and monies appear legitimate. The process of taking monies and other sources of wealth generated by illegal activities from drug trafficking to gun running and putting them through the legal banking systems has had a massive impact on the world economy. Money laundering has been described as the "life blood" of illicit trafficking operations, but it is also the "Achilles heel" of transnational organized crime (Mueller 1999). The ability to sanitize criminal earnings permits drug traffickers and others to live lavishly from their illegal activity. However, the activities required to "rinse" the dirty money and make it clean also provide law enforcement with opportunities to attack criminal enterprises and criminals themselves. Although major crime figures can separate themselves from street-level crime, they cannot and do not separate themselves from the profits that street-level criminal activity generates.

Today, criminals of every sort, ranging from drug traffickers to stock manipulators and corporate embezzlers must launder the money flowing from their crimes for two main reasons. First, the money trail can become evidence against the perpetrators of offenses; second, illegal money itself can be the target of investigation and seizure. Regardless of who puts the apparatus of money laundering to use, the operational principles are essentially the same. Money laundering may be understood as a dynamic three-stage process that requires: (1) moving funds from a direct association with the criminal activity that generated them; (2) disguising the origins of the money to confuse and frustrate any investigative activity seeking to link and connect illicit money with particular individuals; and (3) making the "cleansed" money available to the criminal or criminal enterprise once again, ensuring that the origins of the monies are securely hidden from law enforcement scrutiny (United Nations Office for Drug Control and Crime Prevention 1998). Successful money laundering also helps to support and finance future criminal activity. Estimates about the amount of illicit money laundered vary, and none can be deemed totally reliable in assessing the magnitude of the problem globally, regionally, or nationally. According to one estimate, however, worldwide money-laundering activity amounts to roughly $1 trillion a year, with $300 to $500 billion of that total representing laundered money related to drug trafficking (Kelly 1994).

Laundering consists of an apparatus that places, layers, and mixes legitimate monies with illicit funds. The illegal system is extensive and worldwide. In essence, the rule in successful money laundering is to approximate, as closely as possible, legal transactions. Thus, the mechanisms and techniques used are themselves minor variations on methods employed routinely by legitimate businesses (United Nations 1999). Many methods may be used for laundering money. Among those favored by criminal organizations are "fronts"—seemingly legitimate businesses that mask and hide illegal activity and provide a set of accounts through which illegal money can be "cleansed." These tend to be cash-based businesses such as hotels, casinos, restaurants, financial service firms, travel agencies, bars, and construction agencies whose ostensibly legitimate operations involve substantial cash flow. This makes it difficult for law enforcement agencies to identify illegal proceeds.

Ever since Al Capone was imprisoned for tax evasion in 1932, financially successful criminals have become more sensitive to ways of protecting their "dirty" money. Some have used a cash business such as a vending machine firm to commingle money from illegitimate sources with legitimately earned money. In the state of New Jersey, for example, a drug-trafficking ring opened a casino account for $125,000 and stayed several days but did not gamble. They then left the hotel with checks payable to third parties, who deposited the checks in a securities firm. The money was later withdrawn—laundered (Grabosky 2001). In 1991, several men from Lebanon and Argentina were convicted of laundering $1 billion in Colombian drug profits through the purchase and sale of gold, using jewelry companies in Houston, Miami, Los Angeles, and New York City as fronts.

Money-Laundering Techniques

Taking advantage of the advances in technology and communications, sophisticated money launderers utilize electronic fund transfers. This is a ready instrument for laundering: usually there are no requirements for bank-to-bank transfers. A bank outside the United States may transfer funds to a U.S. bank and then draw on those funds by checks or credit. Schemes of this type usually involve depositing illicit funds into a bank and then transferring these funds to another, often through a number of countries. Electronically, money can be moved anywhere in the world with speed and ease (President's Commission on Organized Crime 1984).

Bulk transfer is a traditional method of laundering money. Covertly smuggling large amounts of cash across borders has reappeared as a method of repatriating illicit funds as a result of the strong anti-money-laundering measures enacted in many nations and among numerous financial institutions. Also, crime groups have improved their methods of obtaining export/import businesses to hide "dirty money." Money is shipped by air, by sea, and by land and is even smuggled out of the United States through the U.S. Postal Service.

Criminal groups also infiltrate banks and utilize safe havens; they use offshore banking centers such as the Cayman Islands, Aruba, the Philippines, Uruguay, Lebanon, and the Bahamas for laundering purposes. Brokerage firms may also launder money. The nature of the securities industry makes it vulnerable to money launderers. It is international in scope; business is conducted by electronic transfer, and the liquidity of securities is attractive to launderers. Temptations for brokers are ever-present: they often disregard the source of capital and do not make detailed inquiries as to its origins because they typically work on commission in highly competitive markets. These offshore banking centers are routinely used to legitimize and transfer criminal proceeds. Huge sums of money are laundered in the world's largest financial markets, such as Hong Kong, Japan, Germany, the United Kingdom, and the United States—even though extensive legislation in the United States and aggressive enforcement make it more difficult and risky to conduct illicit financial transactions (Hess, Myers, Gideon, Gomez, and Daly 1999).

Several factors may make a country particularly vulnerable to money laundering: lack of adequate legislation or appropriate enforcement that can address the problem, inadequate secrecy laws, weak or corrupted financial institutions, and ineffective regulatory oversight of the financial sector. In Latin America, money-laundering investigations are hampered by massive corruption in the state's regulatory apparatus, inadequate legislation to monitor banking activities, and a lack of trained personnel to conduct investigations and carry out prosecutions (Smith 1991). In Russia and the NIS, Western-style market economies and financial sectors are developing. Organized crime groups gained an early and deep foothold in the processes of privatization and in the new segments of the legitimate economy mainly because law enforcement itself was newly developing as, simultaneously, were banking regulations and oversight (Lupsha and Pimentel 1997).

Offshore banking centers typically offer banks corporate secrecy, low tax rates, ease of corporate formation, and low incorporation fees. These provisions or services create incentives for criminals to conduct illicit financial activities in states where such banking centers operate (Shelley 1997). In Southeast and Southwest Asia and the Middle East, for example, parallel informal banking systems, known primarily as "Hawala," "Hundi," or "Hui Kwan," offer an alternative for laundering funds, outside the formal banking system (United Nations Office for Drug Control and Crime Prevention 1998). These financial systems are increasingly being used by criminals, drug traffickers, and even far-flung terrorist organizations of the al-Qaeda network to launder and move illicit funds long distances because they facilitate rapid and cost-effective money transfers and leave virtually no telltale paper trail evidence for law enforcement investigators. The technique is simple and effective: a money broker takes an order for a money transfer to accounts in other locales that may be around the world. A telephone call is made, and money is moved, deposited, withdrawn, and transferred, based on the reputation of the agents making the calls.

Money-Laundering Threats to National Economies

The International Monetary Fund (IMF) has identified some adverse effects that result from money laundering. Among other things, it leads to greater volatility in foreign exchange markets and interest rates; and it distorts market expectations. Although the economic stability of the United States has not been seriously threatened by money-laundering activities, federal and state governments have been hindered in their efforts to collect taxes and to regulate the banking sector, financial markets, and the business environment at large. In other nations money laundering can destabilize a state's entire economy. In the mid-1990s, for example, widespread money-laundering schemes orchestrated by Mafia and Albanian crime groups led to a crisis in Albania that destabilized its economy and disrupted the lives of millions who were ruined financially in the aftermath (National Security Council 1998). The solvency of Albanian banks eroded as public confidence collapsed following disclosure of the fraudulent schemes.

Money Laundering: BCCI, A Case Study

The Bank of Commerce and Credit International (BCCI), referred to facetiously as the "bank of crooks and criminals international," was founded in 1977 by Palestinian and Arab financiers. Incorporated in Luxembourg, a small nation nestled between France and Germany and known for its bank secrecy laws and casual regulations, BCCI emerged as one of the largest private banks in the world, with offices in seventy-two countries (Beare 1995). The bank divided its corporate headquarters between Luxembourg and the Cayman Islands, countries known for their bank secrecy statutes. BCCI also wrapped itself in a mantle of respectability and influence that included associations with former President Jimmy Carter and a former presidential adviser and head of the Department of Defense, Clark Clifford. In 1992, it was revealed that influential former U.S. senator, Stuart Symington, sought to protect BCCI against accusations that it operated as a full-service bank for drug traffickers and terrorists such as Abu Nidal, the notorious head of "Black September"—a Middle Eastern terrorist group that slaughtered the Israeli Olympic team at the 1972 Olympic games in Munich, Germany. Nidal maintained a $60 million account at the London branch of BCCI. BCCI also served the banking needs of Hezbollah, the Iranian-backed terrorist group operating out of Lebanon.

BCCI also laundered drug money for the Medellín cocaine cartel in Colombia and for the opium warlord, Khun Sa, of the Golden Triangle region in Southeast Asia. The U.S. government alleged that the bank laundered $14 million for the Medellín cartel by accepting cash and placing it in certificates of deposit in its European, Central American, and South American branches. Using certificates as collateral, bank officials created accounts accessible through loans at other branches that permitted the drug traffickers to withdraw the funds. The bank repaid the loans with funds from the certificates of deposit. BCCI activities ended in 1991 when regulators seized the bank's branches in the United States, the United Kingdom, and several other countries.

Types of Money Laundering

In some schemes, money launderers use "smurfs" (persons who convert cash into money orders and cashier's checks that do not specify payees). Transactions are held to less than $10,000 to avoid the need to report the transaction as required by law through a Currency Transaction Report (CTR). One ring of money-laundering smurfs operating out of New York City employed dozens of persons who used about thirty banks in New York and New Jersey to launder nearly $100 million a year for the Cali cartel in Colombia. The checks were pasted between the pages of magazines and shipped to Cali. From there the money was transferred to banks in Panama (Potts, Kocham, and Whittington 1992). As bank technology becomes increasingly electronic, enormous amounts of cash across the globe can be transferred instantaneously, which makes proper accounting exceedingly difficult.

In addition, as we have noted, there are banking safe havens—"offshore" banks such as those in Cayman Islands, which, despite their claims of innocence, service the needs of global criminal enterprises and the illicit wealth they generate. The population of Cayman Islands depends on tourism for income and its unique banking system. The islands have 500 banks and 20,000 registered companies, firms, and business corporations. The financial district has the highest density of banks and fax machines in the world. Most of the banks are "plaques" or postal box offices that lack vaults, tellers, security guards, and all the paraphernalia of a banking enterprise. Cayman Islands is administered by Great Britain, and virtually anyone can establish a "shell" company for a few thousand dollars in legal fees, open an account, and hide behind a wall of strict secrecy. In the framework of money laundering, an attorney acting on behalf of a client can create a paper (a "boilerplate") company in such a haven that has strict privacy statutes. Funds to be laundered can be transferred physically or wired to the firm's account in a local bank. The company then transfers the money to the local branch of a large international bank. The paper company is subsequently able to borrow money from any branch of this bank, using the overseas deposit as security (Walter 1990).

Controls and Law Enforcement Responses to Money Laundering

Given the insidious impact of money laundering on the banking and financial sectors of state economies, one would suppose that efforts to reform the banking industry would take precedence in the struggle to contain money laundering within limits. Thus, measures to increase international attention to money laundering have led many countries to implement money-laundering legislation and other preventive measures. International standards are being established to increase banking transparency and to reduce bank secrecy that disguises asset ownership.

In 1994, not more than fifty countries required their banks (and foreign banks doing business in the host state) to maintain uniform financial records. These statutes of the Federal Act on the Prevention of Money Laundering in the Financial Sector, Money Laundering Act of October 10, 1997, are modeled on the American Bank Secrecy Act of 1972 and the Money Laundering Act of 1986. These legislative weapons have undergone revisions as the laws have matured over time. Also, some international standards are being established to increase banking transparency and to reduce the banks' secrecy and other ruses that hide asset ownership. As of 1998, eighty-five countries required their banks (and foreign banks) to maintain uniform financial records. Although more countries are beginning to establish controls over nonbanking financial institutions, much more needs to be done. In June 2000, the U.S. government issued advisories to U.S. financial institutions noting that the anti–money laundering regimes in these countries cited above were deficient. Control of the problem is best handled by uniform and harmonized laws operating across the world.

Drug Trafficking

Despite the "war" on drugs, illegal narcotics are cheaper, more potent, and more readily available than ever before. The United Nations reports that in recent years, illicit drug consumption "has become a global phenomenon" (Lohr 1992). The growth of the drug problem is not necessarily the sole consequence of failed antinarcotics efforts; in fact, as discussed in Chapter 1, it is also a result of post–Cold War policies that have opened up economic markets, societies, and technologies. Briefly, as societies have democratized and liberalized their economies, they often find themselves facing serious problems with the abuse of illegal narcotics. The rise in drug problems is attributable to many factors, including those that are characteristic of legitimate economic activities that shape market operations in free, democratic societies. For example, criminal markets and black-market entrepreneurs copy entrepreneurial activity that exists comparatively unfettered in democratic societies. Markets, legal or illegal, cater to consumers. Also, the evolution of modern business technology (cell phones, faxes, computers, and the Internet) operating in the legitimate marketplace function most effectively in illegal markets.

Despite decades of intensified eradication programs and aggressive drug control and enforcement efforts, more drugs are being produced and distributed. Gauging the quantities of heroin, cocaine, marijuana, and related substances is difficult because of the illegal nature of producing and trafficking in these drugs. Moreover, consumption of drugs takes place in environments that scarcely lend themselves to public scrutiny. Clearly, this complicates any rigorous assessment of the economic, social, and psychological consequences of illicit drug activity. Indeed, the problem's relentless spread throughout the world has given rise to a greater awareness of the enormous negative effects of drug abuse and trafficking on the economic and social fabric holding societies together. The growth of drug use has occurred within many international statutory structures whose laws and criminal codes have been designed to contain it. In the United States, with nearly a $275 billion investment in drug control programs funded at federal, state, and local government levels for more than two decades, the drug business goes on and has even thrived (U.S. Department of State 1998).

Aside from being more available and affordable today, drugs represent one of the world's largest and most lucrative markets. Estimates of its value run as high as $500 billion. Marketing narcotics and trafficking has become truly global: drug seizures of cocaine manufactured in South America and heroin originating in Southeast and Central Asia and Latin America have occurred increasingly in areas outside the United States. Virtually every nation reports that drugs are more available now than at any other time.

The vaunted "war on drugs" appears to have failed in many respects. This failure may be related to the continual reliance on ineffective antitrafficking strategies. In the United States, for example, the drug trade thrives in states where controls are weak or nonexistent. Such states are often too corrupt to take action to stop the cultivation of drug raw material within their borders. Furthermore, with international trade rising sharply, it is not difficult to mix illicit narcotics into the huge tide of legitimate goods, services, and people across national borders; and it is most improbable that drug seizures will occur that will have a significant impact on the drug-using population (Office of National Drug Control Policy 1997).

Drug-Trafficking Impacts on Nation-State Stability

The expansion of drug trafficking has contributed to social turbulence in many nations. The profits from trafficking are enormous and provide terrorists, insurgents, and criminals with the resources to buy weapons, hire gunmen, and intimidate state agencies. Officials are corrupted by massive amounts of drug money, as a result of which the legitimacy of political and judicial institutions is undermined. Social cleavages can only be sharpened and deepened by illicit profits circulating throughout the economic underground of nations teetering on the brink of economic collapse.

Economic and Social Consequences of Illicit Trafficking

The illicit drug industry outside the United States, which is very destructive to the economy and social welfare of the indigenous societies in which drugs are cultivated, constitutes a great threat as well to the welfare and social stability of the United States. Drug addiction carries a terrible human cost in terms of social, economic, and health concerns, including HIV/AIDS, which especially afflicts users of illicit narcotics (Fuentes and Kelly 1999). The negative effects of addiction on family cohesion poses lifelong negative consequences for the lives of children, the quality of community life, and the workplace in terms of man-hours lost to illness and distress (Kelly 1991). Results from the National Household Survey on Drug Abuse, conducted in 1995, indicated that 14.8 million Americans, or about 6.7 percent of the population twelve years or older, were current users of illicit drugs. Moreover, in 1999, according to a study sponsored by the Office of National Drug Control Policy (ONDCP), Americans spent $63 billion on illegal drugs. The National Institute for Drug Abuse estimated that the total cost of drug abuse in the United States, including health care and lost productivity, was $110 billion in 1995. In terms of decreased productivity and lost earnings, drug use is estimated to cost $77 billion a year (Inciardi and Saum 1996).

Illicit Drug Production

The most dangerous drugs abused in the United States are cocaine (and crack), heroin, methylenedioxymethamphetamine (MDMA) (known popularly as "ecstasy"), and methamphetamine (speed). According to the Drug Enforcement Administration (DEA), the bulk of "ecstasy" and "speed" is manufactured in Mexico and distributed in the United States. The source countries for heroin and cocaine are in Asia and Latin America. Cocaine is produced in the South American Andean countries of Colombia, Peru, Bolivia, and Ecuador. The United States constitutes the largest market for cocaine and its byproducts such as "crack."

Drug-Trafficking Networks

International drug-trafficking organizations have extensive networks of suppliers and front companies that facilitate narcotics smuggling and the laundering of illegal earnings. In the Western Hemisphere, Mexican and Colombian trafficking organizations have dominated the drug trade. Colombian cartels supply most of the cocaine through Mexican transshipment syndicates that arrange distribution in the huge American market. In the Asian source regions, heroin production is dominated by large trafficking groups. The Asian trafficking networks are more diffuse than their drug organization counterparts in Latin America: heroin shipments from Asian sources (southeast or central regions) typically change hands among many criminal organizations on their way to their destination. Trafficking patterns in general are more like the Asian groups, which are capable of smuggling not only drugs but also people and other contraband (United Nations International Drug Control Programme 2001). In general, the trends indicate that traffickers in many countries are rejecting traditional types of criminal partnerships with similar ethnic and racial groups and are increasingly collaborating in the purchase, transport, and distribution of illegal drugs with different types of organizations, including rebel armies, terrorist groups, and other ethnic criminal organizations that can protect turf and generate revenue.

Taking advantage of more open borders and modern telecommunications technology, drug trafficking has quickly adapted to law enforcement pressures by finding new methods for smuggling, new routes, and new mechanisms to launder money. In many of the major cocaine- and heroin-producing countries and states and among those that are transit routes for smuggling, traffickers have acquired significant power and influence through the use of violence, intimidation, and the bribing of corrupt officials (Chin 1999). These states include Colombia, Peru, Albania, Bulgaria, Poland, Russia, Cuba, and Nicaragua. They have also experienced a significant rise in drug addiction that is a result of their direct or indirect involvement in the drug trade. In some countries, large segments of the population are also stricken by HIV/AIDS, which further undermines economic growth. The social, economic, and political stresses associated with these problems are felt across national borders and contribute to regional tensions and problems (Bryant 1990).

Drug Market Structure and the Trafficking Industry

In the illegal drug market, the cocaine cartels link the points of coca growing with the street user of crack (a cocaine derivative), a chain that is sometimes described as stretching from "the nose to the pipe." One of the most important features of the drug industry concerns the consumers who form markets for the products. They have little power over price or the quality of the product partly because of the illegality of purchasing and using narcotics. The fact that so many users of these illegal drugs are addicted and dependent on their availability further diminishes the product consumers' capacity to affect quality, price, and availability. Nevertheless, it is their demand for illegal drugs that has stimulated the emergence and growth of powerful criminal organizations engaged in this form of enterprise crime (United Nations International Drug Control Programme 2001).

The supply side of the cocaine industry has been dominated by Colombian cartels, which have not only turned cocaine into

Latin America's most successful export product but have also provided the most successful focus for economic integration among the three countries most involved in the cocaine trade: Peru, Bolivia, and Colombia. There is clear specialization among the three, with Peru, which has over 285,000 acres under cultivation, being the most important cultivator. Bolivia has between 88,000 and 110,000 acres for coca cultivation. Colombia is not an important producer of coca but is both the largest producer of cocaine hydrochloride and the corporate headquarters of the Andean cocaine industry. The emergence of Colombian cartels as the major organizers and suppliers of cocaine may be explained in terms of geographic location. Colombia is adjacent to the major coca growers and has access to the Caribbean and Central America, including Panama, which has extensive money-laundering facilities, a long entrepreneurial tradition, and the availability of a network of Colombians in the United States who provide access to retail markets. The Colombian drug-trafficking organizations have been transnational from the outset. They developed in the 1970s from small smuggling groups into major enterprises partly because they figured out that smuggling increasingly significant loads of cocaine into the United States could mean huge gains. To do this they utilized aircraft, which enabled them to smuggle more volume.

The cartels also developed an increasingly sophisticated set of organizational arrangements in which cooperation among various groups with different specializations greatly enhanced their combined effectiveness, efficiency, and resistance to disruption. The Cali cartel, in particular, had developed a highly specialized and compartmentalized set of operations in which some of the tasks such as money laundering were implemented by what were, in effect, specialized service organizations. The industry has also experienced considerable vertical integration, with the cartels taking responsibility for collecting the coca leaf or coca paste from the peasants, acquiring precursor chemicals, processing them into cocaine hydrochloride, transporting to the United States, supervising wholesale distribution, and even handling some retailing. The industry itself was a particularly profitable one partly because there was little threat from substitute products. The peasants who sell the coca leaf are relatively weak (except in Bolivia, although even there, these efforts are directed mainly against government attempts at eradication rather than at getting a better deal from the traffickers). Drug consumers are also in a weak position because their activity is illegal and they are fragmented as a group.

Although certain benefits come from the illicit nature of the industry, in other respects it resembles legal industries. It is not particularly demanding technologically, but there is considerable product innovation. The development of crack cocaine in particular was a brilliant marketing move, albeit one that has had disastrous consequences for many cities in the United States. In assessing the cocaine industry, therefore, it is necessary to acknowledge that it is based on strong market principles but is run by organizations that combine conventional business skills with considerable ruthlessness and a total disregard for laws and rules (Williams 1992).

The illicit drug industry has also undergone some significant changes. In the early 1980s, it was dominated by the Medellín cartel in which Pablo Escobar, the Ochoa family, and Carlos Lehder played key roles. The Medellín cartel initiated a frontal assault against the Colombian state. Anxious to eliminate the extradition treaty with the United States, the cartel murdered politicians, members of the judiciary, and government officials who opposed its activities. With the capture of Lehder and the effective abandonment of the extradition treaty (a shift in governmental policy that encouraged traffickers to turn themselves in), the Medellín cartel was gradually weakened. Even before the killing of Pablo Escobar in December 1993, the other major Colombian cartel, located in Cali, had established itself not only as Colombia's premier drug-trafficking organization, but also as the Third World's most successful transnational corporation, albeit an illicit one. Most recently, a number of small independent illicit firms and inroads made by law enforcement officials have challenged the position of the Cali cartel. Nevertheless, the organization has been resilient and robust—not least because it has coopted rather than confronted the local and regional, if not the national, power structure. No less importantly, the Cali cartel also initiated an important process of diversification, moving into the more lucrative heroin trade (Lee 1992).

The heroin industry differs from the cocaine trade in that the growing and refining areas are more diverse. The major regions where opium is grown are the Golden Triangle of Burma, Thailand, and Laos, and the Golden Crescent of Iran, Afghanistan, and Pakistan, along with Mexico (which produces *injectable* black tar heroin). The opium itself comes from the poppy plant and is refined into morphine and either heroin-3, which is smokeable, or heroin-4, which is dissolved in water and taken intravenously. Burma and Afghanistan are the most important opium growers in the world, and much of the processing of opium into heroin is done in Burma and in locales in Southwest Asia before it is shipped to European and American markets.

Efforts to disrupt the heroin industry at its source have proved impossible, partly because Burma lacks a strong legitimate government. Indeed, the country has long been characterized by considerable internecine strife in which opium warlords and ethnic insurgents who desire autonomy from the Shan State (the center of the opium growing region) are remnants of two Kuomintang armies that fled into Burma when Chiang Kai-shek was defeated by the Chinese communists in 1949. Perhaps most famous of all is Khun Sa. With his Shan United Army, he has been one of the most important drug lords in Burma.

Related to the changing fortunes of individual trafficking groups has been a geographic shift; in recent years, the focus of much activity has gone from the Burma-Thai border to the Burmese border with China's Yunnan Province, where a considerable amount of refining is also done. Some of the heroin coming out of the Golden Triangle goes through Bangkok, where it is routed directly to Western Europe for the United States, or transshipped through Malaysia and Singapore. There is also an overland route from Burma through China's Yunnan Province to Hong Kong, which seems to have taken on increasing importance (Fuentes 1998).

As discussed in Chapter 1, the Chinese Triads based mainly in Hong Kong play a crucial role in the heroin-trafficking industry. The Triads, as already suggested, are secret societies that engage in many types of criminal activities, including drug trafficking, extortion, large-scale human smuggling, and gambling. Hong Kong provides an excellent distribution center from which heroin can be sent to destinations in the United States and Western Europe. Triads control much of the trafficking in illegal immigrants and heroin that comes from Hong Kong through New York, representing the largest Chinese gateway for illicit trafficking into the United States; much of the trafficking in heroin is also routed via Vancouver and Toronto, Canada, both of which have significant Chinese populations, utilizing cells and networks in these target "host" locales (Flynn 1998).

Another important opium-growing country is Afghanistan.

Much of its opium is refined in Pakistan, especially in the Northwest Frontier Province. The government has little control over this area, which has been described as a sanctuary for heroin manufacturers and, more recently, al-Qaeda and Taliban terrorists. Although significant amounts of heroin are consumed locally by a substantial and growing addict population, heroin is also exported to Europe and the United States. Pakistani trafficking groups play a crucial role, but perhaps as significant are the Turkish criminal organizations that exploit Turkey's geopolitical location between Southwest Asia and Europe and operate transshipment points in the trafficking phase of the drug smuggling.

Smuggling Nuclear Materials and Arms

India and Pakistan are now both nuclear states; therefore, recent tensions between them are all the more threatening (Margolis 2000). Also, Iran and North Korea have proclaimed nuclear infrastructure capabilities; and Sudan, Syria, and the Palestinian Islamic jihad are actively designated on the United States government's terrorist list. Nonstate groups such as Osama bin Laden's al-Qaeda terrorist network have been trying to develop nuclear capacities, as has Aum Shinrikyo, the Japanese group that carried out a sarin nerve-gas attack in the Tokyo subway system in 1995. Although the technological obstacles against building long-range nuclear weapons equipped with reliable delivery systems (i.e., ballistic missiles) remain high, the bar is low for acquiring "dirty" nuclear devices. These devices may consist of small amounts of radioactive materials, whether bomb grade or not, and as such could create immense havoc. In one recent incident along these lines, a Chechen separatist group obtained a small amount of radioactive material (apparently from a nuclear lab in the former Soviet Union) and left it in Gorky Park in the heart of Moscow as a warning to Russian authorities that their demands for the political autonomy of Chechnya must be taken seriously.

According to John Deutch, a former director of the U.S. Central Intelligence Agency (CIA):

> The chilling reality is that nuclear materials and technologies are more accessible now than at any other time in history, due primarily to the dissolution of the former Soviet Union and the region's worsening economic conditions. The protection of fissile materials in

the former Soviet Union has become even more critical at the same time that control has become more difficult . . . the breakup of the Soviet Union, the opening of Russian society, and its economic difficulties have subjected the security system to stresses and risks it was not designed to withstand.

As nations have retreated and their governance has slackened and lost control of vital national resources, organized criminals stepped in to fill the void. Criminal groups have created an active black market in nuclear materials. Highly enriched uranium and plutonium, beryllium, radium, palladium, and lithium are just some of the component materials of nuclear weapons trafficked out of the former USSR and Warsaw Pact countries (Deutch 1996). Much of the smuggling appears to be *supply driven;* that is, it has been prompted by the collapse of internal state protection mechanisms rather than by the demand of specific customer needs at the time of theft. However, given the availability of materials, the expertise to assemble components, and the difficulties surrounding Russia's law enforcement capabilities, a great deal of smuggling into countries such as Iran and Palestinian territories is on the rise. In addition, materials utilized in civilian nuclear power and research facilities are even more vulnerable to theft and smuggling (Zimmerman 1995).

Weapons of Mass Destruction

Since 1987, the proliferation of weapons of mass destruction (WMD), mainly nuclear weapons, has been a formidable and growing problem. Relatively weak states can gain enormous stature by acquiring nuclear, chemical, or biological weapons. Such capabilities are seen as particularly dangerous when they are acquired by states that do not share the norms and conventions of international society. North Korea and Iran, for example, are regarded as particularly unpredictable and dangerous nations. North Korea has openly declared that it possesses nuclear bomb capabilities. In order to prevent these states from acquiring WMD, the international community has attempted to implement a series of nonproliferation standards and protocols. These standards have not only been imperfect, but have been undermined by the operation of a market that includes both licit and illicit business. The participants in the WMD market from supply networks are able to circumvent complex, multilayered export control regimes and thereby move the most advanced technology to the consumer state with virtual impunity.

The commodities of weapons proliferators are the equipment, materials, and land technology used in the production of WMD. Except in rare cases, WMD are not available on the international market. When a state takes the decision to develop WMD capability, it must create a research and development infrastructure and then rely on indigenous production. Once the process engineering and production capacity has been installed, the state must import—or produce—the raw materials needed for the weapons. The actual manufacture of the weapon is in most cases independent of the international market and is outside of the area of focus. It is the creation of the domestic capacity that is dependent on transnational organizations.

Nuclear Theft and Smuggling: The Threat

The dissolution of the Soviet Union made large quantities of weapons susceptible to theft or diversion as the security of production and storage facilities diminished. Never before had an empire disintegrated while in possession of multiple nuclear weapons in its military arsenal, including at least 40,000 tons of chemical weapons and significant biological weapons capability. Adding to the danger was the fact that thousands of scientists, engineers, and technicians were left adrift, unsure of income. The momentous political event of 1989—the fall of the Berlin Wall—created a vast supermarket of nuclear weapons (Lee 1998). Moreover, the threat is a multifaceted one. The supply of nuclear materials attractive to terrorists and criminal groups resides in just a handful of states, but the demand is widespread and may include substate groups (al-Qaeda) in addition to "rogue" states such as North Korea. Nuclear material in the former Soviet Union has become increasingly susceptible to theft. Political and social turmoil worldwide has simply increased the appeal of nuclear material as a means of amassing power, exerting influence, or seeking retribution.

How serious is the problem? An accurate assessment of the problem would be difficult at this juncture, although the United Nations International Atomic Energy Agency (IAEA) has identified nearly 150 confirmed incidents of international nuclear smuggling between 1993 and 1996 (Allison, Cote, Falkenrath, and Miller 1996). Such a view could be very misleading, however, since it is based on incomplete data (IAEA 1996). New criminal trade channels are likely to open up new opportunities in view of the political unrest in Central Asia and in several former Soviet republics. Russia is experiencing a particularly serious problem as regards diverting sensitive nuclear materials inasmuch as the specialists and scientific/technical elements in the military/industrial complex find themselves without jobs or future career prospects. Apparently, two main markets for nuclear materials have arisen in postcommunist Eurasia and the oft-disputed borders created by the Himalayas. In addition, there are the disorganized, supply-driven, and amateurish trade patterns that converge through myriad smuggling routes, and the shadow market organized by professionals and brokered by criminal and corrupt officials with huge illicit trafficking infrastructure resources. The shadow market presents a particular danger, representing a direct challenge to Western security (Williams and Woessner 1996).

The Impact of Change

The centers of weapons design and production in the former USSR, which had been known as "secret cities," were off limits to foreigners and anyone not cleared for access. With the collapse of Soviet control structures, the KGB was replaced with the fledgling Russian Federal Security Services (FSS); these "cities" experienced an influx of thieves, criminals, and profiteers, which catalyzed the spread of nuclear-related crime. In the post-Soviet era, borders became porous and guards were easily bribed, as a result of which most of the theft and trafficking originated with opportunistic insiders in the nuclear complex. Some acted individually, whereas others mobilized a number of accomplices when the components required technical expertise to disassemble, transport safely, and reassemble. A breakdown in discipline and moral standards, coupled with motives of personal gain, helped to create an atmosphere conducive to nuclear materials trafficking.

In such dire circumstances, even government agencies may be susceptible to corruption and conspiracy to traffic: powerful bureaucracies and agencies employing thousands might be more interested in generating revenues and protecting the livelihood of employees than in promoting countertheft policies. Economically hard-pressed government employees may emphasize profits and survival in a crisis and turn a blind eye to violations of their own export control and enforcement policies. Generally, conditions in Russia and the NIS have favored the growth of nuclear material and weapons trafficking.

Biological and Chemical Weapons

Biological warfare—or germ warfare, as it was known in the 1950s—is associated with massive, unpredictable, and potentially uncontrollable consequences. With the onset of the Cold War following World War II, the development of germ warfare in the United States, the Soviet Union, and in other countries was frenzied, often poorly planned, and of course shrouded in secrecy. Unlike nuclear weapons, biological weapons are tactical, not strategic, because a large quantity of a chemical weapon is required to destroy a small number of enemies. In 1972, the United States signed the Convention on the Prohibition of the Development, Production, and Stockpiling of Bacteriological (Biological) and Toxin Weapons and on Their Destruction, commonly known as the Biological Weapons Convention. The Soviet Union supplied much of the language of the treaty and became one of the three so-called depository states for the treaty. (The other two signatories were the United States and Great Britain.) The convention solidified the international venue for oversight of biological warfare.

In the chemical weapons field there are two key acquisition goals: (1) to accumulate precursor chemicals, and (2) to stockpile corrosion-resistant manufacturing equipment. The basic components of the nerve agents—oxygen, phosphorus, hydrogen, carbon, fluorine, and sulfur—all exist, in one form or another, in every country in the world. The state seeking a chemical weapons capability therefore needs time and energy to turn these basic building blocks into the complex molecules that can be used as weapons agents. The industry is so structured that some firms produce precursor chemicals while others utilize the intermediaries to make final commercial products. The trade in precursor chemicals is extensive, involving hundreds of millions of tons per year. In most countries, the precursors that are of greatest utility for chemical weapon manufacture are controlled by export restrictions. Yet the vast legitimate application of these compounds makes it relatively easy to hide their illegal movements. A state seeking a chemical arsenal must develop sources of precursors that can meet its weapons production requirements. Precursor chemicals are considered "commodity chemicals" in the industry in that there is little product differentiation between producers, the cost is uniform across producers, and production is undertaken by several manufacturers. Supply networks for precursors of an illegal chemical weapon site, however, are essentially the same as the networks utilized by commercial manufacturers for legal chemical products. In the commercial case, chemical manufacturers often multisource their precursors even if they have to pay a little extra for one of the sources. Such an approach ensures continued supply even if a particular precursor manufacturer encounters production problems. For the chemical weapons producer, the same multisourcing technique is a logical response to the threat of export enforcement efforts. Many of the chemical weapons agent production techniques require the use of specialized pipes, fittings, and reactor vessels. Such equipment is difficult to manufacture, and only a handful of countries have the domestic capacity for their construction. Consequently, supply networks for special chemical manufacturing equipment must be developed to link the countries that have the available manufacturing technology to the end user. Once the network has been assembled, it facilitates the movement of the equipment to the consumer.

Yet another proliferation concern is the spread of advanced missiles. Like nuclear weapons, guided missiles require a significant industrial infrastructure if indigenous production is to succeed. Missile airframes, engines, pumps, valves, guidance, and telemetry systems are just a few of the sophisticated components that must be developed. As with chemical weapons, however, states that seek to procure weapons are not forced to perform all the manufacturing steps themselves. Iraq, for example, purchased SCUDs from the Soviets in the 1980s and then modified them in ways that extended their range during the Gulf War in 1991. Even local modification, however, required a significant domestic infrastructure, based on foreign manufacturing and testing equipment. Iraq purchased machine tools, inspection equipment, and testing systems abroad. The acquisition of these technologies was supported by the same network as used for its WMD programs.

The programs described here share many of the same technologies used in nuclear medicine, machine tool manufacturing, pesticide production, and the like. These industries operate in a set of legitimate markets that are supported by their host nations. The companies that research, develop, produce, market, and distribute these technologies do so in search of profits. They work hard to expand their customer base and to develop new markets for their products. Of course, the majority of these legitimate national and multinational firms rarely cross the line to include criminal behavior. Nonetheless, the profit-driven market structure facilitates the transnational supply of weapons technologies to pariah and rogue states, even when the international community and domestic export restriction legislation seek to deny these technologies to such states. The legitimate firms in the market provide the source of equipment and materials for these states, which desire weapons-use front companies and *prime contractors* to connect their nefarious technology needs with those of law-abiding companies. Ironically, legitimate firms are not necessarily aware of the end use of their product and so find themselves inadvertently dealing with criminal firms masking the purpose of their activities.

The trafficking process applicable to biochemical weapons technologies is similar to that involved in narcotics trafficking. Both processes attempt to move a product from a willing seller to a willing end user without the knowledge of, or interference from, other parties. Although both markets keep the contents of shipping materials secret, for the biochemical weapons technology market it is the destination rather than the source that is sensitive.

During the early 1990s, Iraq was believed to have come close to using anthrax (a single-celled bacterium that feeds on meat) on the Allied coalition forces. If Iraq had laid down a strain of anthrax during the first Gulf War, Allied casualties might have been the largest sustained by any army in history. Also during the Gulf War of 1991, the Iraqis made large quantities of botulinum toxin or botulism, which is one of the most powerful toxins known. The Iraqi government admitted that it had manufactured enough botulism to kill every person on earth a thousand times over. The intrigues and mysteries of stockpiles of Iraqi chemical munitions remain unsolved as a result of the corruption in the current wartime Iraq. Anthrax spores were sent through the U.S. mail immediately after September 11 to major politicians, officials, and leading figures in the news broadcasting industry. The dried anthrax spores had the potential for becoming lodged in the lungs and eventually migrating into the bloodstream. Indeed, death followed quickly for at least two of the exposed victims.

One consequence of the increasingly interconnected nature of the present world is that minor outbreaks of disease in a remote region could result in pandemics. Terrorists, of course, aware of this fact, seek to take advantage of this vulnerability and sow the seeds of a devastating disease. A bioterror attack involving infectious particles can be stored in a small vial, which is much easier to smuggle into a country than a nuclear device. A smallpox plague initiated by such means could produce enormous social unrest and political instability. Bioterrorism is indeed a matter of heightened concern, as highlighted by the warning by the Centers for Disease Control (CDC) to New York public health agencies, in the wake of 9/11, to be on the lookout for disease entities.

There are some important similarities in the drug-trafficking and biochemical-trafficking markets. In summary, the participants in the drug and biochemical technology markets operate in a hostile environment designed to prevent, obstruct, or disrupt their activities. In both the drug- and biochemical-trafficking cases, the organizations involved tend to display considerable resilience, impressive adaptive capabilities, great ingenuity and skill in circumventing law enforcement and export control efforts, and garner more and more profits in spite of the obstacles they encounter. The results can be seriously damaging to national and international security. Drug abuse and violence are closely related, and the drug-trafficking organizations both thrive on and exacerbate political chaos in countries such as Burma and Afghanistan. In a similar vein, biochemical weapons supply networks can undermine international regimes and provide capabilities to states hostile to the values of the UN member states, such as the EU and the Organization of American States.

Law Enforcement and Control Efforts

In the case of biochemical weapons, the poles of the market should be the prime target of law enforcement and control efforts. This means reducing incentives for states to acquire biochemical weapons technologies, notably by rendering such capabilities unnecessary through more satisfactory security arrangements. Success in this effort is particularly difficult, however, with pariah states such as North Korea. The alternative is to impose such high costs on circumventing international regimes to acquire prohibited technologies that such a course of action no longer appears attractive. This is of course easier said than done.

Illicit Arms Trafficking

If international networks of weapons producers and supplies were not available, many regional and national armed conflicts would not be possible. Ethnic, religious, and nationalist wars as well as the proliferation of arms trafficking are attributable to the openness of markets for buying and selling weapons. The profitability of arms manufacturing and the collapse of Cold War national alliances, with the consequent loss of the services provided by national police and military organizations, greatly diminished the safety and security of many regions of the world. As a result, tribal, religious sects, clans, and extended family groups have been called upon to perform many of the public safety and order functions formerly assigned to state agencies (Timmerman 1990).

Local conflicts and clashes can disrupt economies by destroying civil order and domestic life and can also set the stage for perpetuating age-old conflicts as warlords, gangs, and bandits alongside guerrilla terrorist organizations compete for control. In many regions of Southeast Asia (Burma, Laos, Thailand, Kashmir, Pakistan, and the Philippines), East Africa (Somalia, Eritrea, and Yemen), Central Africa, the Middle East, and the Andean countries of South America, the presence of illicit arms promotes conflict and terrorist violence. Indeed, in Somalia, Vietnam, Peru, Colombia, Sierra Leone, and numerous other countries in the world, entire generations possess skills that are primarily military and violent; when legitimate economic opportunities disappear, they will naturally turn to criminal activity for survival's sake. Warlordism thrives in places where the distinction between crime and politics is murky. Theft, extortion, and contraband traffic enrich criminal groups and also enable ethnic and religious groups to push their goals and objectives through warfare, jihad, and terrorism. And they can do so today on a scale that has been made possible by the prevalence of weapons of all sorts and of all levels of sophistication and destructive power.

A historic fact has been shattered by the post–1989 world in which globalization is the increasingly dominant economic and political reality. During the Cold War conflicts between the two superpowers, small-arms trafficking, including technologically sophisticated automatic infantry weapons and rocket-propelled grenade rifles (RPGs)—the weapon of choice of al-Qaeda and terrorist organizations worldwide—was early on a system of weapons manufacture and procurement controlled by the two powers. Together, the United States and the USSR could adjust the political temperature in their Third World "client states" by expanding or contracting access to the gun and weapons markets. The controls were generally of two sorts. On the supply side of the market, the major powers influenced and even controlled the movement of weapons ammunition and spare parts around the world (Williams 1997). On the demand side, the ability to obtain weapons, whatever the cause or purpose, depended greatly on the ability to pay. Today, neither constraint obtains: weapons are now available to all who can pay, and the means of paying have become possible for a diverse group of terrorists, militants, religious sects, paramilitary forces, and organized criminals. Despite comprehensive treaties and international agreements that control arms transfers, illegal arms proliferation and transfer remains a serious threat.

Dynamics of Arms Trafficking: The Cold War

In past eras, at the conclusion of a major war, arms production would fall rapidly and the availability of weapons would decline sharply. These conditions affected the durability and intensity of guerrilla wars, political insurrections, colonial liberation struggles, insurgencies, and the capacities of criminal groups to engage in sustained violence. In the aftermath of World War I, the view emerged that the responsibility for the massive carnage and violence of the war lay with the manufacturers of weapons who secretly instigated political crises in order to sell their lethal merchandise. Efforts were therefore made at the national and international level to impose controls on the manufacture and distribution of weapons, but these efforts failed. Only in the wake of World War II did international agreements emerge that would at least regulate arms production and sales. But none of these could amount to much because so many weapons of all kinds lay in numerous battlefields across the world. With the exception of China, which, in the immediate post–World War II period was engaged in a major civil war that loomed across its mainland from 1946 through 1949, there was no serious concern beyond immediate civilian safety in war-torn countries to round up, inventory, and control the dissemination of small arms and other weapons designed for conventional warfare.

The United States was preoccupied with the spread of atomic weapons to the Soviet Union—America's principal antagonist in the emerging Cold War. The Marshall Plan was designed to rebuild the countries destroyed during the war, and was concerned with discovering and confiscating land mines and arms that were being smuggled into regions of Western Europe, the Balkans, and southeast Mediterranean countries where communists were a potential threat in the outbreak of civil wars.

In the post–Cold War period meetings of the North Atlantic Treaty Organization (NATO) treaty signatories, the G7 states, SEATO members, the OAS council, and the United Nations attempted to examine their control agency efforts against arms and weapons smuggling. A restrictive protocol common to all agreements concerns export licenses. These would be issued on the condition that a purchaser of arms must produce an end-use document specifying that the weapons would be employed solely for the use of the country's military forces and would not be transferred to third parties without the permission of the country of origin. At the same time, during the Cold War, the United States and the Soviet Union produced sophisticated equipment for their own forces, allies in NATO, and the Warsaw Pact, respectively. Both powers gave away or transferred second-hand materials to Third World satellites.

For several decades after 1945, it was generally accepted that it would be difficult to restrict light weapons (hand guns, infantry weapons). Major weapons systems (missiles, aircraft, tanks, and heavy ordnance) were subject to political controls by the NATO and Warsaw Pact alliances concerning the universal acceptance of the end-user certificate. Still, gun runners managed to figure out ways around these regulations. In the 1960s, wars of colonial liberation in Africa attracted entrepreneurs and adventurers into the arms supply trade. Later, with world production accelerating in the 1970s, the black market began to disintegrate, especially in the light-weapons business. By the 1980s, the market collapsed completely. The United States, the USSR, and other major industrial countries decided to keep arms production at wartime levels (Naylor 2001), and the end of the Cold War did little to reverse the trend.

A nation has many reasons for creating and keeping its own arms industry operational. A domestic arms-producing sector is often considered essential to assure survival of the nation-state and to provide diplomatic clout in international relations. Equally important, the arms industry may become an important and irreplaceable source of jobs and economic growth (Naylor 1995). The expansion of technological development has meant that more arms are produced than can be absorbed by the arsenals of the producing countries' own armed forces. The result has been that arms-producing countries have promoted arms exports. Today, the arms business has been almost completely commercialized just at the point when arms are their most lethal (Ratner 1996).

Arms Trafficking in the Post–Cold War Era

In the contemporary scene, the sheer mass of second-hand equipment, the strong pressures to curtail the legal obstacles to unloading it, and the downward trends in prices resulting from the glut of weapons taken together constitute ominous signs of chronic violence in many regions of the world. For example, an AK-47 automatic, considered one of the best weapons ever made, used to cost about $125 factory-fresh in the USSR. Now, it can be purchased for only $30 to $40 in a Russian flea market. In Uganda, the weapon costs about the same as a live chicken; on the Cambodian black-market, it may go for as little as $8.00— about the same price as a pair of fake designer jeans (Howe 1980). In the past, weapons were supplied or trafficked in at least three ways: (1) they were sold legally and openly to other states following procedures and export controls; (2) they were sold illegally and covertly to other states by diverting weapons through third parties; or (3) they were secretly supplied to other parties working in criminal black markets. All of these methods exist today, but a fourth deadly factor has been added: the arms bazaar feeds the needs of narco-militias, mafias, and paramilitaries (throughout the Balkans, Central Africa and Afghanistan, for instance).

Weapons "Supermarkets" and Conflict Zones

The availability of weapons has also resulted in large part from the spillover effects of the Vietnam War, which raged for more than a decade and ignited related conflicts in Southeast Asia where violence and warfare were stoked by demands for arms and ammunition. In recent years, the Tamil Tigers in Sri Lanka, the Muslim separatist guerrilla Abu Sayyaf in the Philippines, Burmese drug armies, and others turn to Thai arms merchants to replenish their stocks.

There are yet more examples of weapons-trafficking networks in the last three decades of the twentieth century. Within two years of the outbreak of the civil war in Lebanon in 1975, arms dealers from all over the world flocked into the country. Identifiable conflict attracted weapons entrepreneurs who perceived the war as a business opportunity. And when the war ended, Lebanese militias, French Corsican gangsters, and others began selling arms to the breakaway Republic of Croatia in the Balkans (Yudken 1992). Also during the 1970s and extending into the 1980s, the Horn of Africa was ablaze in war and civil unrest. Weapons of all sorts flooded into Ethiopia, Eritrea, and Somalia, and then into Afghanistan after the Soviet Union invaded that country. During the 1980s, $10 billion worth of weapons poured into Afghanistan in support of the antigovernment Mujahideen forces. Weapons dealers from Pakistan, Kashmir, and India pushed guns to the rebels, including Osama bin Laden and the Taliban. Once the government in Kabul fell, the Soviet tanks, RPGs, and other weapons ended up in the same cauldron.

The collapse of the Warsaw Pact in the late 1980s, however, has had the greatest impact on the weapons black markets. With the withdrawal of the Red Army from Eastern Europe, a huge amount of military equipment and stocks became available. The collapse of the USSR, though a cause for celebration in many parts of the world, proved catastrophic and extremely dangerous: in some cases, entire military units sold their weapons in exchange for basic supplies of food, clothing, and shelter (Gamba 1996). Cities in Russia took over local arsenals; and the Ukrainian-Serbian Commodity Exchange switched from selling grain and oil to selling fighter planes, tanks, and antiaircraft weapons systems. The infamous "Kaliningrad Yard Sale" followed. (Kaliningrad was a city with a large military complex attached to it serving as a satellite military base for Moscow, and the entire military arms industrial city went on sale as a sort of "supermarket" of illicit arms.)

Because enormous sums are to be made in arms trafficking, many of the political impediments that states might have imposed on commercial trade have been eliminated or temporarily lifted. Importantly, arms dealing and trafficking fit neatly into black-market transactions at large. Weapons might be sold for cash, exchanged for hostages, bartered for heroin or cocaine or stolen art and precious stones, or traded for grain or oil. Then deals may be conducted not by military men or ex-professional soldiers but may be handled by middlemen who are equally at home smuggling rubies, dumping toxic waste in Central Africa, or stealing computer chips in the United States (Light 1996). Transportation of illicit weapons can be entrusted to a phony corporation registered in the Cayman Islands; to haul the arms, ships can be hired that are registered to one of many states that ignore arms trade embargoes and the rights of seamen. Payments can be moved clandestinely through coded bank accounts in networks of shell companies protected by the banking and corporate secrecy laws of financial safe havens scattered throughout the world.

The Machinery of Arms Smuggling

Effectively curbing arms trafficking involves coping with a number of obstacles and problems. A restriction on the flow of weapons in and out of countries has not slowed down trafficking activities partly because countries and groups seeking arms develop their own groups and production capacities sooner or later. In the tumultuous climate of post–Cold War tensions which have given rise to ethnic nationalism, new states' liberation movements, and transnational organized crime, the demand for weapons is high and unlikely to diminish in the immediate future. As is true of another demand-driven product, narcotics, if weapons traffickers get caught, they are easily replaced. So the real problem is not so much the greed of the trafficker who is merely an intermediary. Indeed, before a trafficker can smuggle in weapons, it is necessary to have access to weapons to sell and a buyer who is eager to purchase arms legally or illegally.

Given this reality, a possible place of interdiction in the smuggling may be on the supply side—where the weapons are produced and manufactured. However, in view of the profits that can be had, governments may opt for financial expediency and turn a blind eye to practices that produce substantial revenues. However, as the United States has learned so painfully, selling weapons to the Afghan rebels in the 1970s came back to haunt them and some of their allies, for those very weapons have been turned against the United States in the present conflict against terror. The problem involved in greatly reducing the production of weapons that have wound up on the black market is that for decades governments in both the West and East used military expenditure as a means of stimulating their economies when they were threatened by recession. The unfortunate consequence was an increase in the productive capacity of the arms industry accompanied by the insidious constant supply of weapons to a rapacious marketplace of smugglers, brokers, and international dealers.

The Gray Arms Market

The U.S. government estimates that military equipment worth several hundred million dollars is sold annually on the illegal arms market to countries under UN arms embargoes. Most illegal arms sales are conducted through the so-called gray arms market, which has been dominated by individual brokers and their firms during the past decade (Naylor 2001). Gray market firms are often legitimate companies operating illegitimately by providing false paperwork to disguise the buyer and the military characteristics of the goods involved. Obtaining licenses, even when fraudulent, allows gray market players to make deals that seem legitimate and in compliance with export regulations and international shipping protocols.

In some cases, large illegal arms shipments arranged by traffickers will be smuggled as contraband. Illegal arms transacted with Afghan rebels and Yugoslav ethnic fighters in the 1970s and 1980s were often disguised as "humanitarian aid." Illicit arms trafficking fuels conflicts and undermines the political and military efforts of the United States to promote stability in several regions of the world. Weapons trafficking helped to arm combatants in the Balkans and on the African continent. Nations under UN or other international arms embargoes in which the United States participates are major clients in the illicit arms markets. Purchases of ordnance and weapons of all kinds by insurgents and factions in civil wars and guerrilla/terrorist activities increase the risk to U.S. military personnel and others operating in hostile environments.

Genuine supply-side reduction of arms production and conversions from weapons manufacturing to other products are both difficult to achieve. The reasons are partly technical and partly the absence of a corporate orientation among weapons producers for domestic industrial production in the civil sector. Furthermore, governments have offered few incentives to cover the huge overhead costs of conversion. Hence, it is not easy to slash military spending when it is a convenient mechanism for economic stability and jobs, even when peacetime conditions constrain military expenditures. Getting industries to cease manufacturing weapons is akin to curing a drug addict or alcoholic: these industries need to be weaned away from war commodities of the military-industrial complex. That is a tall order, however. The stock of weapons that have been manufactured over the six decades since the end of World War II have flooded the world. Putting an end to weapons production is not likely in an environment where peacekeeping is based largely on the certainty of retaliatory destruction. Parading around arsenals of sophisticated weapons only heightens fears and drives impoverished paranoid states like North Korea and Pakistan to arm themselves to the maximum, even though there are masses of people in both countries that are in abject poverty (in the case of North Korea, starvation and famine in past years). In addition, buybacks of weapons and amnesties to encourage voluntary surrender of weapons has a spotty success history. All too often only the worst junk is handed in. Furthermore, the most dangerous elements of society, those most prone to use their weapons, are the last to give them up, if they ever do.

Any global attempt to solve the problem of weapons proliferation and smuggling requires attention to the supply side—encouraging industrial conversion so that fewer weapons are manufactured and attempting to implement the voluntary self-disarming of populations. None of these alternatives will work miracles, nor will they have discernible long-range effects unless attention is focused squarely on the demand side of the illicit arms market. This may well require a major political/sociological reorientation of peoples globally. In this era of globalization, shifting loyalties away from the clan, the sect, and the tribe in forms of building and rebuilding, secular civil societies that are multicultural (meaning that they are more tolerant of social, religious, and ethnic differences) will also help reduce gross inequities and animosities in the global (and local) distribution of income and wealth. If such an environment can be realized, weapons will become irrelevant (Cukier 2001).

Trafficking in Precious Stones

The highly profitable market in diamonds, gold, and precious gems has always attracted professional thieves and organized crime. It has also become a significant source of revenue for warlords and insurgent groups in the war-torn diamond-rich areas of Africa (Cusimano 2002). Nearly 75 percent of the world's rough diamonds—valued at about $5.2 billion on the open market—are mined in Africa (Mueller 1999). Russian, Chinese, Italian, and African criminal groups are particularly involved in the illegal trade of precious metals and gems. Russian crime groups are believed to have infiltrated the legitimate diamond and gold industries in Russia in order to smuggle precious gems out of the country. Russian crime groups illegally extract and sell 300 metric tons of amber worth an estimated $1 billion each year (National Security Council 2000). In South Africa, criminal syndicates stole 20 metric tons of gold and diamonds valued at $350 million in 1996 (Theobald 1994). In Southeast Asia, smuggling of precious gems was a major source of revenue for the Khmer Rouge insurgency in Cambodia (Kampuchea) and remains a secondary source of income for drug-trafficking insurgent armies in Burma (Ebbe 1997).

Trafficking in Human Body Parts

One of the most shocking trafficking crimes is surely the trade in human body parts, including lungs, kidneys, livers, and hearts. They are sometimes obtained through coercion of prison inmates or from "donors" who are slaughtered for the benefit of affluent "recipients" who can afford illegitimate transplants. The trade appears to be internationally organized and is linked to the first kidney transplant in 1954, the first lung transplant in 1963, and the first heart transplant in 1967. Approximately a half million kidneys have been transplanted in these subsequent years; transplantable organs are stimulating a very large industry indeed. At any given moment, thousands of people worldwide are waiting for a transplant, while the potential of an adequate number of donors is constantly problematic. Thus, demand far outstrips supply, setting the conditions for illicit activity and giving rise to an illegitimate industry that makes organs available—for the right price (Finkenauer 1999).

Kidneys are the most sought-after organ worldwide. With populations living longer because of nutritional, medical, and hygienic improvements in most countries, kidney disease has increased dramatically. Dialysis machines and other medical/pharmaceutical technologies extend the lives of many, but by and large, people in developing countries do not have access to expensive machines and so survival there is dependent on kidney transplant—providing a kidney is available along with the monetary and political (often illicit) access to receive a transplant. Organs for transplant are in short supply almost everywhere in the world. One reason for the shortage is that many people are apprehensive about donating organs after death—some because of religious or cultural reasons. Orthodox Jews, some Asians, and Muslims, for example, are hostile to the idea of organ donations. As a consequence, the waiting list to obtain a kidney from a cadaver is a long one. In the United States, the waiting period is two to three years; in other areas of the world, the wait may be much longer, if a waiting list is kept at all (Rothman and Rothman 2003).

The other alternative in obtaining an organ involves a living donor. Ordinarily a spouse, sibling, relative, or friend may be the donor; in the United States and Europe, live donors provide nearly 40 percent of donated kidneys. But when relatives and others are unwilling to serve as donors for religious or personal reasons, what then? Many may seek out organs by purchasing them in the flourishing and largely unregulated international trafficking rings. Estimates of the size of the illicit organ markets are not precise, but evidence suggests that they have grown dramatically each year and will continue to do so. Demand will increase commensurate with the response to pressure: as supply shrinks relative to an aging global population and as transplant technology is spreading everywhere, the result has been a growth in the illicit trafficking markets. Other factors promoting the illegal trade involve the prohibition of commercial trafficking by numerous international transplant societies, including the World Medical Association (World Medical Association 2000). Unfortunately, these protocols and guidelines are rarely enforced and, consequently, no effective international regulatory system of guidelines is in place.

Selling organs can be highly profitable. In Thailand and the Philippines in particular, a great many impoverished peasants in the countryside and slum dwellers in the cities are prepared to sell their kidneys. Illicit trade flourishes in the poorer countries because generally they lack the professional and civic organizations that will oppose the trade in organs. In most cases, the medical and legal organizations in these countries merely respond to complaints, they do not initiate investigations. Misdeeds occur, and action is taken only if disgruntled staff members bring these incidents to the attention of regulators. The enforcement and regulatory agencies that are in place in countries like Thailand have been successful in uncovering and ending some of the illicit transplant activities. However, the weaknesses in the enforcement engine are flagrant: Thailand has no central registry for organs, and private hospitals are not effectively supervised by a state medical authority. The result is that physicians and medical administrators are relatively free to set up their own deals with families and would-be donors.

Singapore's government, unlike many of its neighbors, carefully regulates organ distribution and appears to have avoided financial corruption (Radcliffe et al. 1999). However, because Singapore's citizens, like most other Asians, object to removing organs from deceased relatives, the result is a long waiting list for kidneys. Many of those who need transplants may travel to China to get the organs of executed inmates in the correctional system. Some succeed. For some, the system has a ghastly efficiency: capital punishment is carried out in Singapore by hanging; the moment the trapdoor swings open and the neck is snapped, orderlies hurry the body to an adjoining operating room to have the organs removed while they are fresh and still functional. In 1987, Singapore enacted the Human Organ Transplantation Act (HOTA), a law that is unique in Asia. It provides that everyone who is in a fatal accident is presumed to be a kidney donor, unless there is written documentation on file that the deceased objects to the removal of the kidneys at death.

In the Philippines, pollution, poverty, and slums ring the cities of the archipelago's islands. Not surprisingly, many slum dwellers are willing to sell their kidneys. How are the organs harvested? Kidneys are sold openly and legally. For example, many residents of a squatter community called Tondo in Manila, which is located on the top of a huge garbage dump, have sold their kidneys. Medical teams go out to the slum, perform blood and tissue tests, and store the results until a recipient arrives for a transplant. Usually the medical team gets in touch with a *broker* who connects them with someone whose blood and tissues provide the best match for a transplant. Many of those who sell their kidneys do not improve their lot economically. Often, the organ sellers can no longer do heavy lifting, and so they lose their jobs; others suffer disabilities as a result of kidney removal.

In India, the practice of organ sales has generated a market in which organ brokers intensify the search for sellers. Similarly, creditors become more aggressive in calling in debts, and relatives of patients become more reluctant to donate kidneys when a seller's market expands (Cohen 1999). With the development of more sophisticated transplant technology, the illicit trade and market has expanded but follows the same demand and supply situation as in overpopulated and poverty-stricken areas. The situation regarding organ trafficking has become a great concern to the parliamentary assembly of the Council of Europe, which issued a declaration on forbidding the trafficking in organs. The Council, like other international bodies, lacks the power to enforce its edicts. Nevertheless, it insists that the flourishing trade in kidneys globally promotes criminal organ transplants and a thriving commerce in organ selling that cannot be safely regulated under current conditions. The Council noted that the television and print media provide the principal and often sole investigations of these practices. It also urged that member states tighten their laws on organ donation and make the medical profession accountable for monitoring irregularities and sharing information about medical practitioners who violate the law (World Medical Association 2000). Furthermore, the Council sees the need to amend criminal codes to punish organ trafficking, which should include sanctions against brokers, intermediary agents, hospital and nursing staff, and laboratory personnel who participate and collude in conspiracies to violate the law. The Council has encouraged its members to deny national medical insurance reimbursements for illegal transplants.

Will such initiatives succeed? It remains to be seen how governments address the issue. When patients become desperate, unfortunately, some hospitals and surgeons cannot resist these lucrative opportunities for cash-paying patients and cash-desperate donors. The fact is that human organ brokers and criminal middlemen are energetic and quick to see that poor people are vulnerable to exploitation. At the international level, it would be helpful if the medical profession on its own, and not just in response to external pressures, would seize the initiative and promote a universal commitment to organ transplant policy and standards (Chang 1995). This may be a vain hope.

The Illicit Trade in Art and Cultural Objects

Art theft and the plundering of archaeological treasures have occurred for centuries, but as demand for objects has soared, there has been a proliferation of the market. New to the illicit art market are international networks that smuggle art objects into the museums and auction houses of developed countries. They target particular museums, archaeological sites, and churches worldwide. The trafficking networks participate in the theft of art works, and they tend to be linked with transnational criminal organizations that have found art theft profitable (Conklin 1994). Traditional transnational criminal organizations such as the Italian Mafia and Colombian drug cartels use stolen art to facilitate other illicit transactions, thus linking art crime to other types of organized crime such as drug trafficking and money laundering (Bernick 1999).

No country is safe from crime organizations that strip cultural sites, which represent the heritage of a nation. Traffickers/ smugglers typically act as the intermediaries between the actual thieves and the dealers. Most smugglers have connections with the underworld of thieves and looters, and some auction houses willingly traffic in stolen property. Thefts of this kind require considerable expertise in handling, packing, and transporting objects, as well as knowledge of import/export law. In addition, they usually have access to corrupt government officials (Alsinsla 1995).

The data on transnational criminal organizations' involvement in art and antiquities smuggling leaves many issues unresolved. Do the networks engaged in this type of crime cooperate with each other? What are their connections to the legitimate art and museum world? One fact is clear: the demand for antiquities and other art objects dwarfs the legitimate supply. Porous borders, weak law enforcement, and economically distressed regions all combine in facilitating the trafficking. Most significant of all, however, is the presence of transnational networks that actually stimulate such crime endeavors.

Theft of Intellectual Property

The stealing of industrial trade secrets, copyrights, trademarks, and patents is typical intellectual property rights (IPR) crime that is affecting business worldwide. Criminal violations of IPR, particularly the sale of counterfeit or illegally manufactured products, distort international trade, undermine the legitimate marketplace, and result in significant business revenue losses. Because the United States leads the world in the creation and export of intellectual property, primarily in computer software, motion pictures, sound recording, and book publishing, American commercial enterprises and industries are especially vulnerable to such crimes and are hardest hit by counterfeiting and varied forms of copyright and patent infringements (Kelly 1989). These industries stimulated more than $300 billion, or approximately 4 percent of the gross domestic product (GDP) in 1986. Copyright industry products have surpassed agricultural products as the single largest export sector in the U.S. economy. The United States' three largest software companies are currently worth more than the steel, automotive, aerospace, chemical, and plastic industries combined (National Security Council 2000). Many of the illegal products that violate intellectual property rights are exported to the United States, but most are circulated in markets abroad in direct competition with the legitimate products of American firms (Sell 1989).

IPR violations are a global phenomenon. Most countries have laws protecting IPR, but few devote sufficient resources to suppress the criminal activity. Because of ineffective laws and weak enforcement, intellectual property violations have not been reasonably suppressed. Moreover, law enforcement personnel are inadequately trained, and public officials turn a blind eye to such crimes in the interest of boosting trade and providing indigenous business firms with a competitive edge (Grau 1989). Southeast and East Asia are primary regions of IPR violations that result in significant losses to U.S. businesses. China and Hong Kong harbor criminal operations that duplicate toys and clothing manufactured in Western countries. Firms in Malaysia, Singapore, and Taiwan copy U.S. audio, video, and software products. In Eastern Europe, Ukraine has emerged as the leading producer of illegal optical discs, and Latin America is the third-largest market for illegal duplication of CDs, videos, and cassettes (Grabosky 2001).

Organized Crime and IPR Crimes

Although many IPR crimes are committed by ostensibly legitimate foreign manufacturing, business, and import/export entrepreneurs, criminal organizations are becoming participants in all aspects of IPR crime, from manufacture to distribution. Product piracy and counterfeiting are attractive to criminal organizations because of the absence of strong criminal counterfeiting laws and the potential for huge profits in the counterfeit goods market. Some criminal and terrorist groups utilize the proceeds from producing and selling counterfeit brand-name consumer goods to fund crime and terror in the United States and elsewhere. In New York City, for example, ethnic Chinese crime syndicates produce counterfeit consumer products as a source of tax-free income. The Vietnamese gang, "Born to Kill," relies on the sale of counterfeit Rolex and Cartier watches to fund gang activities (Chin 1996). In 1995, the Los Angeles Police Department discovered several Chinese crime groups, including the Wah-Ching, the Big Circle Boys, and the Four Seas Triad, engaged in manufacturing floppy disks and CD-ROMs (Kelly, Chin, and Fagan 1997). Past press reports indicate that the Provisional Irish Republican Army funded some of its terrorist activities through counterfeit perfumes, home videos, computer software, and pharmaceuticals (Kelly and Schatzberg 1995). The problem is chronic and one of increasing significance. The stealing of trade secrets from the U.S. government and from U.S. businesses through economic espionage, in addition to industrial theft, is a growing threat to U.S. global economic competitiveness.

Alien Smuggling: Trafficking in Human Beings

People move in reaction to a variety of social, economic, and personal pressures. Issues of politics, the ups and downs of economies, livelihoods lost and gained, wars, conflicts, natural disasters—all play a role in precipitating the flow of migrants and refugees. The Middle East crisis is a good example of multifaceted social unrest.

The slave trade made up most of the migration activity from the sixteenth century to the early decades of the nineteenth century (Kane 2000). Europe, the Middle East, indeed the Western Hemisphere, was populated by the migrations of people in small or large roaming bands. Migration creates problems but also solves them. It reduced overcrowding in Europe during the eighteenth and nineteenth centuries, and it helped to populate North and South America and Australia, but it also subjected millions of people to the tragedy of slavery and colonialism. The biography of nations can be understood in terms of the great migratory shocks they experienced during their formative periods. The profound effects of migration on a region are apparent today as more people worldwide move about in one year as have moved in past centuries (Anderson 1991).

The end of the Cold War and the breakup of the Soviet Union have resonated like a powerful earthquake across the world. The consequent realignment of political forces, the rise in ethnic and social conflicts, the assertion of new nationalist aspirations, and the economic desperation across Africa and Latin America have produced crime, violence, and millions of refugees. Economic and demographic stresses are also major factors stimulating illegal migration, especially from China, India, Mexico, Central America, and the Caribbean in the Western Hemisphere (Chin and Kelly 1999). Illegal immigrants, like legal immigrants, seek the "better lives" they believe await them in the United States and Canada; they share the same motives as legal immigrants: economic security and opportunities for a better life for their families. However, as noted in Chapter 1, among the illegal immigrants smuggled into the United States, Western Europe, and Canada are many criminals and terrorists. Upon arrival they "disappear" into the ethnic and racial migrant communities, insulating themselves from the probing eye of the larger community.

Estimates of undocumented aliens vary, but the U.S. Immigration and Naturalization Service (INS) indicates that there may be nearly 10 million living and working in the United States. These numbers represent about 2 to 5 percent of the total U.S. population. Although it is not known with any precision, it is estimated that more than 2 million illegal immigrants come into the United States yearly through alien smuggling networks. Approximately another half-million enter without the help of smugglers. Most illegal aliens enter via Mexico and Canada. Ironically, smuggling not only persists but tends to rise even though U.S. immigrant policies are among the most lenient in the world (U.S.

Immigration and Naturalization Service 1999). By far, the United States is the largest recipient of international migrants, with about 3.5 million foreign-born residents at the end of the 1990s. Migrants come from everywhere and go everywhere; the largest numbers of migrants come from Asia. The United States is the major recipient followed by other parts of North America, Europe, Third World countries in Latin America, and Africa (U.S. Department of State 2001).

Demographically, migration streams became feminized toward the latter decades of the twentieth century. That is, heretofore immigration was primarily a male phenomenon. Many of the modern female immigrants—legal or illegal—are relocating as the principal wage-earners rather than as passive, economically dependent family members.

During the 1990s, many world leaders identified alien smuggling and trafficking as major issues that should be addressed by the United Nations. In 1993, the UN General Assembly adopted Resolution 48/102 on the prevention of alien smuggling. It urged states to change the laws by increasing the penalty for migrant trafficking, criminalizing the activity, developing more sophisticated procedures for detecting forged documents, and aggressively monitoring airports and seaports.

Alien smuggling is becoming one of the most profitable activities of organized crime groups. From 700,000 to 2 million women and children are trafficked globally each year (United Nations 2000). The number of all migrants including men and women of all ages is unknown, but every observer believes that the numbers are increasing as the pace of globalization accelerates in every region of the world. This smuggling of people tends to be an organized process that takes different forms. In the case of Chinese alien smuggling, it is increasingly professionalized with "Snakeheads"—as the smuggling organizations are known—linked to crime syndicates on an intercontinental basis. These syndicates provide links to local networks of gangsters, employers, and facilitators who provide a full range of services from transport to safe houses, jobs, and false documents (U.S. Department of State 1999).

Female Migrants

Nearly one-half of migrants worldwide are women. Although most still accompany families, increasing numbers migrate on their own and are the principal wage-earners for themselves and their families. Women migrants, especially from underdeveloped regions where they do not enjoy men's rights, tend to be vulnerable to deprivation, abuse, and discrimination because of their status as migrants and because of their gender. As such, they have limited access to legal, lucrative employment and generally earn less than men and even native-born women.

The trafficking of women for sexual exploitation is a serious problem that is growing worldwide. Some observers contend that the profits from the sex trade in women and children are among the highest sources of illegal income in America, ranking just below drugs and gun dealing. But unlike drugs or guns, human trafficking deals in reusable and resaleable commodities—people. Smuggled into prostitution rings in the United States equipped with faked visas, women aliens have often been kidnapped or lured by false stories of great opportunities and then find themselves trapped in the sex trade industries in a foreign country. Removed from the protection of family and friends, and held captive in apartments in strange cities, they are forced to engage in unspeakable sex acts with complete strangers (Chin 1999). Although there is nothing new about this (traditionally termed *white slavery*), since the 1980s, sex trafficking has become a well-organized international criminal enterprise. It flourished in the Philippines and Thailand after the Vietnam War by catering to soldiers and then broadened its appeal and accessibility to tourists from North America, Japan, and Europe who found a wide variety of sexual activities available in South Asian brothels (Edwards and Harden 2000).

Prior to the 1990s, many of the women trafficked came from Asia (U.S. Population Division 2000). Many of them share similar social backgrounds and profiles: often they are desperate young people in search of opportunity and livelihood and even a means to survive. The breakup of the Soviet Union in December 1991, the economic revolution across the globe, the porous borders, and the expansion of criminal syndicates are landmark events leading to the profound economic upheavals affecting young women and families. Before 1991, sex trafficking was conducted mainly through mail-order brides and recruitment activities in Thailand and across Asia. Once the Soviet Union collapsed, a new sex market emerged, facilitated by criminal groups operating internationally. The main smuggling routes cover much of Africa, Southeast Asia, Eastern Europe, and South America. Apart from the criminal exploitation of women, men, and children, other dangers are associated with human trafficking, notably HIV/AIDS, Hepatitis C, and the full range of blood pathogen and sexually transmitted diseases.

The growth of sex trade trafficking has prompted the United States Congress to propose legislation to monitor and combat this crime worldwide. The Victims of Trafficking and Violence Protection Act of 2000 became law in November 2000. The United Nations General Assembly Resolution of January 31, 2001, reaffirmed that sexual violence and trafficking in women and children for purposes of economic exploitation are serious violations of human rights. The United Nations supports efforts by governments to develop local and regional action plans against trafficking in persons, especially women and children (Sheldon 2003).

The People's Republic of China, the largest country in the world in terms of population, also provides the largest source of unskilled labor in East Asia. Estimates on Chinese international migration are as high as 400,000—with 200,000 unauthorized migrants leaving China each year through Snakehead organized smuggling rings (United Nations 2001). Of interest is not just the volume of alien trafficking but the role of the criminal organization, which appears to have turned smuggling people into a multibillion dollar business that challenges the integrity of the borders of all nations, particularly the United States. Like all governments, the Chinese government condemns unauthorized migration. Numerous antitrafficking laws have been executed to crack down on this type of organized crime and the victimization it causes (Chin 1999).

The cost of arranging migration is substantial, in excess of $30,000 per person. This illegal migration is likely to be restricted to families with access to resources. Since the sums demanded by the smugglers usually exceed a family's capacity to pay, Snakeheads will advance the sums of money and enforce collection. There is no super, all-powerful syndicate running the operation from numerous locales, but small-scale groups that at times operate alone and other times in association with other smuggling syndicates. Upon arrival at the destination, migrants are often kept as virtual prisoners or bonded labor in the sweatshops of the Chinatowns of some American and European cities (Kelly, Chin, and Fagan 1997).

General Observations: Looking Ahead

Relaxation of tensions following the Cold War led to a weakening of safeguards against both weapons of mass destruction and small arms falling into clandestine hands. Until then, nuclear, chemical, and biological terrorism was never likely. Not only are weapons complicated, intricate, and, therefore, formidable to manufacture, transport, and conceal, their use requires an elaborate support apparatus from a segment of a population within the targeted state. The retaliatory capacity of the United States and the former USSR made that risk dreadful to contemplate, such that a doomsday terrorist apocalypse had to be taken seriously within a war plan but was not very probable given the likely outcome of mutual destruction (Elshtain 2003).

The irony of the Cold War logic, which drained the resources of the major protagonists, was that its end meant that sovereign states would not be interested in becoming involved in combating terrorism on a global scale. After all, terrorism did not pose a strategic threat that could escalate to global confrontation. At least for a time a decade ago that threat had all but disappeared. During the Cold War, terrorist campaigns were often seen as proxy wars between the superpowers. Events in Cuba, Vietnam, Indonesia, Korea, or Afghanistan therefore took on global strategic dimensions. With the end of the Cold War, however, as the second Iraq War illustrates, governments are increasingly asking how a terrorist campaign in some remote region of the world affects their vital interests. We believe that these new realities in international relationships have emboldened dissident organizations to adopt terrorist tactics on the assumption that the great powers will first consider if their self-interest warrants an intervention and justify a military action before actually committing themselves to take up arms. Indeed, what has improved the environment for terrorism has also benefited illicit trafficking in the post–Cold War world. With the symbolic Berlin Wall tumbling down, the greatest change has been the marked increase in the capacity of people and materials to avoid surveillance in crossing international borders (Kelly 2001). Those permanent—often deadly—fixtures in our landscapes and mentalscapes did not close off perceptions of East and West, opulence and squalor. Instead, the boundaries and borders locked the destinies of the "haves" and "have nots" into a passionate grip of desire and hatred.

Facilitated by political, economic, and cultural changes, including most importantly the globalization of trade (open economies), transportation, and financial systems, and the fast-paced revolution in communication and information technologies, organized crime and illicit trafficking on a transnational scale are in full swing. National strategies are inherently inadequate in responding to challenges that cross many borders and invoke many participants. Although governments largely still operate in a bordered world based on antiquated notions of sovereignty (that may be symbolically appealing, though they have lost much of their substance) to inhibit crime, terror, and trafficking, few governments are able to cope effectively with organizations that can simply suspend their activities or shift them to other locales to recover losses and to evade pressure or scrutiny.

Illicit trafficking is linked with international relationships among nation-states. The war on illicit trafficking is not going well because controls rest almost entirely on the coercive arm of the state. Drug trafficking is a good example of the problems connected with the control and containment of trafficking activities. Most of the world's illicit drug supply is cultivated within states that are weak or failing and thus lack effective law enforcement capacities and agencies. Even in strong states, the drug trade and consumption take place in economic and social realms where liberal democratic states have the least ability to intercede. Police cannot randomly break into houses to apprehend drug users; this would be a grievous infringement on civil liberties. Interdiction efforts also run directly counter to legal market forces, making it increasingly difficult to find the needle of contraband in the huge haystack of legal goods, services, and people that now vanish across national borders as a consequence of globalization.

Turning around the war on drugs, organized crime, terrorism, and smuggling of goods, services, and people may require some novel, even radical, responses to these issues. As the evidence of chronic persistent problems involving trafficking indicates, the reactive policies of nation-states, such as increased border patrol and interdiction, may be futile. Fundamental solutions to these problems of refugees, illegal aliens, transnational organized crime, and smuggling demand proactive policies that will enable people to avoid flight and mitigate push-and-pull factors. State-centric responses to illicit trafficking issues appear to be less effective than responses to international threats. Technology and its networks of nonstate, nongovernmental actors can act swiftly to bridge gaps in existing state-sponsored programs and political will. Given the state's limited regulatory and oversight roles, non-state NGOs may constitute powerful allies in battling trafficking problems. However, as states "contract out" to NGOs, accountability may be lost and may adversely impact problems that mutually affect states. At the same time, state-sponsored responses to illicit trafficking problems cannot be utterly abandoned in favor of NGO solutions. The issue of increasing law enforcement efforts against international crime, which constitutes the machinery that delivers goods and services—licit and illicit—is of practical concern for the future. Most prescriptions along these lines focus on state-centered responses, including the improvement of police training, routing out corruption, expanding intelligence gathering and analysis (Maghan 1994; 2004), generating anticrime conventions and norms, and harmonizing legal and regulatory regimes (like RICO) across national boundaries.

The era of big government, as President Clinton put it, is dead (Clinton 2004). What he meant was that when a country's political, economic, and development activities become globalized, the national government may no longer be the dominant entity as transnational cooperation has emerged at all levels of government (national and subnational) and among all types of organizations (public organizations, multinational organizations, and NGOs). Global changes are creating new, complex, decentralized systems of networks that are different from the conventional systems of governance that once controlled the process of international activities and decision making.

Likewise, criminal threats today are diffuse and decentralized; the existence of groups like La Cosa Nostra, the Triads, the drug cartels in Asia and Latin America, and terrorist groups such as al-Qaeda poses few questions of hegemonic forays guided by an ideology of world domination. The problems—as with the numerous advantages modern technologies bestow—lead to more dangerous forms of illicit trafficking because they easily transgress borders and are facilitated by the open global economy, which most societies desire and modern technology promotes.

What has unfortunately emerged as a growing and foreboding aspect of the twenty-first century is widespread, transnational organized crime, which appears to be an offshoot of modern technologies that interact with and overlap terrorism. Terrorists are keenly aware of and utilize the networks, collusions, and coalitions that make up transnational crime in acquiring needed funds, munitions, and resources to augment their control of illicit markets through the regulatory mechanisms of fear and the threat of credible violence. The threat is further heightened by the ugly reality that there are groups prepared to kill randomly, and who are skilled in the use of chemical weapons, ballistic devices, and biological weapons, which they seem eager to use. With these threats in mind, it is not far-fetched to classify such lethal instruments of mass murder and genocide as weapons of mass destruction. The daunting realities of terrorism and transnational organized crime, when wedded together, are quite alarming. Despite our apprehensions, it is evident that nations have little choice but to act together in order to frustrate the spread of these social viruses.

References

Allison, Graham T., Owen Cote, Richard Falkenrath, and Steven Miller. 1996. *Avoiding Nuclear Anarchy: Containing the Threat of Loose Russian Nuclear Weapons and Fissile Material.* Cambridge, MA: MIT Press.

Alsinsla, Konstantin. 1995. *Beautiful Loot: Soviet Plunder of Europe's Art Treasures.* New York: Random House.

Anderson, Benedict. 1991. *Imagined Communities: Reflections on the Origin and Spread of Nationalism.* New York: Verso.

Beare, Margaret E. 1995. "Money Laundering: A Preferred Law Enforcement Target for the 1990s." In Jay S. Albanese (ed.), *Contemporary Issues in Organized Crime,* pp. 171–188. New York: Willow Trees Press.

Bernick, Lauren L. 1999. "Art and Antiques Theft." In Stanley Einstein and Menachem Amir (eds.), *Organized Crime: Uncertainties and Dilemmas,* pp. 317–344. Chicago: Office of International Criminal Justice.

Bryant, Robert. 1990. "Chinese Organized Crime Making Major Inroads in Smuggling Heroin to the United States." *Organized Crime Digest* 11 (7): 1–6.

Chang, Dae H. 1995. "A New Form of International Crime: The Human Organ Trade." *International Journal of Comparative and Applied Criminal Justice* 19 (1): 1–18.

Chin, Ko-lin. 1996. *Chinatown Gangs: Extortion, Enterprise and Ethnicity.* New York: Oxford University Press.

———. 1999. *Illegal Chinese Immigration in America.* Philadelphia: Temple University Press.

Chin, Ko-lin, and Robert J. Kelly. 1999. *Human Snakes: Illegal Chinese Immigrants in the United States.* Washington, DC: National Science Foundation, Final Report, Grant SBR 93–11114.

Chin, Ko-lin, Sheldon Zhang, and Robert J. Kelly. 2001. "Transnational Chinese Organized Crime Activities: Patterns and Emerging Trends." In Phil Williams and Dimitri Vlassis (eds.), *Combating Transnational Crime,* pp. 127–154. London: UN Crime Prevention Program and Frank Cass.

Clinton, William J. 2004. *My Life.* New York: Random House.

Cohen, Lawrence. 1999. "Where It Hurts: Indian Material for an Ethics of Organ Transplantation." *Daedalus* 128 (4) (Fall): 135–165.

Conklin, John. 1994. *Art Crime.* Westport, CT: Praeger.

Cukier, Wendy. 2001. "Measures to Reduce Illicit Trafficking in Firearms." *Gun Control Alliance.* Toronto: Coalition for Gun Control in Canada. (August).

Cusimano, Maryann. 2002. *Unplugging the Cold War Machine: Rethinking U.S. Foreign Policy Institution.* Thousand Oaks, CA: Sage Publications.

Deutch, John. 1996, March 20. "Testimony before the Permanent Sub-committee on Government Affairs." Washington, DC: *Congressional Journal:* 1–2.

Ebbe, Abi N. I. 1997, October 30–31. "Political-Criminal Nexus: Nigerian Case Study." In Roy Godson (ed.), *Confronting the Security Challenge of the Political-Criminal Nexus,* pp. 19–31. Washington, DC: Research Colloquium, Georgetown University.

Edwards, Catherine, and James Harden. 2000, November. "Sex Slave Trade Centers the United States." *Insight:* 14–17.

Elshtain, Jean Bethke. 2003. *Just War Against Terror: The Burden of American Power in a Violent War.* New York: Basic Books.

Finkenauer, James. 1999. "Russian Organized Crime in America." In Robert J. Kelly, Ko-lin Chin, and Rufus Schatzberg (eds.), *Handbook of Organized Crime in the United States,* pp. 245–268. Westport, CT: Greenwood Publishing Group.

Flynn, Stephen E. 1998. "Asian Drugs, Crime and Control: Rethinking the War." In James Shinn (ed.), *Fires Across the Water: Transnational Problems in Asia,* pp. 18–44. New York: Council of Foreign Relations.

Ford, James L. 1996, March 20. "Nuclear Smuggling: How Serious a Threat?" Testimony to the Permanent Subcommittee on Investigation of the Senate Committee on Government Affairs. Washington, DC: 48–53.

Fuentes, Joseph R. 1998. The Impact of Managerial Style on the Colombian Distribution of Cocaine to the Wholesale Level. Ph.D. dissertation, The Graduate Center, City University of New York.

Fuentes, Joseph R., and Robert J. Kelly. 1999, November. "Drug Supply and Demand: The Dynamics of the American Drug Market and Some Aspects of Colombian and Mexican Drug Trafficking." *Journal of Contemporary Criminal Justice* 15 (4): 328–351.

Gamba, Virginia. 1996. *Managing Arms in the Peace Process.* New York: United Nations Institute for Disarmament Research.

Godson, Ray, and Phil Williams. 2000. "Strengthening Cooperation Against Trans-Sovereign Crime: A New Security Imperative." In Maryann K. Cusimano (ed.), *Beyond Sovereignty: Issues for a Global Agenda,* pp. 111–146. Boston: St. Martin's Press.

Grabosky, Peter. 2001. "Crime in Cyberspace." In Phil Williams and Dimitri Vlassis (eds.), *Combating Transnational Crime,* pp. 195–208. London: Frank Cass.

Grau, Joseph J. 1989. "Managing Trade Secrets." *Legal Studies Forum* 13(4): 391–406.

Hess, David, Kenneth Myers, Michele Gideon, Sal Gomez, and John Daly. 1999. "Money Laundering." In S. Einstein and M. Amir (eds.), *Organized Crime, Uncertainties and Dilemmas,* pp. 64–97. Chicago: Office of International Criminal Justice.

Howe, Robert W. 1980. *Weapons: The International Game of Arms, Money and Diplomacy.* New York: Doubleday.

IAEA. 1996, December. "Inside Technical Cooperation." *Reuters Review.*

Inciardi, James, and Christine A. Saum. 1996, Spring. "Legalization Madness." *The Public Interest* (123): 43–59.

Kane, Hal. 2000. "Leaving Home: The Flow of Refugees." In Maryann K. Cusimano (ed.), *Beyond Sovereignty: Issues for a Global Agenda,* pp. 74–91. Boston: St. Martin's Press.

Kelly, Robert J. 1989. "Introduction." *The Legal Studies Forum* (Special Issue on Intellectual Property Rights) 13 (4): 335–341.

———— 1991. "AIDS and the Societal Reaction." In Robert J. Kelly and Donal E. J. MacNamara (eds.), *Perspectives on Deviance: Dominance, Degradation and Denigration,* pp. 47–63. Cincinnati, OH: Anderson Publishing.

————. 1994. "Turning Black Money into Green: Money Laundering." In Robert J. Kelly et al. (eds.), *Handbook of Organized Crime in the United States,* pp. 311–330. Westport, CT: Greenwood Publishing.

————. 2001, July. "Twelve Years After: The Berlin Wall as Will and Idea" *Journal of Social Distress* 10 (3): 217–233.

Kelly, Robert J., Ko-lin Chin, and Jeffrey Fagan. 1997. "Lucky Money for Little Brother: The Prevalence and Seriousness of Chinese Gang Extortion." In P. J. Smith (ed.), *Human Smuggling: Chinese Migrant Trafficking and the Challenge to America's Immigration Tradition.* Washington, DC: Center for Strategic and International Studies.

Kelly, Robert J., Patrick J. Ryan, and Rufus Schatzberg. 1995, December. "Primitive Capitalist Accumulation: Russia on a Rocket." *Journal of Contemporary Criminal Justice* 11 (4): 257–275.

Kelly, Robert J., and Rufus Schatzberg. 1995. "From Pistols to Ploughshares: The IRA's Farewell to Arms." *International Journal of Comparative and Applied Criminal Justice* 17 (2): 165–177.

Lee, Rensselaer. 1992. "Colombia's Cocaine Syndicates." In Alfred McCoy and Alan Black (eds.), *War on Drugs*, pp. 93–124. Boulder, CO: Westview Press.

———. 1998. *Smuggling Armageddon: The Nuclear Black Market in the Former Soviet Union and Europe.* New York: St. Martin's Press.

Light, C. Smith. 1996. "Weapons and the International Arms Trade." In *Small Arms Management and Peacekeeping in Southern Africa.* Geneva: United Nations Institute for Disarmament Research.

Lohr, Steve. 1992, March 29. "When the Money Washes Up: Offshore Banking in the Cayman Islands." *The New York Times Magazine.* pp. 26–52.

Lupsha, Peter, and Stanley Pimentel. 1997. "The Nexus of Organized Crime and Politics: Mexico." In Roy Godson (ed.), *Confronting the Security Challenge of the Political-Criminal Nexus*, pp. 87–136. Washington, DC: National Strategy Information Center.

Maghan, Jess. 1994, Winter. "The Correction Connection: Intelligence Gathering in Prisons." *Low Intensity Conflict and Law Enforcement* 3 (3): 548–557.

———. 2004, September. "The Post 9/11 Prison, Interagency Intelligence Coordination." *Crime and Justice International* 20 (83): 7–14.

Margolis, Eric S. 2000. *The War at the Top of the World: The Struggle for Afghanistan, Kashmir, and Tibet*, pp. 91–92, 192–208. New York: Routledge.

Millson, Anita. 2001. "International Atomic Energy Agency Programme Against Illicit Trafficking in Nuclear Materials and Radioactive Sources." In Phil Williams and Dimitri Vlassis (eds.), *Combating Transnational Crime*, pp. 315–320. London: Frank Cass.

Mueller, Gerhard O. W. 1999. "Transnational Crime: An Experience in Uncertainties." In S. Einstein and M. Amir (eds.), *Organized Crime: Uncertainties and Dilemmas*, pp. 3–18. Chicago: Office of International Criminal Justice.

National Security Council. 1998, May. "Money Laundering." *International Crime Threat Assessment.* Washington, DC: U.S. Government Printing Office.

———. 2000, May. *International Organized Crime.* Washington, DC: NSC.

Naylor, R. T. 1995. "Loose Cannons: Covert Commerce and Underground Finance in the Modern Arms Black Market." *Crime, Law and Social Change* 25: 67–81.

———. 2001. "The Rise of the Modern Arms Black Market and the Fall of

Supply-Side Control." In Phil Williams and Dimitri Vlassis (eds.), *Combating Transnational Crime*, pp. 209–236. London: Frank Cass.

Office of National Drug Control Policy. 1997. *National Drug Control Strategy, 1996: Programs, Resources and Education.* Washington, DC: U.S. Government Printing Office.

Potts, Mark, Nicholas Kocham, and Robert Whittington. 1992. *Dirty Money: BCCI: The Inside Story of the World's Sleaziest Banks.* Washington, DC: National Press Books.

President's Commission on Organized Crime. 1984. *The Cash Connection: Organized Crime, Financial Institutions and Money Laundering.* Washington, DC: U.S. Government Printing Office.

Radcliffe, Richards J., et al. 1999, June 27. "The Case for Allowing Kidney Sales." *The Lancet* (254): 113–139.

Ratner, Steven R. 1996. *The New UN Peacekeeping: Building Peace in Lands of Conflict After the Cold War.* New York: St. Martin's Press.

Rothman, Sheila M., and David J. Rothman. 2003, October 23. "The Organ Markets." *The New York Review* 50 (16): 69–75.

Sell, Susan K. 1989. "Intellectual Property as a Trade Issue: From the Paris Convention to GATT." *Legal Studies Forum* 13 (4): 407–422.

Sheldon, Ronald. 2003. "Trafficking: A Perspective from Asia." *International Migration, Perspective on Trafficking of Migrants and Trafficking in Human Beings.* 38 (3): Special Issue, Vienna, United Nations Office on Drugs and Crime.

Shelley, Louise. 1997. "The Political-Criminal Nexus: Russian-Ukrainian Case Studies." In Roy Godson (ed.), *Confronting the Security Challenge of the Political-Criminal Nexus*, pp. 1–31. Washington, DC: National Strategy Information Center.

Smith, Eugene. 1991. A Study of the Banking Secrecy Act. Ph.D. dissertation, Graduate Center, City University of New York.

Theobald, Robin.1994. "Lancing the Swollen African State: Will It Alleviate the Problem of Corruption." *The Journal of Modern African Studies* 32 (4): 701–706,

Timmerman, Kenneth G. 1990. *The Poison Gas Connection: Western Suppliers of Unconventional Weapons and Technologies to Iraq and Libya.* Vienna: Wiesenthal Center.

United Nations. 1999. *1998 World Drug Report.* New York: UN Secretariat.

———. 2000. *World Migration Report, 2000.* Susan F. Martin (ed.). New York: International Organization for Migration, United Nations.

United Nations, General Assembly. 2001. *Resolution Adopted by the General Assembly, Resolution 48-804-01.* New York: United Nations, *217-A III.*

United Nations International Drug Control Programme. 2001. "Economic and Social Consequences of Drug Abuse and Illicit Trafficking." Vienna: United Nations.

United Nations Office for Drug Control and Crime Prevention. 1998. "Financial Havens, Bank Secrecy and Money Laundering." In *Global Programs Against Money Laundering.* New York: Secretariat, United Nations, V3-V11.

U.S. Department of State. 1998. *International Narcotics Control Strategy Report.* (INCSR-2001). Washington, DC: U.S. Government Printing Office.

———. 2001, July. "Human Smuggling and U.S. Policy." *International Information Program: East Asia Issues.* Washington, DC: U.S. Government Printing Office.

U.S. Department of State, Bureau of Intelligence and Research. 1999. *International Trafficking in Women to the United States: A Contemporary Manifestation of Slavery and Organized Crime.* Washington, DC: Center for the Study of Intelligence.

U.S. Immigration and Naturalization Service. 1999, May. *The Triennial Comprehensive Report on Immigration.* Washington, DC.

U.S. Population Division. 2000. *Replacement Migration: Is it a Solution to Declining and AgingPopulations?* New York: United Nations.

Walter, Ingo. 1990. *Secret Money: The World of International Financial Secrecy.* New York: Harper.

Williams, Phil. 1992, Winter. "The International Drug Trade: An Industry Analysis." *Low Intensity Conflict and Law Enforcement* 2 (3): 397–420.

———. 1997. "Drug Trafficking, Weapons Connection and the Political Criminal Nexus." Washington, DC: Georgetown University Conference, Private Communication.

Williams, Phil, and Paul N. Woessner. 1996, January. "The Real Threat of Nuclear Smuggling." *Scientific American* 274: 40–41.

World Medical Association. 2000, October. *Statement on Human Organ and Tissue Donation and Transplantation.* 52nd World Medical Association Assembly, Edinburgh, Scotland.

Yudken, Jay. 1992. *Dismantling the Cold War Economy.* New York: Basic Books.

Zimmerman, Tim. 1995, October 21. "The Russian Connection." *U.S. News and World Report*: 28–29.

3

Chronology

1949   The United Nations consolidates earlier treaties into the *Convention for the Suppression of the Traffic in Persons and the Exploitation of the Prostitution of Others*, a hallmark event that officially recognized an ancient problem. However, the 1949 convention is problematic in that it does not elaborate a definition of trafficking, but rather simply equates trafficking with prostitution. Consequently, this initial definition of trafficking centers primarily on trafficking for prostitution and excludes vast numbers of women and other persons from its protection. Nonetheless, it lays a framework for the first documentation of *illicit trafficking* undertaken for several purposes, including, but not limited to, prostitution or other sex work; domestic, manual or industrial labor; and marriage or adoption.

1956   The International Criminal Police Commission (IPC) headquartered in Vienna, Austria, is reinstituted into the International Criminal Police Organization (INTERPOL). Functioning as an IGO by the United Nations, its mission is to promote the widest possible *mutual assistance* among all police authorities of the world. Interpol cooperates with NGOs that deal with exposing and interdicting illicit trafficking in persons, smuggling migrants, weapons, body parts, precious stones, and drugs.

1957   On November 19, a meeting of sixty organized crime bosses in Apalachin, New York, is uncovered by the New York State Police. The meeting had been summoned for a number of reasons, including the arrangement for drug trafficking into the United States by members of the Sicilian and Corsican Mafias. As a result of these decisions a drug pipeline, known as the "French Connection," begins smuggling heroin into Canada and the United States.

1969   The countries of South America form the Council of the Cartagena Agreement (JUNAC) and sign the Andean Regulation on improved management of migration flows through bilateral and multilateral action. Under the agreement, the countries of South America and the United States are joined in a coalitional and centralized oversight center to monitor legal and illegal migration patterns.

1970   Congress passes the Racketeer Influenced and Corrupt Organizations (RICO) Act, Title 18, United States Code, Sections 1961–1968. At the time, Congress's goal was to eliminate the ill effects of organized crime on the nation's economy. The law as enacted allows prosecutors to go after whole criminal enterprises, not just stray individuals or low-level criminals. Under RICO, any two of several dozen defined crimes over a ten-year period can convict an individual of taking part in an ongoing rackets enterprise; anyone planning or discussing a crime is considered as guilty as the actual perpetrator. Different crimes by different criminals can still point to a single criminal organization. Crime bosses are no longer insulated from subordinates acting on their orders. RICO also enables law enforcement authorities to seize any stolen loot through property forfeitures. It takes about a decade to apply the new legal tools. In effect, RICO creates a new crime categorization. Belonging to an enterprise engaged in racketeering activities—or illicit trafficking that has emerged in the three decades since the enactment of RICO—comes under the reach of the law. RICO makes it unlawful to acquire or operate a business that receives income from racketeering. In the modern context, virtually every type of illicit trafficking comes under the purview of the RICO statutes. Many countries have adopted versions of RICO to fight all forms of organized crime, including varieties of illicit trafficking that confront developing states in Eastern Europe, Southwest Asia, the Far East, as well as African nations struggling with decolonialization and modernization.

1972   U.S. and French law enforcement initiate a series of successful indictments against the French Connection, a Marseilles-based industry controlled by Corsican gangsters and the U.S. Mafia; heroin trafficking is impaired on the U.S. East Coast.

1973   The "Palermo Connection" is implemented by Mafia heroin smugglers after the French Connection is broken up by the Federal Narcotics Bureau. This drug trafficking network operates successfully throughout the 1980s.

President Nixon establishes the Drug Enforcement Administration, a "superagency" to handle all aspects of the drug trafficking problem. The DEA consolidates deployment of agents from the Bureau of Narcotics, Customs, and the CIA in the war on drugs.

On April 3, the modern mobile telephone is introduced in New York City. Mobile phones began to proliferate through the 1980s with the introduction of cellular networks, including the first automatic roaming cellular network in Saudi Arabia in September 1981, followed by the installation of automatic cellular roaming between the Nordic countries. The first digital cellular phone call is introduced in the United States and Europe in 1990. At the beginning of the twenty-first century, satellite mobile phone systems, with full service Internet capabilities, are now publicly available. Cell phones have fundamentally shifted telecommunication to the individual person and away from landline-determined place, thereby facilitating

1973
(cont.)
immediate universal communication, even in the most remote locations. Simultaneously, cell phones are, by default, furthering a massive increase in illicit criminal activity.

1979
On December 24, the Soviet Defense Ministry orders troops into Afghanistan, where commandos seize strategic installations in Kabul; resistance intensifies with various Mujahideen groups fighting Soviet forces.

1980
The United States, Pakistan, China, Iran, and Saudi Arabia supply money and arms to the Mujahideen groups.

1979–1980
Carlos Lehder, a key member of the alliance that would become the Medellín cartel, revolutionizes the cocaine trade with his purchase of 165 acres on the Bahamian island of Norman's Cay. Lehder is the first to use small planes for transporting the drug. The alliance between Mexico's Ochoa family, Pablo Escobar, Carlos Lehder, and Jose Gonzalo Rodriguez Gacha evolves into the "Medellín Cartel." Later, in 1981, the United States and Colombia ratify a bilateral extradition treaty (which they had previously approved in 1979), and extradition becomes the greatest fear of the Colombian traffickers.

1980
The Andean Pact is established to govern migration by providing for the administration of labor movements and the regularization of migrants in the 1970s and 1980s. In the late 1980s, the enforcement and application of the Andean Regulations weakens and loses its authority of interdiction. Concurrently, the "war" of the narco-traffickers against regional governments in Venezuela, Peru, Colombia, Ecuador, and Bolivia devolves into massive corruption and government inertia in its law enforcement agencies. Migration policies in the Andean region continue to be characterized by a double standard: governments increase restrictive measures against illegal migration and smuggling while these states simultaneously allow

porous borders to sustain an internal economic balance affected by increased oversight of illegal migration/immigration.

1987   The so-called Pizza Connection—twenty-two Mafia defendants and their associates—are tried and convicted in one of the largest international heroin and cocaine trafficking operations in the United States. As a result of these convictions the Mafia drug pipeline is severely disrupted and one of its key organizers, Tommaso Pouscetta, becomes an important informant against the Sicilian Mafia and its associates in North and South America.

1988   The U.S. Congress passes the Anti-Drug Abuse Act of 1988 (P. L.100–6900) and establishes the High Intensity Drug Trafficking Areas (HIDTA) program to operate under the direction of the Office of National Drug Control Policy. The HIDTAprogram provides federal assistance to better coordinate and enhance drug law enforcement efforts of local, state, and federal law enforcement agencies in areas where major drug production, manufacturing, importation, or distribution flourish. In 1990, Federal funds are specifically appropriated to five areas of the United States that are considered the most critical drug trafficking "gateways" into the nation.

1989   In February, the USSR announces the departure of the last Soviet troops from Afghanistan. The civil war continues as the Mujahideen push to overthrow Soviet-backed Afghanistan President Najibullah, who is eventually toppled in 1992. The Taliban era begins and illicit drug trafficking becomes a main source of money and arms for its members.

The Berlin Wall is torn down, symbolizing the disintegration of the Soviet Bloc and the end of the Cold War. Eastern European countries within the orbit of the former Warsaw Pact treaty are initially left vulnerable to massive waves of corruption and illicit trafficking in arms, illegal immigration, drugs, and white slavery.

1989 (cont.)	The United States charges Panamanian general and the country's de facto military leader, Manuel Noriega, with drug smuggling. Noriega declares Panama in a state of emergency in the wake of a failed coup, then declares a "state of war" in the face of increased threats by American law enforcement officials and policymakers. The United States invades Panama in 1989 under Operation Just Cause, and ousts Noriega. The U.S. Federal Court for the Southern District finds Noriega guilty of eight counts of drug trafficking, racketeering, and money laundering in April 1992 and sentences him to forty years of imprisonment in a U.S. federal prison in Miami; on December 4, 2004, he is moved to an undisclosed Miami federal prison hospital after suffering a very minor stroke.
1994	Operation Steady State is jointly inaugurated by the Drug Enforcement Administration (DEA) with local authorities in Peru and Colombia to stem drug production and trafficking. The program lasts two years and gives rise to Operation Selva Verde, conducted by Colombian law enforcement and military groups to destroy drug laboratories or the processing of cocaine and the cartels' trafficking apparatuses. The operations continue to the present.
1995	Presidential Decision Directive 42 by President Clinton declares international crime a threat to the national security interest of the United States. The directive orders the Departments of Justice, State, and Treasury, the Coast Guard, National Security Council, Intelligence Community, and other federal agencies to integrate their efforts against international crime syndicates and money laundering. A key component of this presidential directive is the imposition of sanctions under the 1995 International Emergency Economic Powers Act (IEEPA), which blocks the assets of the leaders, cohorts, and front companies of identified Colombian narcotics traffickers in the United States and in U.S. banks overseas. The IEEPA authorizes the Secretary of the Treasury to impose sanctions, including freezing assets held in U.S. financial institutions,

against nations and entities posing a threat to the national security, foreign policy, or economy of the United States.

On October 21, President Clinton amplifies and extends the purview of significant foreign narcotics traffickers centered in Colombia, noting that the unparalleled violence, corruption, and harm that they cause constitutes an unusual and extraordinary threat to the United States' national security and economy. U.S. individuals and companies are barred from engaging in financial transactions or trade with those identified individuals or enterprises linked to the Colombian Cali cartel.

In Operation Zorro II, a joint counter-drug operation is launched by the United States and Mexico against traffickers and growers. As a major interdiction effort, it lasts through 1996.

Operation Marathon Pacific/Prompt Return goes into effect near Wake Island in the Southwest Pacific in an effort to catch Chinese boat people being smuggled into the United States and elsewhere.

1996   The Illegal Immigration Reform and Immigration Responsibility Act is codified, inaugurating a watershed year for implementation of U.S. policy on immigration and illicit trafficking in persons. Three major laws are enacted that aim to accelerate the deportation of criminal immigrants, reduce access of immigrants to welfare, and step up efforts at reducing illegal immigration. These acts authorize more Border Patrol agents, fences, and lighting along the U.S.-Mexican border.

The International Crime Control Act (ICCA) of 1996 establishes a comprehensive package of legislation formulated to substantially assist U.S. law enforcement agencies in their efforts against drug traffickers, terrorists, and other international crime syndicates as well as to counter money laundering. The ICCA is

1996
(cont.)

devised to enhance U.S. efforts to investigate and prosecute violent international criminals, including the ability to deprive them of their money and deny them access through America's borders.

The International Organization for Migration (IOM) and the Organization for Security and Cooperation in Europe (OSCE) organizes a world conference to address the problems of refugees, displaced persons, and trafficking of women in the Commonwealth of Independent States (CIS) and relevant neighboring states.

1997

On January 15, the U.S. Treasury Department identifies twenty-one businesses and fifty-seven individuals determined to be directly involved with illegal traffickers and their seemingly legitimate business fronts. Bringing a total of 359 businesses and individuals whose assets have been blocked since 1995 under authority of Presidential Decision Directive 42 (PDD 42), this action consolidated the interagency deployment of measures against international criminal cartels.

1998

In June, migration ministers from more than thirty countries meet in Budapest, Hungary, for a special conference on illegal migration through southeastern Europe. The meeting urges the imposition of stricter controls on migration at the borders in countries surrounding Western Europe. In September, the EU announces a plan to tighten border controls, fingerprint all unauthorized and detained foreigners, and increase penalties on employers who hire unauthorized migrants. Also the EU launches "Operation Odysseus" to combat unauthorized immigration by financing new border control initiatives both within and outside the EU and supporting training and police cooperation throughout the EU.

2000

High-level Political Signing Conference for the United Nations Convention against Transnational Organized Crime meets in Palermo, Sicily, on December 12–15.

The convention marks an unprecedented step in the history of the struggle against organized crime. Transnational organized crime is identified as the key infrastructure in global illicit trafficking. By signing the protocols of the convention's declaration, the world community of more than 140 signatory nations begins to free itself of the decades-old failed solution of attempting to address international crime with local, parochial solutions and perspectives. The UN Convention highlights the fact that organized crime today forms the dark side of globalization, which reaches across nations and continents by exploiting today's open borders, new technologies, and massive movement of peoples.

2001   On September 11, a series of attacks by al-Qaeda occur against the United States in Washington, D.C., at the Pentagon and in New York City at the World Trade Center. The United States retaliates with attacks in Afghanistan against the Taliban, continuing its search for Osama bin Laden and its operations for liberating and securing Afghanistan. The United States establishes the Department of Homeland Security (DHS), consolidating domestic security of transportation and infrastructure, surveillance of borders, intelligence operations, and illicit arms and terrorist interdiction strategies. Global illicit trafficking markets maneuver to more sophisticated modes in response to consolidated security initiatives in the United States and Europe.

2004   The twelve nations bordering the Indian and Pacific oceans experience massive infrastructure damage and suffer the death of approximately 280,000 persons as a result of a tsunami produced by an undersea earthquake, registering 9.0 on the Richter scale below the southwest Pacific Ocean area on December 26. In Thailand and sections of northern Indonesia, children orphaned by the catastrophe are vulnerable to kidnapping and child traffickers. These child slaves are sold in the region's sex industries or put to work on

2004
(cont.)   fishing vessels, in factories, or in manufacturing businesses. The tsunami disaster also disrupts a range of
large-scale illicit trafficking networks in the region
and will have a profound influence on exposure and
surveillance of these illicit networks.

4

Biographical Sketches

Al Kassar, Monzar (1945–)

Place of origin: Nabek, Syria

Monzar Al Kassar is involved in known arms sales with Argentina, Austria, Bosnia, Brazil, Bulgaria, Chad, Croatia, Guatemala, Iran, Lebanon, Nicaragua, Panama, Poland, South Africa, Sri Lanka, Syria, the United States, and Yemen, as well as large-scale trafficking in cocaine, hashish, and stolen cars. He speaks Arabic, English, and Spanish, and these language skills have helped him to conduct illicit trafficking across the globe. Al Kassar has been the subject of ongoing investigations for arming various Palestinian terrorist groups and for involvement in terrorist attacks during the 1980s. He offered cruise missile technology to Iran in 1997 and was involved in brokering the sale of $1.11 billion worth of submarines by the Argentine Defense Ministry. He has been falsely accused of involvement in the bombing of Pan Am Flight 103 over Lockerbie, Scotland. Al Kassar has had dealings with the International Bank for Credit and Commerce (BCCI); former Argentine President Carlos Menem; Popular Front for the Liberation of Palestine-General Command (PFLP-GC), and its leader, Ahmad Jibril; Abu Abbas, leader of another Palestine Liberation Organization (PLO) extremist splinter group; and the Palestine Liberation Front (PLF), which orchestrated the *Achille Lauro* hijacking. He has also been tied to Abu Nidal, leader of the Fatah Revolutionary Council, a.k.a. *Black September* or *Arab Revolutionary Brigades.* Currently, he travels freely, claiming that he has not sold weapons in twelve years. In 1992, his Swiss bank accounts were frozen at Spain's request. He continued to be the subject of investigations conducted for gun running and for money laundering, false documents, and false foreign certificates. He was arrested in Spain in 1993 on charges of piracy and providing weapons for the hijacking of the *Achille Lauro* in which the American tourist Leon Klinghoffer was murdered. In 1993, he was released, after serving nine months, on $15.5 million bail. In 1995, Al Kassar was acquitted of all charges in the *Achille Lauro* case. In 2000, he was indicted in Argentina for obtaining documents under false pretenses in the course of his 1992 acquisition of an Argentine passport with the help of high-level Menem administration officials.

bin Laden, Osama (1957–)

Place of origin: Riyadh, Saudi Arabia
Osama bin Laden gained a following principally because of his mostly financial commitment to the anti-Soviet jihad (holy war) in Afghanistan in the 1970s. In Kenya and Tanzania, he bolstered his credentials as an Islamic warrior by destroying U.S. embassies in the capitals of those African nations. On September 11, 2001, terrorists connected with bin Laden's al-Qaeda network hijacked four American commercial airliners at U.S. airports and flew three into the World Trade Center and the Pentagon. A fourth plane, diverted by resisting passengers, crashed into a field in Sharpsburg, Pennsylvania. The combined attacks killed approximately 3,000 people including hijacked passengers, the 19 suicidal terrorists, hundreds of police, firefighters, emergency service workers, and building occupants. Prior to the World Trade Center and Pentagon attacks, bin Laden and his associates were sought by the United States on charges of terrorism in connection with the 1998 bombings of American embassies in Africa and the attack on the battleship USS *Cole* in Yemen in 2000.

Bin Laden grew up in great wealth. His father made a fortune in engineering construction in Saudi Arabia, and as a youth, bin Laden fully indulged himself in the West but soon grew bored with the Western lifestyle. Through an arranged marriage to a distant relative, a young Syrian girl, he returned to Saudi Arabia and enrolled in the King Abdul Aziz University in Jeddah to study management and civil engineering. It was at the university that bin Laden developed his militant beliefs.

In the late 1970s bin Laden's father died and reportedly left his son more than $450 million as his inheritance. In 1979, Leonid Brezhnev ordered Soviet troops into Afghanistan. At this point, bin Laden began to use his wealth to create training networks of Muslim fighters across the world to protect the Islamic Afghan people from the infidel invader. With his money he created recruitment centers around the world enlisting, sheltering, and transporting thousands of individuals from more than thirty-five countries to Afghanistan to fight the Soviets. In Afghanistan, bin Laden himself built roads, storage depots, tunnels, and hospitals to move, shelter, and manage supplies and support anti-Soviet fighters.

Bin Laden's political celebrity helped his family businesses enormously. In 1983, bin Laden Brothers for Contracting and Industry secured the most important contract in its history: a $3 billion deal to restore Mecca and Medina, the two holiest sites in the Islamic world. At the end of the Afghan War, bin Laden became involved with Algeria's radical Islamic movement, the Islamic Salvation Front. His role was that of financier and organizer as well as frontline soldier. His organization, al-Qaeda ("The Base"), became international, and he himself something of a major leader who was increasingly radical in his religious and political beliefs.

In 1994, because of his activities in weapons smuggling, the Saudi authorities revoked his citizenship. Bin Laden took up residence in Khartoum, Sudan, the home base of Sudan's Islamic revolution in 1989, and became the leader of the country's ruling National Islamic Front.

In an August 1998 indictment, Osama bin Laden and his organization, al-Qaeda, were alleged to have conspired in the killing of American military personnel in Saudi Arabia and Somalia. They were also indicted for the bombings of the American embassies in Kenya and Tanzania. In Nairobi and Dar es Salaam, 220 people were killed and 5,000 wounded. A $5 million reward was offered by the American government for information that would lead to his arrest and conviction. Bin Laden also marked for assassination Middle Eastern leaders whom he opposed, such as Crown Prince Abdullah of Jordan and President Hosni Mubarak of Egypt. American missile attacks on Sudanese and Afghani locales in retaliation for his acts of murder obliged the Sudanese to force bin Laden out of the country. Even as he moved from Sudan back to Afghanistan, al-Qaeda prepared more attacks. On June 25, 1996, nineteen American servicemen were killed in an explosion in Dharan, Saudi Arabia. In 1998, bin Laden met with Islamic and Taliban leaders (Afghan Islamic radicals) to discuss building a broad coalition against the West and the regimes in the Islamic world which they despised. Bin Laden and his associates in al-Qaeda perceive the United States as a hostile force of evil. They advocate the destruction of America because they view it as the chief obstacle to radical reform in Muslim societies.

When confronted by journalists in 1999, bin Laden claimed that he did not consider it a crime if he tried to obtain nuclear, chemical, and biological weapons. In the same interview, he claimed that should he acquire such weapons from rogue scientists in the East or West, he would use them without hesitation against the West and all of the infidels in the East. Bin Laden's financial resources are so diversified and well hidden that they are not readily immobilized and frozen. His followers on the Pakistan-Afghanistani border are numerous and loyal; therefore, detection and the possibilities for arrest and prosecution have proven to be extremely difficult. Bin Laden's current location is unknown. He previously resided in Parmir Mountains, Tajikistan, and Afghanistan

Bout, Victor (1967–)

Place of origin: Dushanbe, Tajikistan
Victor Bout's background is Tajik. He attended the Soviet Military Institute of Foreign Languages in Moscow, earning a degree in economics. He speaks six languages fluently. He served in a military aviation regiment until 1991. It is said that he worked for the KGB in Angola when the Soviet Union dissolved on December 25, 1991. In 1992, he struck his first business deal. He bought three Antonov cargo planes for $120,000 and then brokered their services for long-haul flights from Moscow, leasing the planes both "wet" (with a crew) and "dry" (plane only). His maiden voyage was to Denmark. In 1995, his air freight services were expanded west to Ostend, Belgium, and to Odessa in the Ukraine.

Ostend served as a transit point for weapons in the Iran-Contra operations. From Shariyah, United Arab Emirates, and South Africa, Bout tapped into what Africa and the Middle East needed in terms of arms. It may have been true in the Cold War that control of arms shipments was merely a matter of international diplomacy. Traffickers were often no more than subcontractors feeding the proxy conflicts sponsored by Washington and Moscow. After the fall of the Berlin Wall, the exclusive club of arms brokers coalesced. Some still worked at the behest of governments and intelligence agencies, but most went entrepreneurial, becoming free-lancers who sold weapons without regard to ideology, allegiance, conscience, or consequences, with profit being the ultimate goal.

In the wake of the Cold War, adapting meant exploiting the chaos of the Soviet east. The Soviet Army's massive arsenal ended up in the hands of former Soviet republics. Desperate for hard currency, they sold off weapons the same way they sold off other resources and products they inherited from the defunct Soviet Empire. Of all the republics outside of Russia, Ukraine obtained the most and most lethal weapons—enough conventional fire-power to sustain a million troops. However, the Ukrainian gov-ernment made a public show of transferring its vast nuclear arse-nal back to Russia. The Ukrainian military degenerated into a tool for revenue by a cache of politicians who took advantage of the factories and used them to manufacture and ship weapons for money to anyone who wanted them and could pay. Representa-tives from Iraq, Iran, Somalia, Yemen, Afghanistan, and Pakistan joined in this illicit trafficking market, as well as North Korea, by way of Pakistan and al-Qaeda through the Taliban.

In the hands of Victor Bout and others, Ukraine became the epicenter of global boldness in illicit arms. Bout had access to the former Soviet Union's Cold War weapons supply network along with its clandestine transport system and shipping pipelines. By 2000, according to the arms investigators of Human Rights Watch, Bout was the top arms trafficker in the world. Skirting the United Nations embargo on weapons by going to Africa where weapons smuggling was vigorous, Bout employed false end-user certificates required for any legal sale of weapons to a legitimate government. False certificates can be purchased from corrupt governments for under $100,000. Arms traffickers like Bout adroitly disguise their smuggling with what appears to be legiti-mate business activity. Weapons shopping lists are quietly passed through webs of people who fill orders, usually for cash on de-livery. Bribes are paid to military officers and officials to look the other way, and soldiers are paid to act as warehouse stock clerks. Crates of ammunition are sometimes labeled as perishable fruit. Waiting freight handlers switch cargo at "refueling" stops; a pilot may fly into an airport under one registry number and depart under a different one—and all is bogus. Payments are wired from a buyer's shell company into a seller's shell account in money-laundering havens like Dubai or the Cayman Islands. Bout's pro-curement and logistics network was fully integrated.

For Bout, arms cargo hauling is no different than transporting aspirins. He claims it is not his business to know the contents of the crates he hauls; after all, rebels very often become legitimate governments, he reasons. There is simply not enough law on arms trafficking to deter the process. Since 1990, not one UN arms embargo has resulted in the conviction of an arms trafficker. The United Nations has no power to arrest. Interpol, which basically is an information-sharing organization, depends on the co-operation of local authorities. Astonishingly, the United States, despite its having the toughest arms-trafficking laws in the world, has not prosecuted a single case of arms trafficking. As Bout is noted for stating, what is for many observers the most repugnant kind of commerce is usually not illegal at all.

Capone, Alphonse, a.k.a. "Big Al," "Snorky," and "Scarface" (1899–1947)

Place of Origin: Brooklyn, New York

Capone, a major crime leader in the United States in the 1920s, belongs to that handful of successful criminals who enjoy a kind of public admiration during their careers, despite the repugnance of their profession. Al Capone was a master criminal who stands second only to Jesse James. And just as Jesse James's popularity benefited from the Civil War tragedy, Capone's celebrity derives in large part from the war between the government and the people over Prohibition. It is estimated that in 1927, when he was only twenty-eight years old, his organization took in some $105 million. In 1930, students at the Medill School of Journalism in Chicago chose Capone as one of the most outstanding persons in the world, along with Mahatma Gandhi, Albert Einstein, and Henry Ford. Countless films, melodramas, and books have been done about Capone. He believed that he symbolized the public's discontent with social and cultural policies (Prohibition) and economic trends (the 1929 Wall Street collapse). He was a master in manipulating the media to both entertain and mislead the public.

Al Capone was born into a working-class family in Brooklyn, New York, in 1899. Typically, the family was large and close-knit. Al was a bright pupil but had little use for school. Minor squabbles with the law and his work as a bouncer in a saloon–house of prostitution produced the scar on his left cheek. As a young man, he learned the way of the streets in Brooklyn and joined a gang run by a slightly older man, Johnny Torrio, who would later play a fateful role in Capone's life in Chicago. Torrio and his partner Frankie Yale operated a brothel in Brooklyn and hired the burly young Capone as a bouncer. Within two years, Capone was facing murder charges and Torrio had relocated in Chicago to join his uncle "Big Jim" Colosimo to fend off Black Hand extortionists who wanted a piece of Colosimo's profitable prostitution empire. The Black Hand (La Mano Nera) was simply a crude method of extortion with a long Italian (chiefly Sicilian) tradition, transplanted to America during the mass immigrations of the 1880s. By the time Capone arrived in Chicago, Torrio was at odds with Colosimo over bootlegging. Torrio realized that Big Jim would have to be eliminated. Together with Capone, Torrio arranged Big Jim's assassination. Capone's position with Torrio was strengthened after Colosimo's murder.

Bootlegging dragged the gangsters to center stage. As Capone himself noted, manufacturing, importing, and serving alcohol brought him into contact with virtually every level of society, from the spacious penthouses along Lake Shore Drive to the crowded shacks on the South Side. The visibility proved, in the long run, to be a tremendous liability, exposing Capone to unrelenting law enforcement scrutiny. It was as if Prohibition had been an allure and a gigantic trap to ensnare the racketeers.

The Torrio-Capone gang moved quickly to take over criminal territories by crushing competitors. Capone organized black bootleggers, protected them from the police, and shared profits equitably with them. His willingness to work with blacks demonstrated his ability to build a broad-based economic coalition, which contributed to his political power.

In 1920, Torrio put together a bootleg syndicate, which included all the major gangs in Cook County and the Chicago suburbs. The idea was to create a business out of Prohibition; street gang leaders owned and operated breweries and distilleries, but by Torrio's gang treaty, they were to receive their supplies from Torrio as well as protection of deliveries, shipments, and trucks. The syndicate would furnish gunmen, when needed, corrupt law enforcement, where needed, and intimidate saloon keepers and "speakeasies" (illegal bars) into buying beer and whisky from the syndicate.

In the election of 1924, Al and his brother Frank brazenly led a group of 200 gunmen into Cicero to ensure the victory of local Republican candidates with a record of "accommodation" to the bootlegging underground. In the melee with police, Frank

Capone was killed, but Cicero became the headquarters of the syndicate—and remained so throughout Capone's career.

As gang war raged against the North Side gangs under Earl "Hymie" Weiss, Capone inherited an organization that was multi-ethnic, with loose ties to the local Mafia organization. Gang wars were bad for the image of the bootlegger and bad for business. So in 1926, a truce was arranged among the warring gangs, principally between Vincent ("The Schemer") Drucci, Bugs Moran—both leaders of the North Side gang—and Capone's forces.

Capone's rackets employed hundreds, if not thousands, of people caught up in the misery of the Great Depression. Indeed, the entire city of Chicago required the services of the Capone organization, in one way or another. The police needed his payoffs because they could not survive on their civil service salaries, nor could they be expected to keep order; newspapers needed the image of "Scarface" with his bodyguards, armored-plated limousine, colorful suits, and big-spending ways to sell papers; and the city's numerous speakeasies needed him to keep them supplied. Most of all, the political machine needed Capone's money and vote-generating ability to stay in office and keep the peace among the murderous gangs. Al Capone, the gangster, bootlegger, gunman, and corrupter, became, paradoxically, a force of public community stability, doing more perhaps in maintaining law and order than the police and civil authorities.

By 1927, Prohibition was entering its tenth year and had turned hundreds of thousands of otherwise law-abiding citizens into lawbreakers. Because of Prohibition, a casual disregard of the law became part of the American way of life. Capone and others like him exploited this cultural malaise. Capone was both Robin Hood and Public Enemy Number One, the villain/hero who fed hungry, out-of-work citizens from soup kitchens operated by retail food suppliers "encouraged" by Capone to provide the bread and the soup. His political power, which was crucial to his racketeering enterprises, was based solely on corruption. As his trial for tax evasion and the detailed newspaper accounts would suggest, although he did an efficient job of redistributing some wealth, he also stole as much from the poor as he did from the rich, very probably more through his control of unions and extortion activities of small businesses. Indeed, his natural victims were the small people, and the glittering wealth he displayed came largely out of the pockets of the working people who were tempted into his speakeasies, gambling dens, and brothels.

The year 1929 was a benchmark in Capone's life and in the nation's history. The racketeering coalition he had built reached across ethnic boundaries and derived illicit wealth from Jews, blacks, Italians, Irish, Polish, and WASP communities; Capone was not only the bootlegger in Chicago, but clearly he was the most dominant trafficker of illegal goods and services in the United States. He was also dominant in the areas of brothels and gambling: Capone's move into large racketeering and his infiltration of legitimate businesses made it difficult to describe him as just another thug or hoodlum. Bugs Moran was a hoodlum, Dion O'Bannion and Spike O'Donnell were gangsters, and Jake "Greasy Thumb" Guzik was a racketeer; Capone appeared to have transcended these labels: He was all of these at one time or another, but he was also something else—a feared political boss with wealth and powerful connections, legal and illegal. No one, including Capone himself, could say what he earned. He naturally avoided banks and saved nothing beyond stashes of cash he kept in his homes. He was a pipeline through which huge quantities of money passed; when he needed funds, he simply dipped into the stream and helped himself. Political circumstances favored him, even though his antihero status and great popularity among the working class and the unemployed was worrisome.

A tax evasion case against Capone was begun in 1929, and by October 1931 he stood convicted and faced a prison sentence of eleven years. In 1932, Capone entered the federal prison in Atlanta. He was transferred to the newly constructed Alcatraz facility in 1934, where it was discovered that he was suffering from an advanced case of syphilis. With his good behavior and illness, he was released in 1939. He was the quintessential illicit trafficker. Capone slowly deteriorated at his Palm Island estate in Miami during his remaining years. On January 25, 1947, he died of cardiac arrest.

Escobar, Pablo Emilio Gaviria, a.k.a. "The Godfather" (1949–1993)

Place of origin: Rionegro, Colombia
In December 1993, Pablo Escobar, leader of the Medellín Colombian drug cartel, was killed in a shootout with police officers. He had escaped from the prison he had built (a vivid example of the intrinsic extortion power of illicit criminals and insurgent forces in Colombia) to ensure his own safety and comfort prior to surrendering to authorities on drug-trafficking charges. Dissatisfied

with prison restrictions, Escobar escaped and was the subject of a countrywide manhunt that ended with his death.

One of the most powerful drug traffickers in the world, heading an organization capable of manipulating the national state through bribes and intimidation, Pablo Escobar and his cartel partners operated a government within a government in Colombia during the 1970s and 1980s. Escobar was physically unimposing: he was a short man, overweight, with a mustache and a shock of black, curly hair. He was not born in abject poverty, nor was he underprivileged as his apologists and imagemakers suggested. He in fact graduated from high school and had some university training.

Escobar's criminal career began in adolescence when he stole headstones from local graveyards and engaged in stealing and fencing (illegal resale) of stereo equipment and auto parts. He was first arrested in 1974 for auto theft, and it was not until 1976 that Escobar was arrested on drug-smuggling charges. During the marijuana-smuggling days of the late 1970s, he would emerge with a reputation in the Medellín underworld not only as a cold-blooded killer but also as a master schemer and an evader of justice.

Escobar was only one of Colombia's many cocaine traffickers who expanded their operations in the late 1970s. The men who became the leaders and biggest allies of the Medellín cartel were, like Escobar, all born between 1947 and 1949 during a chaotic political period in Colombia's history; Jorge Luis Vasquez Ochoa, Jose Gonzalo Rodriguez Gacha, and Carlos Lehder-Rivas would come together to create one of the world's most powerful drug-trafficking syndicates. Escobar's involvement as cocaine trafficker began as a middleman: he obtained small amounts of coca paste from Ecuador and sold it within Colombia. Then, after buying it from newly established laboratories in the Colombian Amazon that converted the paste into cocaine, he started to employ "mules" (couriers) who moved it to traffickers in Panama. In order to earn serious money, Escobar had to make the business vertical—that is, he needed enough money to buy bulk direct from Bolivia and Peru, and he needed enough access to consumer markets abroad. Mustering the cash brought him into partnerships with the Ochoa brothers, whose high-society links ensured a ready supply of investors.

Marijuana smuggling was so structured that many American groups could deal directly with suppliers in Mexico, Panama,

Colombia, and the Caribbean basin islands such as Jamaica. The American mob never had a chance as regards cocaine, however, inasmuch as they were too far away from its source. In any event, aided by the sudden boost of Latin American migration during the 1970s, the Colombians were already developing their own U.S. distribution networks among Cubans and Dominicans. Escobar's first priorities were to gather enough capital in order to import Bolivian and Peruvian coca paste himself—Colombian coca leaf was as yet too low in quality—and to create cocaine in his own laboratories. By the mid-1970s, his criminal activities in car theft, kidnapping, fencing stolen goods, and drug trafficking yielded sufficient profit to establish drug labs and smuggling routes.

The cartel dramatically improved its capacity to move cocaine into the United States when Carlos Lehder bought Norman's Cay, an archipelago in the Bahamas. Lehder equipped the narrow strip of coral reef with electronic equipment and airport facilities for the transport of cocaine. Larger shipments of cocaine began to make their way into the Florida Everglades and locations in the Southwest via Mexico. To operate with minimum interference from authorities, Escobar and Lehder paid bribes to Lynden Pindling, the governor-general of the Bahamas, and Panama's dictator, Manuel Noriega.

Like other Colombian traffickers, Escobar poured his money into land and buildings. Construction in Medellín quadrupled in the 1980s with money from the cartel drug mafia. Escobar's pride and joy was his 8,000-acre ranch equipped with five swimming pools, human-made lakes, a jet aircraft runway, and animal parks and zoos accommodating elephants, lions, buffaloes, zebras, rhinoceroses, and hippopotamuses. The clever Escobar used his zoo animals in his smuggling operations very effectively: animal dung masked the smell of contraband cocaine.

Along with growing political pressure from the United States, internal unrest in Colombia created serious threats to Escobar's drug empire in the late 1980s. Cocaine, and its derivative "crack," saturated American cities, and the outcry that Colombia stop the trade mounted steadily. Within the country, competition and violence among narco-traffickers were heightened by left-wing and communist terrorists such as M-19 and FARC (the Revolutionary Armed Forces of Colombia), who demanded either ransom for kidnapped cartel members or a share of the drug profits.

Escobar would have none of it. He mobilized his enforcement squads, and the Medellín mafia declared war on the guerrillas.

Dozens of top Colombian cocaine traffickers—including those from Cali, Medellín's chief competitor—gathered to develop a strategy of resistance. One Sunday in early December 1981, the cartels bared their teeth. At a soccer match in Cali, leaflets fluttered down from a small aircraft announcing the formation of *Muerte a Secuestradores* (Death to the Kidnappers). The leaflet indicated that Colombian "businessmen" had formed a defense group against the kidnappers, who would be subject to immediate execution and hung from trees in public parks. Within two months assassins killed dozens of M-19 leaders and militants; other guerrillas were turned over to Colombian security forces. The kidnap threat ended in 1982.

Escobar's problems were not over, however. Pressure from the United States on the Colombian government to extradite Escobar on drug-trafficking charges increased. Many within the cartels began to think that Escobar could be a sacrificial lamb to appease the Americans and relax the pressure on the government and the mafias, but "The Godfather" had a different approach to the problem: He arranged for an attack on the Ministry of Justice, where his hit men sought out judges who were marked for death and proceeded to destroy incriminating files. With his private army of 1,000 men, Escobar could easily kill rivals, politicians, police, and informers. During the struggle with the government, it is estimated that he was responsible for 400 deaths. Extradition on drug charges to the United States would become an irrelevant issue for the likes of Escobar.

In 1988, the Cali cartel made an attempt on Escobar's life. The "War of the Cartels," as it came to be called, ended shortly thereafter with eighty people murdered, more than sixty of whom were from Cali. Escobar had much to defend. He had put together a highly sophisticated operation with its own security force, air network, export outlets, mechanics, chemists, and hit men. The trafficking network operated across the United States and Canada and was making inroads in Europe through the Sicilian Mafia. In 1988, when Escobar faced threats from the government and drug competitors, the Medellín cartel was taking in $10 billion a year.

The Colombian government faced a dilemma with powerful traffickers such as Escobar. The U.S. government demanded their extradition, and the traffickers insisted that Colombia assert its independence and ignore American pressure. Bribes, threats, election fraud, and other forms of intimidation persuaded the

Colombians to decide to punish their own and not extradite cartel bosses. Escobar acceded to government decisions and surrendered on condition that he build his own jail to ensure his safety from other inmates.

In late November 1993, Escobar escaped from the prison facility he built and was shot dead on December 2, 1993, in a firefight with police and army units. The press indicated that members of the rival Cali cartel helped police locate Escobar. The question facing both Colombians and Americans, many of whom suffer greatly from cocaine and crack addiction, is whether the elimination or incarceration of the leaders of criminal organizations is enough to frustrate narcotics trafficking. So far, the evidence suggests that a kingpin strategy focused on the leaders has not dramatically affected the availability of cocaine on the streets of American cities.

Herrera-Buitrago, Helmer, a.k.a. "Pacho" (1951–)

Place of origin: Palmira, Colombia
Helmer Herrera, a Colombian cocaine-trafficking boss, was one of the most influential and violent members of the Cali cartel leadership. Herrera was one of the charter members of the Cali trafficking organization and was the last remaining "kingpin" sought by Colombian authorities. At one point he was the subject of an intensive manhunt by both the Colombian National Police (CNP) and the Drug Enforcement Administration of the U.S. government. (In June 1995, a federal grand jury in Miami issued the first RICO indictment against the Cali cartel, charging fifty-nine defendants, effectively smashing the top hierarchy of the Cali cartel. The defendants included the four Cali kingpins—Miguel Rodriguez-Orejuela, Gilberto Rodriguez-Orejuela, Jose Santacruz-Londono, and Helmer Herrera-Buitrago—as well as nine managers, ten lawyers, and several hit men. The indictment charged the Cali cartel with the importation of 200,000 kilograms of cocaine and the laundering of $2 billion dollars from 1983 through 1995. Cali kingpins Gilberto and Miguel Rodriguez-Orejuela were apprehended and jailed in Colombia in 1995. Santacruz-Londono and Herrera-Buitriago were later killed.)

Pacho Herrera started his criminal career selling relatively small amounts of cocaine in New York, where he was arrested in

1975 and again later in 1976. He was a major supplier of cocaine for both New York and southern Florida. The Colombian charges against Herrera were based on the seizure of 3,500 kilograms of cocaine in Tarpon Springs, Florida, in 1988. The violence and suffering caused by Herrera's criminal activities extended from the jungles of Colombia to the neighborhoods of Florida and the streets of New York.

Herrera's organization was large and well organized. He had multiple sources for cocaine base from both Peru and Bolivia and an excellent transportation organization, which delivered cocaine base to numerous conversion laboratories in Colombia. DEA intelligence reports indicate that Herrera had used his close association with various guerrilla groups, including M-19 and the Revolutionary Armed Forces of Colombia (FARC) for the protection of remote laboratory sites. Herrera's organization staged cocaine shipments from clandestine airstrips in Colombia and from north coast ports through Central America and the Caribbean to various U.S. locations. To ensure the rapid return of his cocaine distribution profits to Colombia, he operated one of the Cali cartel's most profitable money-laundering operations in New York. In 1995, Pacho Herrera became the subject of law enforcement investigations in the Eastern District of New York and was indicted on drug-related charges in Federal District court in the Southern District of Florida in June 1995. In September 1995, Herrera was murdered, by an unknown assassin, to prevent him from incriminating other members of the Cali cartel.

Khan, Abdul Qadeer, a.k.a. A. Q. Khan, "Father of the Muslim Atomic Bomb" (1936–)

Place of Origin: Bhopal, India
Since the invention of nuclear weapons sixty years ago, no one has done more as a trafficker of nuclear materials than Khan, whose network flourished across thirty countries. Khan has confessed to transferring nuclear know-how to Iran, Libya, and North Korea. U.S. officials and investigators at the United Nations' International Atomic Energy Agency still continue to search for other customers who possess Khan's blueprints for nuclear equipment and how-to manuals for running uranium enrichment centrifuges.

Pakistan exploded a series of atomic bombs in 1998, bringing it into nuclear parity with India. Khan trained as an engineer at the University of Karachi and obtained metallurgical training in Germany, Belgium, and Holland. In the 1970s, he worked for a consortium funded by the British, Dutch, and German governments that manufactured centrifuges used to make atomic bombs. Khan later stole centrifuge designs and fled to Pakistan in 1976 where he ran the country's nuclear program for the next twenty-five years. In contrast to bin Laden, Khan's whereabouts are well known. He is living under house arrest in Islamabad, the capital of Pakistan, as part of a deal that Pakistan's president Pervez Musharraf unveiled in 2004 with the United States and the global community. That deal pardoned Khan and allowed him to keep the millions of dollars he is thought to have netted from the illicit sales. In exchange, Khan took responsibility for the crimes and agreed to house arrest—a punishment that has forced him to vanish from public life and scientific endeavor.

Khun Sa, a.k.a. Chang Chi Fu, "The Prince of Death" (1934–)

Place of Origin: Burma

Khun Sa was the head of the Shan United Army (SUA), the leading heroin-trafficking group in the Golden Triangle, which comprises the countries of Burma, Thailand, and Laos. Khun Sa and his family have been active in the opium trade for many years. In 1960, the Burmese government organized a self-defense force under Khun Sa to defend itself against ethnic Shan resistance groups in the Shan State. To support his self-defense force, Khun Sa transported opium for major traffickers. By January 1969, he emerged as one of the most powerful ethnic Chinese self-defense force leaders in Upper Burma and the undisputed drug king of the Golden Triangle.

In the 1990s, the Golden Triangle, headed by drug lord Khun Sa, found itself under attack by the Burmese Military Junta. Khun Sa responded by shifting the trafficking of heroin westward to make greater use of Laos, and possibly Cambodia and Vietnam as well. The heroin was then transported to international markets by independent brokers and shippers. These brokers provided connections to ethnic Chinese criminals acting as wholesale distributors in the United States and Europe and to an ancillary pool of Nigerian and West African traffickers, smuggling Southeast Asian heroin through their own criminal group contacts.

Two major developments combined against Khun Sa in 1994: (1) the Thai government closed the country's borders, thus depriving the Shan United Army of essential operational materiel, and (2) the U.S. Drug Enforcement Administration, working with the Royal Thai government, arrested thirteen of Khun Sa's top lieutenants in "Operation Tiger Trap," thus depriving the SUA of cash from heroin trafficking. With their heroin trafficking disabled, the Shan United Army surrendered to the Burmese Army in December 1995, and Khun Sa stepped down from its leadership. However, the Burmese junta of military rulers continues to enjoy the fruits of illicit drug trafficking through sheltering Khun Sa and other drug traffickers in Rangoon. The historical roots and modern-day tentacles of Khun Sa remain deeply rooted in Southeast Asia.

In December 2004, the United States issued indictments of eight major Southeast Asia drug barons, specifically in Burma. As it has consistently been proven, however, the elimination of the heads of large-scale criminal enterprises is not effective, for eventually a new leadership emerges, beginning a new range of nefarious strategies by lower level operatives of the criminal enterprise.

As with the new-generation international law enforcement strategies and tactics, global illicit drug production and trafficking is also adapting to twenty-first-century information technology and strategies in furthering criminal goals. Currently, Khun Sa lives in Yangon, Burma.

Lehder-Rivas, Carlos (1949–)

Place of origin: Colombia
Carlos Lehder-Rivas, a Medellín cartel drug lord, was born in Colombia but lived in Detroit, Michigan, for almost ten years; there he acquired English and knowledge of American culture. In 1973, he became involved with car thieves and was arrested. He skipped bail but was later arrested in Miami on drug possession charges. When he was released in 1975, he was deported. By 1980, he was smuggling cocaine into the United States; business was so profitable that planeloads of cocaine were being shipped into the United States, provided in part by Pablo Emilio Escobar, a leader of the Medellín cartel.

Scoring great success in drug trafficking, Lehder moved into Norman's Cay in the Bahamas, where he bought a luxurious home and constructed an airport to facilitate drug-smuggling operations into the United States. It has been alleged that Lehder bribed the Bahamian prime minister, Lynden O. Pindling, to ignore the smuggling operation. Other members of the Medellín cartel, namely, Pablo Escobar and Jorge Luis Vasques Ochoa, utilized the airstrip for their shipments of cocaine to America. The close relationship among Lehder, Escobar, and Ochoa would develop into a coalition that would rule the cocaine trade and set the terms of organization during the period of its greatest expansion.

In 1981, Lehder was indicted by a Jacksonville, Florida, federal grand jury for drug trafficking and income tax evasion. His extradition was requested, but first he had to be found and arrested. Lehder was obsessed by fantasies of political power and had become violently anti-American. He founded a youth movement and supported candidates for political office in Colombia. While a fugitive in 1985, perhaps because he felt hounded by American law enforcement pressure for his arrest and extradition to the United States for trial, Lehder appeared on Colombian television appealing to Colombian revolutionary organizations, such as the Marxist group known as M-19, to provide protection and resources for the "cocaine bonanza" as an effort to resist American imperialism. Lehder explained to his stunned audiences that marijuana and cocaine could be the weapons of revolution against the power of the North American colossus.

His party newspaper printed articles condemning the DEA, and distributed leaflets in the countryside, urging the peasants to join the guerrillas and traffickers. In a shootout in 1987, Lehder was finally arrested and extradited to the United States. It is rumored that others in the drug cartel may have betrayed him, fearing all the public attention Lehder attracted with his antics. The following year he was convicted of cocaine trafficking and sentenced to life without parole in a federal correctional facility.

"Little Pete," a.k.a. F. C. Peters, Fung Jing Day (1864–1897)

Place of origin: Fung Ching in Kow Gong, Canton, China
Fung Ching, "Little Pete," a Chinese "Godfather" of considerable reputation and prestige, was shot down by an unknown gunman in San Francisco in 1897 in front of his home, despite the extraordinary protection he had arranged for himself. A prosperous

businessman who was highly literate and fluent in English and Cantonese, Little Pete was also the boss of Chinatown crime at the time of his death in one of the biggest cities in the United States—San Francisco. Little Pete was respected and yet hated.

Little Pete was born in Kow Gong, a small town ten miles out of Canton in 1864 and arrived in San Francisco in 1874 at the age of ten. In his early teens he worked hard as an errand boy for a shoe factory and helped to support his family. His ambitions took him to the Sunday School of the Methodist Chinese Mission and its schools where he learned to speak, read, and write proficiently in English—a rare asset among the mass of illiterate Chinese migrants at that time. While still a youth, Little Pete became involved in citywide politics. Handsome, intelligent, and always fastidious in his clothes, he served as an interpreter for the Sam Yup Company which gave him access to all sorts of business information which he shrewdly exploited in his own interests. With money earned as a middleman between the white and Chinese communities, Little Pete was able to establish himself in the shoe business with his uncle and brother. He built upon a thriving wholesale business, and he even hired white sales employees to sell his shoes along the entire West Coast of the United States from Puget Sound to San Diego. Within a short time he was independently wealthy. But he was not content. Little Pete opened gambling dens and formed a fighting Tong, the Gee Sin Seer, to protect his activities in gambling, opium, smuggling immigrants, and prostitution. In time, Little Pete's Tong went to war with the Bo Sin Seer Tongs, so he hired Boo How Day—hatchet men and professional killers known as "Highbinders" because of their use of wood hatchets and meat cleavers and because of their traditional Chinese dress, which included bound leggings worn outwardly on their pants.

In 1887, Little Pete was arrested and convicted in connection with his criminal enterprises, including jury tampering and bribing law enforcement officers. He served five years in Folsom Prison. When he was released, he renewed his role as a criminal entrepreneur and added fixing horse races to his criminal repertoire. At the time of his assassination, he was the mastermind behind many extortion schemes in the Chinatowns of San Francisco and Sacramento and held great power over the Highbinders. He continued with his immigrant trafficking, enabling thousands of Chinese to come to the United States and work.

In 1889, some 30,000 Chinese, mainly males, lived in San Francisco's Dupont Gai, as the Chinese called Grant Avenue. Although they constituted a whole city within a city, the Chinese were never fully accepted during the whole of the nineteenth century; indeed, it was not until after World War I that first-class citizenship was extended to San Franciscans of Chinese heritage. The blame for the exclusion of the Chinese in "Gum San Ta Fow" (Big City in the Land of Golden Hills), as San Francisco was known, did not rest entirely with the host community. For fifty years after the Gold Rush, Chinatown was the Celestial Empire's most far-flung political and cultural outpost. Chinatown was run not exclusively by the mayor of San Francisco, but by the consul general of Imperial China and dubious early Chinese versions of "The Godfather," among whom Little Pete was the most distinguished.

Luciano, Charles "Lucky," a.k.a. "Charley Lucky" and Charles Ross (1897–1962)

Place of origin: Sicily

Charles "Lucky" Luciano was born Salvatore Luciania in Sicily on November 24, 1897. A major La Cosa Nostra boss, he is best known for transforming brawling gangs of thugs into smooth-running crime syndicates. He was the original "Dapper Don" in the New York underworld, smooth and deadly. With the possible exception of Al Capone, Luciano was the most influential Italian American gangster in the twentieth century. In 1931, Luciano played an important role in "Americanizing" organized crime. With Meyer Lansky, Owney Madden, "Moe" Dalitz, and other underworld figures around the country, Luciano helped create a national gambling syndicate and a Mafia Commission to resolve disputes and conflicts among Mafiosi. He also played a significant role in heroin trafficking, prostitution, and illegal alcohol trafficking during Prohibition.

Luciano immigrated to the United States in 1906 with his family. He rarely attended school, and in 1907 he was arrested for shoplifting. Luciano began working legitimately for a hat manufacturer, but his life in the slums of the Lower East Side of Manhattan also equipped him with a set of criminal skills and values that pushed aside the ethic of hard work to which his family and many other immigrants were committed.

Before he was eighteen years old, Luciano had been charged and convicted of heroin possession and served a prison term of six months. By 1916, he was a leading member of the notorious

"Five Points Gang." Apart from its routine criminal activities, the Five Pointers worked for the Tammany Hall political machine and enjoyed its protection.

By 1920, Luciano had emerged as a power in the bootlegging rackets and was closely tied to Meyer Lansky and "Bugsy" Siegel. Through Lansky and Siegel, Luciano expanded his network of friends and associates to include other ethnic gangsters. Ignoring the warning of the old-time Mafiosi about associating with non-Italians, Luciano maintained these ties, believing instead that the "Mustache Petes" (the Old World gangsters) were the problem. At the same time, he became a boss in New York's largest Mafia crime family led by "Joe the Boss" Masseria, for whom he felt contempt but whom he feared—at least until the Castellammarese War erupted between Joe the Boss and his Sicilian immigrant rival, Salvatore Maranzano. Masseria was the main obstacle but was ultimately removed through a plot in which Luciano played a central role. Luciano and his associates were seen as threats to the Mafia kingdom that Maranzano envisioned. Therefore, Maranzano began planning Luciano's death as well as that of another potential rival: Al Capone. But Maranzano failed to act quickly enough, and Luciano learned of his murder plans. With Lansky's aid, Luciano arranged for Maranzano's murder in his office while Maranzano himself awaited the arrival of Luciano, whom he planned to kill.

The "Old World" Mafia lost its foothold in America with the end of the Castellammarese War. Luciano was at the pinnacle of criminal power. Not only did he enjoy the protection and support of La Cosa Nostra crime families (he headed one of several in New York), but his alliance with Jews, Irish, and other ethnics enabled him to accumulate additional power that ensured his virtual domination of American organized crime.

In 1935, Thomas E. Dewey, a rackets-busting special prosecutor, launched a campaign against the big crime bosses in New York. A year later, Luciano was convicted of compulsory prostitution and was sentenced to fifty years imprisonment. The sentence was a cruel twist of fate for Luciano because earlier he had saved Dewey's life: Dewey, unknowingly, had had his life threatened, and he was saved through Luciano's intervention. Luciano realized the infamy of such an act would bring an onslaught of attention and interdiction to the crime syndicate.

During World War II, German U-boats and agents posed a threat to the waterfront facilities on the East Coast of the United

States. Shipping war supplies to the British and Russians was vital for the Allies, and German submarine operations and espionage activities were very active in critical port areas from Newfoundland to the Caribbean. U.S. Naval Intelligence approached Luciano for help. Through Joseph "Socks" Lanza, Luciano instructed his associates in the International Longshoremen's Union to cooperate with the U.S. Navy in reporting incidents of sabotage and by providing information on suspected enemy agents.

In another effort to help his adopted country in 1943, Luciano, through his underboss Vito Genovese (who left the United States before the war to avoid a murder indictment), alerted the Sicilian Mafia bosses to help the Allied invasion of Sicily. As a result of his services to the United States during the war, in 1946 Luciano was pardoned by Governor Thomas E. Dewey but was deported to Italy with the provision that he not return to the United States. Eight months after his departure to Naples, Luciano traveled to Havana, Cuba, and set up a major syndicate meeting in 1947 where drug trafficking and the status of the mob's investment in the Las Vegas Flamingo Hotel construction (being handled by "Bugsy" Siegel) were on the agenda. When U.S. government agents discovered Luciano's presence, he was forced to return to Italy, where he nonetheless continued to issue orders. With protests from the Federal Narcotics Bureau, the Italian government forced Luciano to take up residence in Palermo, Sicily, which, however, did not deter his efforts to set up a heroin pipeline to the United States.

Minin, Leonid, a.k.a. Leon Minin, Wulf Breslav, Leonid Bluvshtein, Leonid Bluvstein, Igor Osols, Vladimir Abramovich Kerler, Igor Limar (1947–)

Place of origin: Odessa, Soviet Ukraine

The arrest in 2000 of suspected arms smuggler Leonid Minin, who is currently in Vigevano prison outside Milan, Italy, is just one piece of a puzzle involving illicit weapons, high-level corruption, and organized crime centered in Ukraine. Minin was charged for violating a UN arms embargo adopted by the Italian parliament, thus becoming Italian law. It is the first such case which does not involve a national law separate from the embargo. Others have been convicted for arms deals to embargoed countries, but the crimes generally have involved national export laws and attempts to obscure the recipient—when the customer is a country under UN embargo. The case is potentially precedent setting and could encourage other prosecutors around the world to bring more cases against embargo busters.

Even after Minin's highly publicized arrest, the conditions for the sales of small arms to embargoed African hot spots remain the same: a massive supply of small arms sits stockpiled in the former Soviet Union; extensive networks of organized gun smuggling are formed and regroup if discovered; government corruption and negligence is the norm in impoverished countries; the system of controls worldwide has little defense against unscrupulous arms brokers; and the demand for arms remains constant.

His known business activities include oil, electricity, timber, small arms, Russian religious icons, diamonds, and gems (Russian and possibly African), consumer goods, and prefabricated homes. He is subject to ongoing investigations in several European countries for money laundering and cocaine trafficking.

A Ukrainian parliamentary inquiry concluded that between 1992 and 1998, Ukraine lost $32 billion in military assets, in part through theft, discount arms sales, and lack of oversight. Although Ukraine's legal arms industry has boomed, the international small arms black market may have proved far more lucrative. Ukrainian arms have been linked to some of the world's bloodiest conflicts and most notorious governments, including the Iraqi regime of Saddam Hussein, the Taliban in Afghanistan, and other hot spots around the globe, from Sierra Leone to Croatia.

Noriega, Manuel Antonio (1934–)

Place of origin: Panama City, Panama

First a friend, then an enemy, of the United States, Manuel A. Noriega, the strongman of Panama, was finally deposed by a U.S. military invasion, captured, and brought to Miami for trial in 1989. Manuel Antonio Noriega was born on February 11, 1934, in Panama City, Panama, the son of an accountant and his maid in a poor barrio of Panama City in 1934. He attended the National Institute, a well-regarded high school, with the intention of becoming a doctor, but lack of financial resources prevented fulfillment of this career choice. Instead, Noriega accepted a scholarship to attend the Peruvian Military Academy. He graduated in 1962 with a degree in engineering. Returning to Panama, he was commissioned a sublieutenant in the National Guard.

Noriega acquired the command of Chiriqui, the country's westernmost province. In October 1968, military conspirators overturned the civilian government of Amulfo Arias. Noriega's troops seized radio and telephone stations in David, the provincial capital. Omar Efraín Torrijos Herrera, the military head of the province, emerged from the coup as the strongman. From that moment, Noriega's career blossomed. In 1971, he became useful to U.S. intelligence and at the behest of the Nixon administration, went to Havana to obtain the release of crewmen of two American freighters seized by Fidel Castro's government. He was already involved in narcotics trafficking at the time. (Panama's National Guard had been implicated in the heroin trade from the late 1940s.) American officials learned that Noriega was the Panama "connection," and a high-ranking drug enforcement officer recommended that President Nixon order his assassination, but Nixon demurred because Noriega was useful to U.S. counterintelligence. As head of G-2, Panama's military intelligence command, Noriega was the second most powerful man in Panama. In 1975, G-2 agents rounded up businessmen critical of Torrijos's dictatorial populist style, confiscated their property, and sent them into exile in Ecuador. Torrijos said of Noriega, "This is my gangster." Torrijos died in 1981 in a mysterious plane crash, and in the ensuing two-year contest for power between civilian politicians and ambitious military officers, Noriega emerged triumphant. In late 1983, following his promotion to general and commander of the National Guard, the guard was combined with the navy and air force into the Panama Defense Forces (which also included the national police). The following year Noriega's choice for president, Nicholas Arditio Barietta, won a narrow victory over Amulfo Arias. But there was widespread fraud in the election, and Noriega forced Barietta out. The reasons for Noriega's actions had less to do with fraud or Barietta's economic policies than with Barietta's alleged threat to investigate the brutal slaying of Hug Spadora, who had publicly accused Noriega of being a drug trafficker. In 1985, G-2 agents had taken Spadora from a bus near the Costa Rican border, and in September of that year, searchers found his tortured, decapitated body stuffed in a U.S. mailbag on the Costa Rican side of the border. In addition, in June 1986, *New York Times* investigative reporter Seymour Hersh reported that Noriega had used his position to facilitate sale of restricted U.S. technology to Eastern European governments. In the process Noriega had earned $3 million.

Noriega denounced these and other allegations as a conspiracy of right-wing U.S. politicians looking for a way to undo the Panama Canal treaties before the canal became Panamanian property on December 31, 1999. Yet more allegations about Noriega now surfaced. During the Reagan administration's covert war against the government of Nicaragua in the 1980s, Noriega helped to supply arms to the Nicaraguan resistance called the Contras. (The U.S. Congress had prohibited any expenditures to bring down the Nicaraguan government.) At the same time, he received arms from Cuba and sold them to Salvadoran leftist guerrillas and supplied Nicaraguan leaders with intelligence reports. Although Noriega was a gunrunner, money launderer, drug trafficker, and double agent, he was still useful to the U.S. government and its policies in Latin America.

In June 1987, a former naval officer accused Noriega in the death of Torrijos. Middle-class Panamanians organized street demonstrations, demanding his ouster. Noriega responded by declaring a national emergency. He suspended constitutional rights, shut down the newspapers and radio stations, and drove his political enemies into exile. Church leaders, businessmen, and students, dressed in white, organized into the National Civil Crusade and went into the streets banging pots and pans. The riot squads dispersed them. By now the Americans were outraged, and in June 1987, the U.S. Senate called for Noriega's removal. Noriega retaliated by removing police protection from the U.S. embassy; subsequently, a pro-Noriega mob attacked the building and caused $100,000 in damages. From that day, the administration of President Ronald Regan began looking for a way to bring Noriega down. U.S. economic and military assistance came to an end, and Panamanian bankers began withdrawing their support (Torrijos had transformed the country into an international banking center). As a result, Noriega rapidly lost favor everywhere except among the Panama Defense Forces.

In October 1989, the firing on U.S. soldiers passing by the PDF headquarters caused the United States to launch a full-scale attack ("Operation Just Cause") with 24,000 troops on December 20, 1989. Noriega evaded capture for a few days and ultimately took refuge in the Papal Nunciature. Under pressure from Vatican officials, Noriega surrendered to the Vatican Embassy in Panama City on January 3, 1990. He was convicted of cocaine trafficking, racketeering, and money laundering and sentenced to forty years in a federal prison. He was also ordered to pay $44 million to the Panamanian government. The trial was not without controversy, however; in late 1995, there were charges of bribery. The DEA was told that the Cali drug cartel had paid a witness, Ricardo Bilonik, to testify about Noriega's ties to the Medellín cartel, Cali's rival. Since then, however, federal prosecutors have determined that the bribery charges were not enough to justify a new trial. In 1999, his sentence was reduced to thirty years, making Noriega eligible for parole in 2006. He is incarcerated in a federal U.S. prison in southern California.

Ochoa, Jorge Luis Vasquez, a.k.a. "El Gordo" (The Fat Man) (1949–)

Place of origin: Medellín, Colombia

Along with Pablo Escobar, Jorge Luis Vasquez, known as "The Fat Man," was one of the original members of the Medellín cartel. After being on the run for years, Ochoa surrendered to authorities in Colombia in January 1991, as did his brothers Fabio and Juan David. All pled guilty, confessed to a few narcotics-related crimes, agreed to pay nominal fines, and went to jail. Ochoa was released in July 1996 after serving five and a half years in custody. He is believed to be one of the world's wealthiest men and is probably worth more than $10 billion. For years prior to their arrests, the Ochoas presided over *la mafia criolla*, the Colombian version of La Cosa Nostra. Medellín was the boiler room of the international cocaine trade, and Ochoa and his family were among a handful of families that dominated it.

Jorge Ochoa and his relatives and friends, including Pablo Escobar and Jose Gonzalo Rodriguez Gacha, controlled a loose federation of underground corporations they called "la compania" (the company), known to the outside world as the cartel. It was well structured and highly organized for efficient and profitable international drug trafficking. With it were groups specializing in obtaining the raw materials needed for the production of cocaine and delivering them to clandestine laboratories throughout Colombia, Panama, Venezuela, Brazil, Argentina, and even the United States. There were groups responsible for security and, if necessary, for subverting law enforcement agents, the military, politicians, judges, and even presidents. Yet other groups handled transportation of the cocaine to markets around the world.

As the cartel grew in wealth and power, Ochoa wanted more, including a stake in the U.S. distribution. In the early phases of trafficking, the cartel wholesaled cocaine to retail distributors in the United States. In the late 1980s, the Ochoas set up thousands of Colombians in "cells," which were small distributing groups in key markets in U.S. and European cities, including Madrid, Paris, London, Rome, Hamburg, Rotterdam, Los Angeles and Miami. The cells were organized by special envoys from Medellín and worked under a strict code of discipline under Ochoa's leadership. The Medellín cartel emerged as a sophisticated and ruthless multinational conglomerate dealing in dope. Ochoa brought Colombia to its knees through violence and corruption and had an impact on other countries far beyond Colombia's borders.

In 1984, Ochoa was arrested in Spain on a charge of conspiracy to distribute cocaine. The DEA pressed the Spanish government to extradite him to the United States. After a year of legal battles, the U.S. extradition petition having been denied, Ochoa was sent back to Colombia on charges of illegal bull smuggling. The American government lost the appeal, following the assassination of the chief witness against Ochoa, Barry Seal, a former air smuggler in the employ of the Medellín cartel.

Ochoa managed to stay free in Colombia on the bull-smuggling charges through the shrewd manipulation of his lawyers. On November 21, 1987, he was arrested for speeding by a traffic cop not far from Cali. The Fat Man tried to bribe the police, offering at one point 100 million pesos ($400,000), but they would have none of it. The government decided to hold him on the bull-smuggling charge and then considered extradition to the United States, but the cartel reacted to Ochoa's capture almost immediately. Within twenty-four hours, twelve gunmen attempted to assassinate Gomez Martinez, editor of Bogotá's biggest daily newspaper, in his home. The attempt failed, but the cartel made it clear that it did not want Ochoa extradited to the United States and threatened total war against the country's political leaders. On January 18, 1988, a candidate for mayor of Bogotá was abducted; a week later, Carlos Mauro Hayos, attorney general of Colombia, was attacked, abducted, and executed. After hiding out while the war between Colombian authorities and the cartel continued, Ochoa surrendered and served a sentence in Colombia. He was not extradited.

Ong, Benny, a.k.a. "Uncle Seven" (1907–1994)

Place of origin: Hong Kong

Benny Ong, the Hip Sing Tong boss and Chinatown "Godfather," personified the two sides of life in Chinatowns throughout America. He lived in both the underworld and upperworld, maintaining that invisible line between the legitimate and the illegitimate, between what tourists see on the colorful streets and what goes on behind the Chinatown storefronts. Many of the Tong leaders who make up the legitimate power of community leaders, merchant associations, district family associations, and burial societies are also sponsors of illegal gambling halls, prostitution services, drug trafficking, and alien smuggling groups.

When Benny Ong died in 1994 there was a funeral procession in the streets of New York's Chinatown. Thousands of people lined the sidewalks as his twelve-car funeral procession made its way through the humid, narrow streets. A large photo of his smiling face, decked out in white carnations and red roses, was mounted in a flower limousine. The words "Big Bucks, Benny Ong" were displayed on flowerpots in keeping with the Chinese tradition of wishing the dead prosperity in the afterlife.

"Uncle Seven," as he was known in Chinatown (because of the number seven signifying the most lucky number and his position as a benefactor to those needing a favor), was well known for his temper and energy even in his old age. As "adviser for life" of the Hip Sing, a powerful Chinatown Tong, Ong was considered one of Chinatown's most important elders. His influence was enormous: Uncle Seven could help an immigrant get a job, settle a dispute between businessmen, secure loans for merchants, and so on. In 1991, a U.S. Senate subcommittee identified Benny Ong as the "Godfather" of organized crime in Chinatown. He allegedly took a percentage of gambling, loan-sharking, and extortion money in the Hip Sing territory, which covered scores of restaurants and retail businesses along the Bowery and Pell and Hester streets. His real claim to power lay in his influence with the Flying Dragons, a vicious street gang affiliated with the Hip Sing for more than two decades. The Flying Dragons protected the Tongs' gambling establishments, exacted extortion payments from businesses in the Tongs' territory—sparing only those with close ties to Uncle Seven—and played roles in his drug-trafficking and alien-smuggling enterprises. The alien-smuggling enterprises supplied "slave labor" for Chinatown's numerous small manufacturing "sweatshop" industries. Anyone daring to question Ong's power did so at great risk.

Riina, Salvatore, a.k.a. Toto "The Beast" (1931–)

Place of origin: Palermo, Sicily

Between 1974 and 1980, Salvatore Riina began building one of the largest, richest, and most violent criminal empires in the world. He ultimately became boss of the Sicilian Mafia. The corpses and maimed bodies that began showing up all over Messina and other parts of Sicily were testimony to his bloody rise to absolute power. Toto Riina was for many the perfect embodiment of evil incarnate; even his fellow Mafiosi were shocked by his willingness to kill. Before his happenstance arrest on the streets of Palermo in January 1993, Riina had been a fugitive for twenty-three years, sentenced in absentia to nine life terms for murder. He was believed to have personally shot or strangled at least forty people and masterminded the liquidation of a thousand others. With cold, relentless efficiency, Riina had eliminated any rival who stood in his way. If the intended victim managed to escape, the guns, knives, ropes, and bombs were turned on his family; he would target mothers and children, bomb their churches, burn their homes.

The murders of Judges Giovanni Falcone and Paolo Borsellino just twenty days apart in May and June 1992 in Palermo were among the most daring and violent in the long, blood-soaked history of the Mafia. Falcone, a Sicilian, had launched a major crackdown on Mafia heroin operations. Testimony in the 1995 "nontrials" established that a $20 billion a year international drug empire stretched from Southeast and Southwest Asia to Western Europe and across the Atlantic to the Americas. Riina was one of the controlling bosses on the heroin network, and he tolerated no obstacles, including magistrates and judges. Falcone and his Sicilian colleague, Paolo Borsellino (also murdered by the Mafia in a car bombing), brought approximately 500 crime indictments that threatened the breakup of the drug empire. Falcone had to be eliminated.

Toto Riina cleverly used the fabulous new wealth of the drug trade to undermine his main rivals. Because members of different families were free to do drug deals together, Riina cultivated rising members of each family and pitted them against their bosses. By 1981, he had planted his own men in all the most important families, and then, with stunning rapidity, he had several of Sicily's most powerful bosses murdered, often by their own soldiers. Murder and internal warfare were hardly new to La Cosa Nostra, but this was no conventional Mafia war: it was a genuine extermination campaign, targeting not only the old bosses but virtually everyone connected with the Mafia families. Hundreds of friends and relatives, women, and children were hunted down and murdered. And once the war was won, Riina had many of his chosen assassins eliminated because they themselves had become too powerful.

Although the great Mafia war ended with the total victory of Toto Riina and the Corleonesi clan, the heart of the Sicilian Mafia who were located in the village of Corleone, the war helped shatter the code of silence, *omerta*, on which La Cosa Nostra's power had long relied. The survivors of the losing clans lived like cornered animals waiting for their own assassination, watching helplessly as friends and relatives were murdered. La Cosa Nostra killed more than a dozen relatives of Tommaso Buscetta, including two of his sons, even though Buscetta, who was then living in Brazil, represented little threat to the Corleonesi. For those men, almost the only hope of survival and revenge lay in cooperation with the police.

The rise of the Corleonesi also altered the balance of power between La Cosa Nostra and the political world. In the past, the Mafia had accepted occasional jail terms as an occupational hazard necessary to allow the government to save face with the public. In compensation, judges rarely sent Mafia members to jail for more than a few years. The old relationship between Mafia and politics was one of negotiation and mediation. Between 1975 and 1978, La Cosa Nostra had killed only one prosecutor; since 1978, however, it has assassinated more than twenty-five public servants involved in the fight against the Mafia. Those killings and the escalation of the drug trade in Italy made it more and more difficult for Sicilian politicians to justify maintaining friendly ties with "men of honor." Besides, many of the "moderate" Mafia bosses who were killed off by Riina in the 1980s were among those who had the closest ties to the political world.

Riina is believed to have been behind the most spectacular political crimes of the last two decades: the assassination of the police prefect of Palermo in broad daylight, General Carol Alberto Dalla Chiesa, in 1982, and the Falcone and Borsellino assassinations in 1992. With such an aura of power it was a shock when after his arrest on the streets of Palermo by the Italian Carabinieri, a short, paunchy, sixty-two-year-old diabetic with crudely cut short hair and inexpensive, ill-fitting clothes appeared before the magistrate. Riina looked like what his fake identity card declared: a Sicilian farmhand on a visit to the big city. The man the Mafia referred to as "the beast" was a model of soft-spoken, Old World courtesy; he stood whenever prosecutors entered the courtroom, and he addressed them deferentially. Insisting he was simply a poor, sick old man, he said he knew nothing about La Cosa Nostra. Riina seems an anomalous, almost impossible figure. In a modern Europe with high-tech bullet trains and First World economies, Riina is a throwback. His capture would mark the culmination of a remarkable reversal for the Mafia, which began after the devastating murders of Giovanni Falcone and Paolo Borsellino.

With its Capo in jail and an ongoing avalanche of defections, the Sicilian Mafia's future was now open to question, In fact, Toto Riina may not even have lost his power. Although he already had two unserved life sentences, Riina was nonetheless tried and convicted of dozens of crimes over the next decade, including the murders of Falcone and Borsellino. In 1998, Riina picked up yet another life sentence for the high-profile murder of Salvo Lima, a politician who had long since been suspected of being in league with the Mafia and who had been shot dead after he had failed to prevent the convictions of Mafiosi in the Maxi Trials of the mid-1980s.

Riina is currently held in a maximum security prison, with limited contact with the outside world, in order to prevent him from running his organization from behind bars as many others have done. Over $125,000,000 in assets were confiscated from Riina—probably just a fraction of his illicit fortune—and his vast mansion was also acquired by the crusading anti-Mafia mayor of Corleone in 1997. In a move that was both practical and symbolic, this mansion was turned into a school for the local children. One of Riina's close friends in the Corleonsi clan, Bernardo Provenzano, is believed to have taken over as head of the organization.

Tijuana Cartel

Once Mexico's deadliest drug-trafficking organization, the now weakened Tijuana cartel merged with the so-called Gulf cartel, led by Osiel Cardenas, in late 2004 to fend off usurpers. The Tijuana cartel leaders continued to manage their organizations from prison. As another sign of intercartel cooperation, Mexican officials reported that the so-called Zetas, specially trained antinarcotics troops who joined the Gulf cartel as enforcers, were believed to have acted as hired killers for the Arellano Felix Organization (AFO). Many law enforcement officials attribute the unusual level of violence in Tijuana to the arrests of major players in 2000. Then-president Ernesto Zedillo issued an ultimatum to the cartel on February 25, 2000. Two days later Tijuana's police chief was ambushed and killed. President Zedillo also dealt another serious blow, sending in federal troops and Mexican soldiers, and federal agents nabbed Ismael "El Mayel" Higuera Guerrero, the cartel's chief lieutenant. Higuera Guerrero has been blamed for forty murders, including the murder of the Tijuana police chief and three antidrug agents. U.S. authorities in San Diego continue to tighten the noose on the cartel. Prosecutors unsealed a ten-count indictment accusing the cartel leaders of shipping large quantities of drugs from Mexico into Southern California and of using violence, intimidation, and bribery to maintain power over its illicit operations in the United States. The virulent forces of the Gulf cartel continue to be evident via shadow illicit drug syndicates. Recent intelligence indicates that Mexico's cartels are behind the almost daily drug-related murders from Cancún, an entry point for Colombian cocaine, to Reynosa and Tijuana, border transshipment centers. It appears that the loss of their imprisoned leaders is invoking internal wars over control of the lucrative drug cartel enterprises.

5

Statistics and Reference Documents

For the researcher just setting out on his or her exploration of illicit trafficking, it is useful to become familiar with the major sources of information. As there are countless sources available, in each section of this chapter we present documents and data from the perspective of the U.S. government, the United Nations, and one major nongovernmental organization that conducts research and monitors developments in the field. Using the web site addresses provided, vast numbers of documents of all types may be accessed. This chapter focuses on four types of trafficking: trafficking in human beings, narcotics trafficking, trafficking in small arms and light weapons, and trafficking in nuclear materials.

Trafficking in Human Beings

Trafficking in human beings is a phenomenon with a long past. For centuries people have been coerced, seduced, and otherwise deceived into leaving their homelands in pursuit of greater economic and social freedoms, only to find themselves enslaved under inhumane conditions. With the collapse of the Berlin Wall and the Soviet Union, this problem appears to be spiraling out of control in Eastern Europe, while it continues unabated throughout Asia and Africa.

Trafficking in human beings is a global busienss:

- Migrant trafficking and smuggling generates huge profits for traffickers and organized crime syndicates.
- There are an estimated 15 to 30 million irregular migrants worldwide at any given time.
- Of these migrants, some 700,000 women and children are trafficked across borders annually.
- Illicit trafficking typically focuses on women and children for sexual and labor exploitation; men are sometimes trafficked for labor purposes.

Characteristics of Traffickers and Their Victims

A variety of factors fuel the traffic in human beings. Frequently referred to as "push" factors—that is, those factors that encourage people, especially women, to look outside their home towns, cities, and countries for opportunities—they focus primarily on the desire to escape difficult socioeconomic conditions.

Some factors that fuel trafficking in human beings include:

- poverty and general weakening of domestic economies
- migrations caused by war
- expansion of prostitution due to militarization
- globalization of the economy
- laws and policies on prostitution
- high profits for organized crime groups
- increasingly difficult governmental budget situations encouraging official corruption
- newly opened borders or increasingly weaker borders
- development strategies (for example, tourism)
- gender-based discrimination

Transnational trafficking of women and children frequently involves deception, seduction, or force. Young women answer advertisements for models, dancers, or other entertainment industry jobs. Once they arrive at their destination, their documents are confiscated by the trafficker or brothel owner, for example; the girls are essentially kept under close watch and held in captivity. Usually with little or no knowledge of the language of their destination country, and too afraid to approach law enforcement authorities, victims have little choice but to remain in their situations. Traffickers frequently tell their victims that they are illegal immigrants and will be put in prison and deported if they approach law enforcement. In retribution for attempted escapes, or simply to maintain control, victims' "owners" administer beatings and threats.

Most trafficking victims do not readily volunteer information about their status because of fear and the abuse they have suffered at the hands of their traffickers. They may also be reluctant to come forward with information because of despair, discouragement, and a sense that there are no viable options to escape their situation. Even if pressed, they may not identify themselves as someone held in bondage for fear of retribution to themselves or family members. However, there are indicators that often point to a person held in slavery. They include:

- malnutrition, dehydration, or poor personal hygiene
- sexually transmitted diseases
- signs of rape or sexual abuse
- bruising, broken bones, or other signs of untreated medical problems
- critical illnesses, including diabetes, cancer, or heart disease
- post-traumatic stress or psychological disorders

Because trafficking in persons is usually an "underground" crime, it can be difficult for law enforcement personnel, the public, or service providers to readily identify a trafficking victim. There have been cases of victims escaping and reporting the situation to the police. However, many are physically unable to leave their worksites without an escort and are not free to contact family, friends, or members of the public.

In addition to some of the obvious physical and mental indicators of trafficking, there are other signs that an individual is being controlled by someone else.

It is possible that a person is being held as a slave if he or she

- does not hold his/her own identity or travel documents
- has very little or no pocket money (trafficker or pimp controls the money)
- is extremely nervous, especially if their "translator" (who may be their trafficker) is present

- suffers from verbal or psychological abuse designed to intimidate, degrade, and frighten the individual
- is subject to heavy security at the commercial establishment, including barred windows, locked doors, isolated location, electronic surveillance
- lives at the same premises as the brothel or worksite or is driven between the living quarters and work by a guard; for labor trafficking, is often prohibited from leaving the worksite, which may look like a guarded compound from the outside
- is kept under surveillance when taken to a doctor, hospital, or clinic for treatment; trafficker may act as a translator

Victims of Sex Trafficking

These victims are often found in the streets or working in establishments that offer commercial sex acts (e.g., brothels, strip clubs, pornography production houses). Such establishments may operate under the guise of:

- massage parlors
- escort services
- adult bookstores
- modeling studios
- bars/strip clubs

Victims of Labor Trafficking

These victims tend to be people forced into indentured servitude and can be found working in:

- sweatshops (where abusive labor standards are present)
- commercial agricultural situations (fields, processing plants, canneries)
- domestic situations (maids, nannies)
- construction sites (particularly if public access is denied)
- restaurant and custodial work

Generally speaking, traffickers are categorized into three types:

- In border regions, occasional traffickers provide internal or international transportation. They are usually owners of taxis, small boats, or trucks that can carry individuals or small groups from a drop-off point on the coast, across a narrow strait, or over a poorly secured border. This type is not organized in any sophisticated or ongoing way.
- Small, well-organized trafficking rings often specialize in trafficking nationals out of one specific country, consistently using similar routing.
- Organized, international trafficking networks are the most sophisticated and, consequently, the most dangerous and difficult to combat. These networks have access to fraudulent and/or authentic, usually stolen, documents or the capability to produce falsified documents themselves. They can change routing and means of transportation when a traditional route is blocked. Members are present worldwide. Lodging and logistical support are at their disposal in countries of transit and destination.

Traffickers are known to travel deep into poverty-stricken rural areas to seduce their targets with promises of high-paying jobs and the easy life, or pretend to fall in love with the girls and promise to marry them. Because of the global AIDS epidemic, traffickers frequently travel to villages in the countryside in search of virgins to provide to high-paying clients. In some cases, parents give little thought to the morality of selling their daughters' virginity or of selling them into a period of prostitution; some of the girls themselves perceive it as a normal business transaction or a way of paying a debt to their parents.

Huge profit at relatively low risk is the primary motivating factor for law breakers (traffickers, brothel owners, pimps). The benefits are so great that many continue in the sex business after being arrested and serving time in prison. Usually the traffickers are drinkers, drug abusers, or gamblers. The traffickers are also frequently women who were formerly the victims of trafficking themselves and realize the profits to be made.

International Organization for Migration

Web site: *http://www.iom.int*

Founded in 1951 as the Provisional Intergovernmental Committee for the Movement of Migrants from Europe (PICMME), the International Organization for Migration (IOM) has become the leading international organization for migration. The IOM assists governments and nongovernmental organizations through rapid humanitarian responses to sudden migration flows, postemergency return, and reintegration programs, rendering help to migrants in distress and training officials. In addition, the IOM pursues extensive research and informational campaigns as well as programs providing counseling and assistance to victims of trafficking. The IOM also aids governments looking to improve their countertrafficking capabilities. At present, the IOM has more than ninety active projects on all continents in the area of countertrafficking.

The IOM has a staff of 3,200, of whom 300 are assigned to its Geneva headquarters; the remainder are posted in more than 160 offices throughout the world. In the United States, IOM has offices in Washington D.C., New York, Miami, Chicago, San Francisco, Seattle, and Los Angeles.

In 2002, as part of its direct assistance projects, the IOM came to the aid of more than 3,000 victims of trafficking. They were assisted to return home, and once in their country of origin, IOM and partner nongovernmental organizations provided reintegration assistance.

Documents

The IOM web site contains an extensive list of documents regarding trafficking in migrants around the world. The following is a small sample of those reports.

"Understanding and Counteracting Trafficking in Persons," 2004, at *http://www.iom.int//DOCUMENTS/PUBLICATION/EN/manuale_finale_cap1–7.pdf*.

"Revisiting the Human Trafficking Paradigm: The Bangladesh Experience," 2004, at *http://www.iom.int//DOCUMENTS/PUBLICATION/EN/Full_BangladeshTrafficking_Rpt.pdf*.

"Trafficking in Unaccompanied Minors in Ireland," 2004, at *http://www.iom.int/iomwebsite/Publication/ServletSearchPublication?event=detail&id=3594*.

"Who Is the Next Victim? Vulnerability of Young Romanian Women to Trafficking in Human Beings," 2004, at *http://www.iom.int/iomwebsite/ Publication/ServletSearchPublication?event=detail&id=3171.*

"Psychosocial Support to Groups of Victims of Human Trafficking in Transit Situations," 2004, at *http://www.iom.int/iomwebsite/Publication/ ServletSearchPublication?event=detail&id=3052.*

"Counter-trafficking in Eastern Europe and Central Asia," 2003, at *http:// www.iom.int/iomwebsite/Publication/ServletSearchPublication?event=detail&i d=2991.*

"Trafficking for Sexual Exploitation: The Case of the Russian Federation," 2002, at *http://www.iom.int/DOCUMENTS/PUBLICATION/EN/ mrs_7_2002.pdf.*

Coalition against Trafficking in Women

Web site: *www.catwinternational.org*
The Coalition Against Trafficking in Women (CATW) is a nongovernmental organization that promotes women's human rights by working internationally to combat sexual exploitation in all its forms. Founded in 1988, CATW was the first international nongovernmental organization to focus on human trafficking, especially sex trafficking of women and girls. CATW is composed of regional networks and of affiliated individuals and groups. It serves as an umbrella organization that coordinates and takes direction from its regional organizations and networks in its work against sexual exploitation and in support of women's human rights.

A major project of the CATW is the publication of *The Factbook on Global Sexual Exploitation,* compiled by Donna M. Hughes, Laura Joy Sporcic, Nadine Z. Mendelsohn, and Vanessa Chirgwin (Coalition Against Trafficking in Women, 1999).

The Factbook on Global Sexual Exploitation was compiled from media, nongovernmental organization, and government reports as an initial effort to collect facts, statistics, and known cases on global sexual exploitation. The information is organized into four categories: trafficking, prostitution, pornography, and organized and institutionalized sexual exploitation and violence.

The idea of the book was to create a sketch of the overall situation in each country to illustrate the harm caused by sexual violence and exploitation throughout the world. Thus, as the authors indicate, sources of information were not contacted to verify the information, and close examination will reveal contradictions in the information presented. All statistics are reported with no attempt made to evaluate which numbers are more likely to be accurate. In any event, the exact numbers in many cases are not known, and estimates come from a variety of sources that use different methods to determine what they report.

As such, the report is an indispensable resource, particularly for the researcher just becoming acquainted with trafficking in humans, because it provides a thorough treatment of the trafficking situation in countries and regions throughout the world. The following are snapshots of the scope of this pandemic extracted from *The Factbook on Global Sexual Exploitation.*

- *Bangladesh:* 200,000 women and girls have been trafficked to Pakistan in the last ten years, continuing at the rate of 200 to 400 women monthly.
- *Burma:* 20,000 to 30,000 prostituted women and girls in Thailand, about 1,000 from Shan state, are in Chiang Mai. As illegal immigrants in Thailand, prostitutes are arrested, detained, and deported back to Burma, with 50 to 70 percent being HIV positive.
- *Cambodia:* Unofficial estimates say that there are as many as 15,000 prostituted people in Phnom Penh and that up to 35 percent of them have been smuggled into Cambodia from China or Vietnam. Brothel owners pay traffickers from $350 to $450 for each attractive Vietnamese virgin sixteen years or younger. Nonvirgins and those considered less beautiful are sold from $150 to $170 each.
- *China:* There is a resurgence of prostitution and trafficking in women and girls all over China, involving a high percentage of children and minors. In 1994, the police handled 15,000 cases involving the sale of women as wives or for prostitution. There are now 70 million unmarried men in China as a consequence of the preference for sons in Chinese families. Many are desperately seeking wives from Vietnam, although marriage arrangements are difficult.
- *Hong Kong:* Fake contracts, often for domestic work, land women in brothels that employ Chinese minders

to prevent runaways. An influx of East European women in high-priced clubs has been noted, with a Russian mafia said to be bringing women to Macau.

- *India:* A quarter of the total number of prostitutes are minors, in over 1,000 red-light districts all over India. Cage prostitutes are often minors, often from Nepal and Bangladesh. In India alone, estimates range from 2.3 million to 8 million women and children involved in prostitution.
- *Indonesia:* The estimated financial turnover of the sex industry ranges from $1.2 billion to $3.6 billion. Estimates of 1994 were that there were 500,000 prostitutes, although only 65,582 were registered.
- *Japan:* This is believed to be the largest sex industry market for Asian women, with over 150,000 non-Japanese women in prostitution, mostly Thai and Filipinas. The sex industry accounts for 1 percent of GNP and equals the country's defense budget. One "sex zone" in Tokyo, only 0.34 sq. km., has 3,500 sex "facilities": strip theaters, peep shows, "lovers' banks," porno shops, sex telephone clubs, karaoke bars, clubs, and so on.
- *Korea:* Around the military bases, there are 18,000 registered and 9,000 unregistered prostitutes. Forms of prostitution include escort and call girls, street prostitution, and from cafes, clubs, cabarets, show cases, massage parlors, and beauty shops.
- *Malaysia:* Estimates put the number of women in prostitution at around 142,000, with from 8,000 to 10,000 in Kuala Lumpur. The main channels are the recreation business, that is, entertainment, fitness clubs, and the like.
- *Nepal:* Every year about 10,000 Nepali girls, mostly between the ages of nine and sixteen, are sold to brothels in Indian cities. According to international social agencies, this flow of Nepali girls into Indian brothels is probably the busiest slave traffic of its kind anywhere in the world. Brokers, especially in rural areas, and even family members sell girls; husbands sometimes sell their wives to brothels.
- *New Zealand:* The majority of the 6,000 to 8,000 prostituted women are Asians. In Auckland, of 4,000

prostitutes, 800 are Thai, and 400 other Asian women. New Zealand is also used by traffickers of Thai women as a departure point for Japan, Australia, and Cyprus.

- *Philippines:* 300,000 women are involved in prostitution, and 75,000 are prostituted children. Government approval of "R and R" privileges for the U.S. Navy sustains a system and infrastructure of military prostitution. Of the 200,000 or so street children in the Philippines, about 60,000 sell their bodies.
- *Sri Lanka:* 15,000 prostitutes work in the streets and in licensed and unlicensed massage parlors and brothels, and 30,000 prostitutes are children; 80 percent of the labor migration in 1994 was of women workers.
- *Taiwan:* 40,000 to 60,000 children are involved in prostitution. Forty percent of young prostitutes in the main red-light district are aboriginal girls. Girls under thirteen have been made to undergo hormone injections by brothel owners to hasten their physical development.
- *Thailand:* Estimates of women in prostitution range from 300,000 to 2.8 million, of which a third are minors and children. Thai women are also in prostitution in many countries in Asia, Australia, Europe, and the United States. Some 4.6 million Thai men regularly and 500,000 foreign tourists annually use prostituted women and girls.
- *Vietnam:* There are between 60,000 and 200,000 women and girls in prostitution, with 6.3 percent under the age of sixteen. Trafficking occurs through kidnapping for brothels, deceptive offers for jobs or tourist trips, and marriage matchmaking with foreigners who sell and resell the women abroad.

Trafficking in women plagues the United States as well. Organized prostitution networks have migrated from metropolitan areas to small cities and suburbs. Women trafficked to the United States have been forced to have sex with 400 to 500 men to pay off $40,000 in debt for their passage. The following are some characteristic incidents of trafficking in the United States as compiled by *The Factbook on Global Sexual Exploitation:*

- Some 14,500 to 17,500 people are trafficked into the United States each year.

- In mid-1997, in Queens, New York, police were informed of more than sixty Mexican immigrants, including twelve children ranging in age from six months to six years, being held in "involuntary servitude."
- The United Nations lists Mexico as the number one center for the supply of young children to North America. Most of the children are sold to rich, childless couples unwilling to wait for bona fide adoption agencies to provide them with a child. Many times the children are snatched while on errands for their parents. Often they are drugged and raped. Most of the children over twelve end up as prostitutes.
- Some 5,000 women of Chinese descent are in prostitution in Los Angeles. Traffickers force Chinese immigrants into indentured servitude—women into prostitution, and men into the restaurant business.
- Traffickers in Miami receive Asian children who are trafficked through Europe by Japanese and Chinese criminal gangs.

CATW's web site has extensive links to articles, documents, reports, statements, and other resources on trafficking of women and children around the world.

The Factbook on Global Sexual Exploitation can be found at *http://www.catwinternational.org/factbook/index.php*.

U.S. Department of State

Web site: *www.state.gov*

The U.S. Department of State is the leading foreign affairs agency of the U.S. government. It is responsible for leading interagency coordination in developing and implementing foreign policy, leading and coordinating U.S. representation abroad, and conveying U.S. foreign policy to foreign governments and international organizations through its network of embassies, consulates, and diplomatic missions. The State Department also assists U.S. businesses in the international marketplace and works to protect and assist U.S. citizens living or traveling abroad.

The United States maintains diplomatic relations with about 180 countries and also maintains relations with many international organizations, adding up to a total of more than 250 posts around the world. In the United States, about 5,000 professional, technical, and administrative domestic employees work alongside members of the Diplomatic Service compiling and analyzing reports from overseas, providing logistical support to posts, consulting with and keeping the Congress informed about foreign policy initiatives and policies, communicating with the American public, formulating and overseeing the budget, issuing passports and travel warnings, and more.

An important part of the State Department's mission is to monitor and work with other governments to counter global problems such as cross-border pollution, the spread of communicable diseases, terrorism, nuclear smuggling, and humanitarian crises. The litany of critical problems exacerbated by increasingly weak national borders, increasingly sophisticated criminal groups, and worsening economic conditions in many parts of the world includes, of course, trafficking in human beings.

At the governmental level, trafficking in humans has raised numerous challenging questions:

- How can the United States assist and influence foreign governments in improving their economies so as to stem the tide of people going abroad in search of better opportunities?
- What should the attitude of the U.S. government be toward victims of trafficking who arrive in the United States illegally? How should the criminal justice system handle victims of trafficking? Should they be arrested, deported, or allowed to apply for citizenship?
- What measures can the U.S. government take to educate people in remote parts of foreign countries about the telltale signs of overtures that frequently lead to trafficking?

In the State Department, the Office of Global Affairs coordinates U.S. foreign relations on a variety of global issues, including democracy, human rights, and labor; environment, oceans, and science; narcotics control and law enforcement; population, refugees, and migration; women's issues; and trafficking in persons. Coming under the jurisdiction of the Office of Global Affairs is the Office to Monitor and Combat Trafficking in Persons (*http://www.state.gov/g/tip/*), which is tasked with coordinating U.S. government activities in the global fight against modern-day slavery, including forced labor and sexual exploitation.

On its extensive web site, the State Department enumerates the various programs administered by the Office to Monitor and Combat Trafficking in Persons, providing brief descriptions of international antitrafficking programs approved for funding by the State Department, the Department of Labor, and the U.S. Agency for International Development. Other programs dealing with domestic antitrafficking are coordinated through the Department of Justice and the Department of Health and Human Services, among other agencies.

In the area of monitoring and fighting trafficking in persons, the State Department is known for its annual "Trafficking in Persons Report." This document is one of the most comprehensive reports on human trafficking around the world and on what governments are doing to end it. The 2004 report includes analyses of 140 countries' efforts to combat trafficking, best practices worldwide, a summary of U.S. action to fight human trafficking at home, and new data on the scope of this phenomenon.

An example of domestic efforts to fight trafficking in humans is the passage of legislation to assist victims of trafficking. On October 28, 2000, President Clinton signed into law the Victims of Trafficking and Violence Protection Act of 2000. Commonly known as the Trafficking Victims Protection Act of 2000 (TVPA), this new law, along with the Trafficking Victims Protection Reauthorization Act of 2003, addresses issues of worker exploitation resulting from trafficking in persons. This law is the culmination of the federal government's efforts through the Trafficking in Persons and Worker Exploitation Task Force, an interagency group that brings together the FBI, Immigration and Naturalization Service, the Department of Labor, and other agencies to assist victims of trafficking.

Highlights of the statute include the following:

- It creates new laws that criminalize trafficking with respect to slavery, involuntary servitude, peonage, or forced labor.
- It permits prosecution where nonviolent coercion is used to force victims to work in the belief they would be subject to serious harm.
- It permits prosecution where the victim's service was compelled by confiscation of documents such as passports or birth certificates.
- It increases prison terms for all slavery violations from

ten to twenty years and adds life imprisonment where the violation involves the death or sexual abuse of the victim.

- It requires courts to order restitution and forfeiture of assets upon conviction.
- It enables victims to seek witness protection and other types of assistance.
- It gives prosecutors and agents new tools to get legal immigration status for victims of trafficking during investigation and prosecution.
- It created the State Department's Office to Monitor and Combat Trafficking in Persons.

Under the TVPA, the U.S. Department of Health and Human Services, through the Administration for Children and Families, is responsible for certifying persons as trafficking victims and helping them access the benefits and services they need to rebuild their lives. To this end, a nationwide network of organizations was created to identify victims through community outreach, provide technical assistance to service organizations, and provide services to victims.

Documents

"The U.S. Government's International Anti-Trafficking Programs," 2003, at *http://www.state.gov/g/tip/rls/rpt/17858.htm.*

"Pathbreaking Strategies in the Global Fight Against Sex Trafficking," *http://www.state.gov/g/tip/c8628.htm.* Documents from a conference held February 23–26, 2003. Among available documents is "Accomplishments in the Fight to Prevent Trafficking in Persons" at *http://www.state.gov/ g/tip/rls/fs/17968.htm.*

"2004 Trafficking in Persons Report," at *http://www.state.gov/g/tip/rls/ tiprpt/2004/.* The web site provides the entire 2004 Report as well as 2005 updates along with other documents.

See also "International Trafficking in Women to the United States: A Contemporary Manifestation of Slavery and Organized Crime," Amy O'Neill Richard, Center for the Study of Intelligence, 2000, at *http://www.cia .gov/csi/monograph/women/trafficking.pdf.*

For additional documents and extensive links on human trafficking, go to the U.S. Department of Justice, Trafficking in Persons Information web site at *http://www.usdoj.gov/trafficking.htm.*

See the Department of Justice's Office on Violence Against Women at *http://www.ojp.usdoj.gov/vawo/about.htm*. The full text of the Trafficking Victims and Protection Act of 2000 can be found at *http://www.ojp.usdoj .gov/vawo/laws/vawo2000/stitle_a.htm*.

"Assessment of U.S. Government Activities to Combat Trafficking in Persons, Multi-agency Report," 2004, at *http://www.state.gov/g/tip/rls/rpt/ 23495.htm*.

United Nations

Web site: *http://www.unodc.org*
The United Nations Office on Drugs and Crime (UNODC), created in 1997, has become a leading agency against international crime with 500 staff members located in its twenty-one field offices throughout the world. The UNODC has numerous counter–drug trafficking operations, including the Illicit Crop Monitoring Programme (ICMP), the Alternative Development Programme, and the Global Programme Against Money Laundering (GPML). In its work against human trafficking, the UNODC has created the Global Programme against Trafficking in Human Beings (GPAT).

To more effectively research and monitor illicit trafficking and other trends in the criminal world, the United Nations established the United Nations Crime Prevention and Criminal Justice Programme Network. The Network consists of a number of interregional and regional institutes, as well as specialized centers, around the world. Its components provide a variety of services including exchange of information, research, training, and public education. We provide this list here so that the researcher might consult with each organization individually to examine programs being pursued in connection with trafficking in persons.

UNODC—United Nations Office on Drugs and Crime, Vienna, Austria

UNICRI—United Nations Interregional Crime and Justice Research Institute, Turin, Italy

UNAFEI—United Nations Asia and Far East Institute for the Prevention of Crime and the Treatment of Offenders, Tokyo, Japan

ILANUD—United Nations Latin American Institute for the Prevention of Crime and the Treatment of Offenders, San Jose, Costa Rica

HEUNI—European Institute for Crime Prevention and Control affiliated with the United Nations, Helsinki, Finland

UNAFRI—United Nations African Institute for the Prevention of Crime and the Treatment of Offenders, United Nations

NAASS—Naif Arab Academy for Security Sciences, Riyadh, Kingdom of Saudi Arabia

AIC—Australian Institute of Criminology, Canberra, Australia

ICCLR and CJP—International Centre for Criminal Law Reform and Criminal Justice Policy, Vancouver, Canada

ISISC—International Institute of Higher Studies in Criminal Science, Siracusa, Italy

NIJ—National Institute of Justice, Washington, D.C., United States

ISPAC—International Scientific and Professional Advisory Council of the United Nations Crime Prevention and Criminal Justice Programme, Milan, Italy

ICPC—International Centre for the Prevention of Crime, Montreal, Canada

Raoul Wallenberg Institute of Human Rights and Humanitarian Law, Lund, Sweden

Documents

The United Nations Convention against Transnational Organized Crime, at *http://www.unodc.org/unodc/en/crime_cicp_convention.html*.

The United Nations Protocol to Prevent, Suppress, and Punish Trafficking in Persons, Especially Women and Children, Supplementing the UN Convention Against Transnational Organized Crime, at *http://www.unodc .org/unodc/en/crime_cicp_convention.html*.

The United Nations Convention for the Suppression of the Traffic in Persons and of the Exploitation of the Prostitution of Others, at *http://www.unodc.org/unodc/en/crime_cicp_convention.html.*

The United Nations Protocol against Smuggling of Migrants by Land, Sea and Air Supplementing the Convention against Transnational Organized Crime, at *http://www.unodc.org/unodc/en/crime_cicp_convention.html.*

The United Nations High Commissioner for Human Rights Principles and Guidelines on Human Rights and Trafficking, at *http://www1.umn .edu/humanrts/instree/traffickingGuidelinesHCHR.html.*

Slavery, Servitude, Forced Labor and Similar Institutions and Practices Convention of 1926 (Slavery Convention of 1926), at *http://www1.umn .edu/humanrts/instree/f1sc.htm.*

The United Nations Protocol Amending the Slavery Convention (1953), at *http://www1.umn.edu/humanrts/instree/f2psc.htm.*

The United Nations Supplementary Convention on the Abolition of Slavery, the Slave Trade and Institutions and Practices Similar to Slavery, at *http://www1.umn.edu/humanrts/instree/f3scas.htm.*

"The Relationship between Organised Crime and Trafficking in Aliens," International Centre for Migration Policy Development (ICMPD), 1999, at *http://www.icmpd.org/uploadimg/OcandTR.pdf.*

"Organised Crime and the Business of Migrant Trafficking: An Economic Analysis," Andreas Schloenhardt, Australian Institute of Criminology, 1999, at *http://www.aic.gov.au/conferences/occasional/schloenhardt.pdf.*

"Report of the Experts Group on Trafficking in Human Beings," European Commission, Directorate-General Justice, Freedom and Security, December 2004, at *http://www.antislavery.org/homepage/resources/PDF/ CAHTEH_2004_INFO6_E.pdf.*

For additional United Nations documents on trafficking, see United Nations Anti-Human Trafficking Unit, Global Programme against Trafficking in Human Beings at *http://www.unodc.org/unodc/en/trafficking_projects .html.*

For additional documents and extensive links on human trafficking, see Michigan State University's Criminal Justice Resources: Human Trafficking, at *http://www.lib.msu.edu/harris23/crimjust/human.htm.*

For additional documents and extensive links on human rights generally, go to the University of Minnesota Human Rights Library, at *http://www1 .umn.edu/humanrts/* or Human Rights Watch, at *www .hrw.org/links.html.*

Narcotics Trafficking

Trafficking in narcotics is a global business.

- Three percent of the world's population, or 185 million people, consume illicit drugs annually.
- Countless more people around the world are involved in the production and trafficking of illicit drugs.
- In the United States, wholesale cocaine prices range from approximately $12,000 to $35,000 per kilogram.
- The availability of South American heroin, produced in Colombia, has increased dramatically in the United States since 1993. It ranges from $50,000 to $200,000 per kilogram.
- Israeli and Russian drug-trafficking syndicates and Western Europe-based drug traffickers are the principal traffickers of methylenedioxymethamphetamine (MDMA), commonly known as ecstasy, worldwide.
- MDMA, primarily manufactured clandestinely in Western Europe, is smuggled into the United States by couriers via commercial airlines, as well as through the use of express package carriers.
- African nations are mainly concerned with a rise in the use of cannabis and opiates.
- In the People's Republic of China, 70 percent of all HIV cases are linked to injected drug use.

Bureau for International Narcotics and Law Enforcement Affairs

Web site: *http://www.state.gov/g/inl/*
The Bureau for International Narcotics and Law Enforcement Affairs (INL) advises the president, secretary of state, other bureaus in the Department of State, and other departments and agencies within the U.S. government on the development of policies and programs to combat international narcotics and crime.

INL programs support two of the Department's strategic goals: to reduce the entry of illegal drugs into the United States and to minimize the impact of international crime on the United States and its citizens. Counternarcotics and anticrime programs also complement the war on terrorism, both directly and indirectly, by promoting modernization of and supporting operations by foreign criminal justice systems and law enforcement agencies charged with the counterterrorism mission.

The International Narcotics Control element of the U.S. foreign assistance program enhances the institutional capabilities of foreign governments to define and implement their strategies and national programs to prevent the production, trafficking, and abuse of illicit drugs. These programs focus on interdiction capabilities, eradication, sustainable alternative development, and demand reduction. This includes reducing drug crop cultivation through a combination of law enforcement, eradication, and alternative development programs in key source countries as well as improving the capacity of host nation police and military forces to attack narcotics production and trafficking centers. It also includes strengthening the ability of law enforcement and judicial authorities in both source and transit countries to investigate and prosecute major drug-trafficking organizations and their leaders and to seize and block their assets.

The International Narcotics Control Strategy Report (INCSR) is an annual report by the Department of State to Congress prepared in accordance with the Foreign Assistance Act. It describes the efforts of key countries to attack all aspects of the international drug trade in the calendar year. The INCSR is a country-by-country two-volume report that describes the efforts to attack all aspects of the international drug trade, chemical control, money laundering, and financial crimes. Part I covers drug and chemical control activities. Part II covers money laundering and financial crimes.

Office of National Drug Control Policy

Web site: *http://www.whitehousedrugpolicy.gov/*
The White House Office of National Drug Control Policy (ONDCP), a component of the Executive Office of the President, was established by the Anti-Drug Abuse Act of 1988. The principal purpose of ONDCP is to establish policies, priorities, and objectives for the drug control program of the United States. The goals of the program are to reduce illicit drug use, manufacturing, and trafficking, drug-related crime and violence, and drug-related health consequences. To achieve these goals, the director of ONDCP is charged with producing the National Drug Control Strategy. The Strategy directs antidrug efforts and establishes a

program, a budget, and guidelines for cooperation among federal, state, and local entities.

By law, the director of ONDCP also evaluates, coordinates, and oversees both the international and domestic antidrug efforts of executive branch agencies and ensures that such efforts sustain and complement state and local antidrug activities. The director advises the president regarding changes in the organization, management, budgeting, and personnel of federal agencies that could affect the nation's antidrug efforts.

The Drug Policy Information Clearinghouse supports the ONDCP. A component of the National Criminal Justice Reference Service (NCJRS), the Clearinghouse is staffed by subject matter specialists and serves as a resource for statistics, research data, and referrals useful for developing and implementing drug policy. The Clearinghouse disseminates ONDCP and the U.S. Department of Justice's Office of Justice Programs (OJP) drug-related publications. Its staff also writes and produces documents on drug-related topics, coordinates with federal, state, and local agencies to identify data resources, and provides information to the public.

Characteristics of Traffickers

One of the most important elements in controlling the trafficking of drugs into the U.S. is the relationship between the United States and Mexico.

Traffickers from Mexico

- Drug traffickers from Mexico are the primary transporters of the major narcotics imported into the United States.
- The U.S.-Mexico border is the entry point for a large percentage of these drugs. Approximately 90 million automobiles, 4.5 million trucks, and 293 million people enter the United States from Mexico annually.
- Traffickers utilize all these modes of transportation as well as high-speed boats and cargo ships. These ships carry more than 400 million tons of cargo. Another 160,000 smaller vessels visit coastal towns.
- Criminal groups operating from Mexico smuggle cocaine, heroin, methamphetamine, amphetamine, and marijuana into the United States.

- Approximately half of the cocaine available in the United States enters the country along the U.S.-Mexico border.
- Mexican traffickers historically have both worked with and competed against the Colombian cartels.
- The majority of marijuana and a significant portion of heroin consumed in the United States emanates from Mexico.
- Costs that the illegal drug trade imposes on the United States have been estimated at $70 billion each year.
- Mexican drug organizations have established methamphetamine laboratories that have been estimated to produce 85 percent of the methamphetamine available in the United States.
- Mexican drug organizations have established labs throughout Mexico and California.

Besides trafficking activities to the United States originating in Mexico, a significant amount of global drug-trafficking begins in Southeast Asia.

- Criminal groups based in Southeast and Southwest Asia smuggle heroin into the United States.
- Afghanistan accounts for 76 percent of the world's illicit opium production as well as being a central point in the illegal trafficking of opiates.
- Heroin is also processed in the so-called Golden Triangle (Burma, Laos, and Thailand).

At the wholesale trafficking level:

- The trafficking process becomes fluid and diversified.
- The process of moving the heroin from its point of origin can involve any number of smuggling groups and brokers.
- Brokers often have close connections with particular producers while also arranging transactions with rival producers.
- Traffickers form limited partnerships with different individuals or groups for the purpose of executing

specific drug transactions. These procedures ensure business flexibility as well as protection.

- Southeast Asian heroin traffickers smuggle bulk quantities of SEA heroin to international markets by the use of commercial containerized cargo.
- Heroin processed in the Golden Triangle (Burma, Laos, and Thailand) is smuggled overland to seaports in Burma, China, Thailand, Malaysia, and Vietnam for transshipment in cargo containers through Taiwan, Hong Kong, Singapore, Japan, and Korea. From these transit countries in Southeast Asia, the heroin-laden containers are shipped to consumer markets in Europe, Australia, Canada, and the United States.

"Mexico and the United States: Neighbors Confront Drug Trafficking," James O. Finkenauer, Joseph R. Fuentes, George L. Ward, *http://www .ojp.usdoj.gov/nij/international/trafficking.html*.

"Southeast Asian Heroin Smuggling Methods: Containerized Cargo," Drug Intelligence Brief, 2001, *http://www.usdoj.gov/dea/pubs/intel/01_022/*.

National Drug Control Strategy 2004 – The White House, *http://www.state .gov/documents/organization/30228.pdf*.

United Nations

Web site: *www.un.org*

Commission on Narcotic Drugs

The Commission on Narcotic Drugs (CND) was established in 1946 by the Economic and Social Council of the United Nations. It is the central policy-making body within the UN system for dealing with all drug-related matters. The Commission analyses the world drug abuse situation and develops proposals to strengthen international drug control.

The International Narcotics Control Board

Web site: *http://www.unodc.org/unodc/en/incb.html*

The International Narcotics Control Board (INCB) is the independent and quasijudicial control body for the implementation of UN drug conventions. It was created by the Single Convention on Narcotic Drugs of 1961 and came into being in 1968.

The INCB is independent of governments as well as of the United Nations; its thirteen members serve in their personal capacity. The Board monitors compliance with the provisions of international drug control treaties and ensures that adequate supplies of legal drugs are available for medical and scientific purposes. The Board also endeavors to ensure that no leakage from licit sources of drugs to illicit trafficking occurs. It identifies and helps to correct weaknesses in drug control systems and determines which chemicals used to illicitly manufacture drugs should be under international control.

Annually, the UNODC publishes an extensive report on illicit narcotics. For the first time, the 2004 World Drug Report was issued as a two-volume edition. The first volume covers market trends and provides in-depth trend analysis; the second volume compiles detailed statistics on all of the drug markets. Together they provide one of the most comprehensive sources on the international drug problem. The report includes trends in production, trafficking, abuse in the opium/heroin, coca/cocaine, cannabis, amphetamine-type stimulants market; as well as production, seizures, prices, and consumption in each of these areas; and it contains numerous maps, statistics, charts, tables, and graphs.

Documents

United Nations 2004 World Drug Report, at *http://www.unodc.org/ unodc/world_drug_report.html.*

United Nations Single Convention on Narcotic Drugs, 1961, at *http:// www.unodc.org/pdf/convention_1961_en.pdf.*

United Nations Convention on Psychotropic Drugs, 1971, at *http://www .unodc.org/pdf/convention_1971_en.pdf.*

United Nations Convention against the Illicit Traffic in Narcotic Drugs and Psychotropic Substances, 1988, at *http://www.unodc.org/pdf/ convention_1988_en.pdf.*

For a collection of United Nations Resolutions on Illicit Narcotics since 1946, go to *http://www.unodc.org/unodc/en/resolutions.html.*

Trafficking in Small Arms and Light Weapons

The proliferation of illicit small arms and light weapons (SA/LW) in regions of the world suffering from political instability and violent conflict has proven a major obstacle to peace, economic development, and efforts to rebuild war-torn societies. In places like Sierra Leone, Kosovo, and Colombia, thousands of innocent civilians have been killed and tens of thousands more displaced by ethnic and civil conflicts perpetuated in large part by easy access to illicit small arms and light weapons.

- At least 1 million civilian firearms are lost or stolen annually worldwide.
- Worldwide, there are at least 200,000 annual non-war-related firearm deaths—the vast majority of which are homicides.
- At least 1,249 companies in more than 90 countries are involved in some aspect of small arms and light weapons production.
- The largest exporters by value are the United States, Italy, Belgium, Germany, the Russian Federation, Brazil, and China.
- Countries that are known to be medium producers of small arms include Iran, Pakistan, and Singapore.
- Iraqi civilians may have gained control of 7 to 8 million small arms.
- Between 1994 and 2003, the U.S. Bureau of Alcohol, Tobacco, Firearms and Explosives responded to over 90,000 requests from foreign governments for assistance in tracing illegal firearms.

Office of Weapons Removal and Abatement

Web site: *http://www.state.gov/t/pm/wra/*
The State Department's Office of Weapons Removal and Abatement (WRA) works to curb the illicit proliferation of conventional weapons of war such as light automatic weapons and rocket-propelled grenades, and removing and destroying others, such as persistent landmines and abandoned stocks of munitions that remain and pose hazards after the conclusion of armed conflict.

The Office develops, implements, and monitors policy, programs, and public engagement efforts that contribute to the prevention and mitigation of conflict, as well as post-conflict social and economic recovery. The focus is threefold: to curb the illicit trafficking, availability, and indiscriminate use of conventional weapons of war that fuel regional and internal instability; to pursue and help manage postconflict cleanup of such weapons in areas needed for civilian use; and to engage civil society to broaden support for mitigation efforts.

The Office promotes U.S. foreign policy goals through the development and implementation of comprehensive programs to address the security challenges and harmful humanitarian effects caused by the illicit proliferation of conventional weapons of war, and the existence of public hazards from such weapons following cessation of armed conflict. The Office works to limit the access of terrorist or criminal groups to such weapons and munitions, and coordinates with other U.S. government agencies as well as nongovernmental organizations, international organizations, and private enterprises.

In the document, "U.S. Measures to Fight the Illicit Small Arms/Light Weapons (SA/LW) Trade" (*http://www.state.gov/t/ pm/rls/fs/2001/3837.htm*), the State Department outlines the various approaches at its disposal for dealing with small arms and light weapons trafficking. The various reports, documents, and organizations mentioned in the following list provide numerous leads for the researcher examining SA/LW issues.

- *International Diplomacy.* The United States works with many nations bilaterally, and with regional and international organizations, to stem the flow of illicit SA/LW trafficking.
- *Arms Brokering Legislation.* U.S. legislation in 1996 was one of the world's first comprehensive laws on arms brokering. The U.S. brokering law covers all U.S. citizens in the United States and abroad as well as foreign nationals in the United States.
- *Transparency in SA/LW.* Through its Section 655 Report to Congress, the United States regulates SA/LW exports under fully transparent procedures. This annual report to Congress provides information on all U.S. arms exports and is available on the Internet.
- *Excess Weapons Destruction and Stockpile Security.* The United States earmarks funds for SA/LW destruction and stockpile security.

- *The Organization of American States (OAS) Illicit Manufacturing of and Trafficking in Firearms Convention.* This agreement among OAS countries strengthens their ability to combat illicit trafficking, while facilitating cooperation among them.
- *Embargo Enforcement.* The United States observes and enforces sanctions and embargoes established by the United Nations Security Council.
- *Cracking Down on Financing of Illicit Arms.* The United States has been actively involved in initiatives to curb the impact of the illegitimate diamond trade on African conflicts.
- *Vigilance at the Borders.* The United States, through the Bureau of Alcohol, Tobacco, Firearms and Explosives and the U.S. Customs Service, intensified interdiction and investigative efforts to prevent illicit trafficking across its borders.
- *UN Transnational Organized Crime Convention "Firearms Protocol."* The United States joined consensus on a legally binding agreement on measures to combat illicit trade in firearms, May 31, 2001.

On November 14, 1997, the OAS adopted the Inter-American Convention against the Illicit Manufacturing of and Trafficking in Firearms, Ammunition, Explosives, and Other Related Materials. This was the first multilateral treaty designed to prevent, combat, and eradicate illegal transnational trafficking in firearms, ammunition, and explosives. As of March 1, 2004, twenty-two OAS member states had ratified the Convention (Antigua and Barbuda, Argentina, Bahamas, Belize, Bolivia, Brazil, Chile, Costa Rica, Colombia, Ecuador, El Salvador, Grenada, Guatemala, Mexico, Nicaragua, Panama, Paraguay, Peru, Saint Lucia, Trinidad and Tobago, Uruguay, and Venezuela), and thirty-three of the thirty-four active OAS member states (including the United States) have signed.

The aim of the Convention is to help shut down the illicit transnational arms market that fuels violence associated with drug trafficking, terrorism, and international organized crime. (See *http://www.state.gov/t/ac/rls/fs/2004/30218.htm.*)

Some key provisions of the Convention include:

- requiring parties to the Convention to establish or

maintain an effective licensing or authorization system for the export, import, and transit of firearms, ammunition, explosives, and other related materials
- obligating parties to require at the time of manufacture the marking of firearms with the name of the manufacturer, place of manufacture, and serial number (similar identifying markings are required for imported firearms)
- requiring parties to adopt laws and regulations criminalizing the illicit manufacture of and trafficking in firearms, ammunition, explosives, and related materials
- encouraging parties to share information on legislative practices and other national measures to combat illicit trafficking; techniques used to combat money laundering related to illicit transfers; routes customarily used by criminal organizations engaged in illicit trafficking; and the means of concealment used and methods for detecting them

Documents

"Background Paper: The U.S. Approach to Combating the Spread of Small Arms," 2001, at *http://www.state.gov/t/pm/rls/fs/2001/3766.htm.*

"Transparency in Arms Sales," 2001, at *http://www.state.gov/t/pm/rls/fs/2001/3780.htm.*

The State Department publishes reports on arms flows to regions of conflict in order to raise public awareness of the illicit small arms and light weapons trade issue. In 1999, for example, the State Department released "Arms and Conflict in Africa," at *http://www.state.gov/www/regions/africa/9907_africa_conflict.html.*

"U.S.-EU Statement of Common Principles on Small Arms and Light Weapons," U.S. Mission to the European Union, Brussels, Belgium, December 17, 1999, at *http://www.state.gov/p/eur/rls/or/3750.htm.*

United Nations

Web site: *www.un.org*
The first ever United Nations Conference on the Illicit Trade in Small Arms and Light Weapons in All Its Aspects, held July 9–20, 2001, in New York, represented a step forward in facing the challenge of small arms around the world. Through the consensus adoption of the Programme of Action to Prevent, Combat and

Eradicate the Illicit Trade in Small Arms and Light Weapons in All Its Aspects, member states expressed their collective will to establish and follow up on a set of universal norms to eradicate the uncontrolled proliferation and misuse of illicit small arms. The Programme of Action identified a variety of national, regional, and global measures, including the following:

- legislation on illegal manufacturing, possession, stockpiling, and trade in small arms
- stockpile management and destruction of weapons confiscated, seized, or collected
- identification and tracing of illicit arms
- international cooperation and assistance to states to strengthen their ability to identify and trace illicit weapons
- public awareness campaigns

The followup to this meeting was the UN Biennial Meeting on the Illicit Trade in Small Arms and Light Weapons in July 2003. (For a complete set of documents to the 2001 meeting, see *http://disarmament.un.org:8080/cab/smallarms/*; for the 2003 meeting, go to *http://disarmament2.un.org/cab/salw–2003.html*.)

UN Institute for Disarmament Research

Web site: *www.unidir.org*
The United Nations Institute for Disarmament Research (UNIDIR)—an intergovernmental organization within the United Nations—conducts research on disarmament and security with the aim of assisting the international community in its disarmament thinking, decisions, and efforts. Through its research projects, publications, meetings, and expert networks, UNIDIR monitors a wide array of disarmament and security-related challenges facing the world. These include tactical nuclear weapons, refugee security, computer warfare, regional confidence-building measures, and small arms. Working with researchers, diplomats, government officials, nongovernmental organizations, and other institutions, UNIDIR bridges the research community with United Nations member states.

Documents

Protocol against the Illicit Manufacturing of and Trafficking in Firearms, Their Parts and Components and Ammunition, supplementing the United Nations Convention against Transnational Organized Crime, at *http://www.unodc.org/unodc/en/crime_cicp_convention.html.*

"National Reports by Member States to the United Nations in Preparation for the First Biennial Meeting of States on the Implementation of the UN Programme of Action on Small Arms and Light Weapons," 2003, at *http://disarmament.un.org:8080/cab/salw–2003.html.*

The national reports are at *http://disarmament.un.org:8080/cab/salw-nationalreports.html.*

For a list of United Nations publications on small arms, see United Nations Publications: Small Arms at *http://www.un.org/Pubs/whatsnew/small arms.htm* as well as *http://www.unidir.ch/bdd/focus-search.php?onglet=5.*

"Report of the United Nations Conference on the Illicit Trade in Small and Light Weapons in All Its Aspects," 2001, at *http://www.state.gov/documents/organization/ 7494.pdf.*

Small Arms Survey

Website: *www.smallarmssurvey.org*
The Small Arms Survey is an independent research project located at the Graduate Institute of International Studies, Geneva, Switzerland. It serves as the principal international source of public information on all aspects of small arms, and as a resource center for governments, policymakers, researchers, and activists. The project has an international staff with expertise in security studies, political science, international public policy, law, economics, development studies, conflict resolution, and sociology. The staff works closely with a worldwide network of researchers and partners.

The Small Arms Survey project is funded by contributions from the governments of Switzerland, Australia, Belgium, Canada, Finland, Denmark, France, Netherlands, New Zealand, Norway, Sweden, and the United Kingdom.

The Small Arms Survey web site contains a wealth of information, documents, reports, and links to organizations around the world specializing in the study and monitoring of small arms. For example, by clicking on "partners" at the Small Arms Survey web site, the researcher will find links to more than twenty organizations.

Small Arms Survey 2004: Rights at Risk (*http://www.small armssurvey.org/publications/yb_2004.htm*) provides original research and updated information on small arms production, stockpiles, and trade. In focusing on the links between small arms and the abuse of human rights, this volume explores the impact of arms exports to areas of conflict, the role of weapons in global violence and crime, and the implementation of human rights standards by police forces worldwide.

For reports and documents on small arms from regions around the world, go to Small Arms Survey's site at *http://www .smallarmssurvey.org/resources/reg_docs.htm*.

Trafficking in Nuclear Materials

International Atomic Energy Agency

Web site: *http://www.iaea.org/index.html*
The International Atomic Energy Agency (IAEA) is a leading agency for monitoring and regulating the nuclear field in the international arena. It was established as "Atoms for Peace" in 1957 within the United Nations organizational structure. The IAEA works with its member states and multiple partners worldwide to promote safe, secure, and peaceful nuclear technologies.

The IAEA Secretariat is headquartered at the Vienna International Centre in Vienna, Austria. Operational liaison and regional offices are located in Geneva, New York, Toronto, and Tokyo. The IAEA runs or supports research centers and scientific laboratories in Vienna and Seibersdorf, Austria; Monaco; and Trieste, Italy. The Secretariat consists of 2,200 multidisciplinary professional and support staff from more than ninety countries. Its budget for 2004 amounted to $268.5 million, and an additional $74.75 million in voluntary contributions was expected. Three main pillars underpin the IAEA's mission: safety and security; science and technology; and safeguards and verification.

The IAEA has compiled an extensive database called "Illicit Nuclear Trafficking Facts and Figures: Illicit Nuclear Trafficking Statistics, January 1993 to December 2003," tracking black-market activities in nuclear and radioactive material. As of December 2003, the database contained 540 confirmed incidents involving illicit trafficking in nuclear and other radioactive materials. Several hundred additional incidents that have been reported in open sources, but not confirmed, are also tracked in the IAEA database but are not included in the statistics that follow. According to the IAEA, the majority of the confirmed incidents involved the deliberate intent to illegally acquire, smuggle, or sell nuclear material or other radioactive material. The database also includes some incidents where actions may have been inadvertent, such as accidental disposal or the detection of radioactively contaminated products.

Of the 540 confirmed illicit trafficking incidents:

- 182 incidents involved nuclear material
- 335 incidents involved radioactive material other than nuclear material
- 23 incidents involved both nuclear and other radioactive materials

As of December 2003, the IAEA database included 205 confirmed incidents since January 1, 1993, that involved nuclear material. Of these incidents with nuclear material, less than 10 percent (seventeen incidents) involved highly enriched uranium (HEU) or plutonium, materials that could be used for the fissile core of a nuclear explosive device.

During the first half of the 1990s, quantities of a kilogram or more of HEU were seized in a few cases, and in one case about 0.3 kg of plutonium was seized. By contrast, no confirmed theft or seizure from 1995 to today has involved more than 1 or 2 percent of what would be needed for constructing a nuclear bomb. Even when small quantities of such material are seized, the question remains whether they might have been samples of larger quantities available for illicit sale. Trafficking in such materials, of course, might occur undetected. This data generally corresponds with the findings of Rensselaer Lee in his book, *Smuggling Armageddon* (see Chapter 7 of the present volume).

According to the IAEA, the overwhelming majority of confirmed nuclear trafficking involved lower grade materials. Although the quantities of these lower-grade materials that have been stolen or seized have been too small to be significant for nuclear proliferation, these cases sometimes are indicative of gaps in the control and security of nuclear material.

The IAEA database includes 358 confirmed incidents since January 1, 1993, that involved radioactive material other than nuclear. In most of the cases, the trafficked radioactive material was in the form of sealed radioactive sources, but some incidents with unsealed radioactive samples or radioactivity-contaminated materials such as scrap metal also have been reported to the illicit trafficking database and are included in the statistics. Some countries are more complete than others in reporting incidents, and open-source information suggests that the actual number of cases is significantly larger than the number confirmed to the IAEA.

Radioactive sources involved in confirmed trafficking demonstrate a wide range of activity levels. The vast majority of them have been too weak to cause serious health problems if used for malicious acts.

The Center for International Security and Cooperation

Web site: *http://cisac.stanford.edu/*
Another major database on the illicit trafficking in nuclear and radioactive materials has been compiled by the Center for International Security and Cooperation (CISAC) at the Stanford Institute for International Studies (SIIS). Called the Database on Nuclear Smuggling, Theft and Orphan Radiation Sources (DSTO), this resource was compiled from databases, technical journals, newspapers, and other sources since 1999 to derive a picture of illicit trafficking of nuclear material worldwide. DSTO is divided into twenty-one categories, including type of incident, type of material, suspected origin, perpetrators involved, reported destination, and intended use. The database also categorizes the reliability of information used and identifies major routes of illicit trafficking and how they have changed during the last decade. For example, in the early 1990s, Western Europe was the place to sell nuclear material. Now the market has apparently shifted to Central Asia, the Caucasus, and Turkey.

DSTO combines information from the IAEA's Illicit Trafficking Database and the Newly Independent States' Nuclear Trafficking Database at the Center for Nonproliferation Studies (CNS) in Monterey, California. The IAEA database is based on state-confirmed incidents, and CNS's database is confined to incidents in the former Soviet Union. The DSTO team also uses additional, independently obtained information. As a result, DSTO lists 830 entries including:

- A total of 643 nuclear smuggling incidents that include thefts and seizures of nuclear and other radioactive material have been documented.
- There are 107 sources of "orphaned" radiation (orphaned radiation sources refers to material that has been lost intentionally or by mistake).
- More than 80 cases involving fraud or malevolent acts using radioactive material to commit murder, deliberate exposure and blackmail, and poisoning of food and water supplies have been reported.
- Every year, the U.S. Nuclear Regulatory Commission receives 200 reports of lost, stolen, or abandoned radioactive sources.
- About 40 kilograms of weapons-usable uranium and plutonium have been stolen from poorly protected nuclear facilities in the former Soviet Union during the last decade; most of it has been retrieved.
- Two kilos of highly enriched uranium stolen from a research reactor in the Republic of Georgia are still missing.

Generally speaking, a few kilograms of plutonium and less than 20 kilograms of highly enriched uranium are required to make a nuclear bomb.

DSTO gives an example of how even relatively low-level radiation exposure can risk public health and create major problems for society. In 1987, in Goiania, Brazil, scavengers dismantled a metal canister from a radiotherapy machine at an abandoned cancer clinic. Soon afterward, a junkyard worker opened the lead canister and discovered a pretty blue, glowing dust: radioactive cesium–137. In the days following, scores of people were exposed to the substance—some parents painted their children with it and sold tickets to neighbors to watch them dance. As a result, 112,000 people had to be monitored. Of those, 249 were contaminated; 28 suffered radiation burns, and 4 people died. More than 67 square kilometers were monitored, large areas had to be decontaminated, and 3,500 cubic meters of radioactive waste were generated.

The Database on Nuclear Smuggling, Theft and Orphan Radiation Sources is accessible only to carefully vetted researchers cooperating with the team at Stanford.

Nuclear Threat Initiatives

Web site: *http://www.nti.org*
Concerned that the threat from nuclear weapons had fallen off most people's radar screens after the initial period following the collapse of the Soviet Union, CNN founder Ted Turner asked former senator Sam Nunn in the spring of 2000 to help assess the need for a private institution to monitor the nuclear threat from the former Soviet Union and make recommendations for action. In January 2001, Turner and Nunn founded the Nuclear Threat Initiative (NTI).

NTI's goal is to strengthen global security by reducing the risk of use and preventing the spread of nuclear, biological, and chemical weapons. This is done primarily through programs and research focusing on the United States and the former Soviet Union and the various nuclear, biological, and chemical concerns between the two countries.

The value of NTI's web site to the researcher is its briefing papers on a wide range of issues within the area of nuclear, biological, and chemical weapons, including the illicit trafficking of nuclear materials. In addition, the site has extensive links to documents issued by nongovernmental organizations, the U.S. government, and international organizations such as the United Nations, NATO, and the European Union.

Some of the data provided by NTI outlines the scope of the problem:

- After the Cold War, in Russia alone there were approximately 30,000 nuclear warheads and enough highly enriched uranium and plutonium to make 60,000 more.
- After the Cold War, tens of thousands of scientists in the former Soviet Union with weapons expertise no longer had assured jobs.
- In more than forty countries around the world, there are more than 100 research reactors with highly enriched uranium, some of which is inadequately secured and vulnerable to theft.
- Threat-reduction programs are believed to have made progress in securing vulnerable weapons and materials in the former Soviet Union. However, only 43 percent

of rapid cooperative security upgrades and 22 percent of comprehensive cooperative security measures are in place.

United Nations Convention on the Physical Protection of Nuclear Material, 1980, at *http://www.unodc.org/unodc/terrorism_convention_nuclear_material.html.*

"Measures against Illicit Trafficking in Nuclear Materials and Other Radioactive Sources," International Atomic Energy Agency, Report by the Director General, 1997, at *http://www.iaea.org/About/Policy/GC/GC41/Documents/gc41–21.html.*

International Standard to Combat Nuclear Trafficking, at *http://www.standards.org.au/newsroom/tgs/2004–08/trafficking/trafficking.htm.*

For extensive links to documents on nuclear security-related issues compiled from various sources, go to Russian American Nuclear Security Advisory Council (RANSAC) at *www.ransac.org.*

6

Agencies and Organizations

Amnesty International
1 Easton Street
London WC1X 0DW
United Kingdom
Tel: +44-20-74135500
Fax: +44-20-79561157
Web site: www.amnesty.org

Human trafficking is one of the many abuses that Amnesty International (AI) campaigns against in its pursuit to advance human rights throughout the world. Founded in 1961 by British lawyer Peter Benenson, the organization has spread to over 150 countries and territories with the involvement of over 1.8 million people. Politically, religiously, nationally, and economically independent, AI conducts research, surveys, and engages in a variety of other projects focused on preventing and ending grave abuses of the rights to physical and mental integrity, freedom of conscience and expression, and freedom from discrimination. Major policy decisions are taken by AI's International Council.

Historically, the main focus of AI's campaigning has been to free all prisoners of conscience, to ensure a prompt and fair trial for all political prisoners; to abolish the death penalty, torture, and other cruel, inhuman, or degrading treatment or punishment; and to end extrajudicial executions and "disappearances." Over the years, Amnesty International has expanded this mandate to encompass human rights abuses committed by nongovernmental bodies and private individuals. It opposes abuses by armed political groups (in control of territory or operating in opposition to governments), such as hostage taking, torture, and unlawful killings. Amnesty International sends fact-finding missions to assess situations on the spot. The delegates might interview prisoners, relatives, lawyers, witnesses to human rights violations, and local human rights activists. They may also observe trials and meet government officials. The organization monitors newspapers, web sites, and other media outlets.

Anti-Slavery International

Thomas Clarkson House
The Stableyard
Broomgrove Road
London SW9 9TL
United Kingdom
Tel: +44-(0)20-7501-8920
Fax: +44-(0)20-7738-4110
E-mail: info@antislavery.org
Web site: http://www.antislavery.org

Established in 1839, Anti-Slavery International is the world's oldest international human rights organization. It works to eliminate human trafficking along with child labor, forced and bonded labor, and traditional slavery. The methods of Anti-Slavery International include lobbying governments, supporting research, and increasing public awareness and education. In addition, Anti-Slavery International honors individuals or organizations for courageous long-term campaigning against slavery with its annual Anti-Slavery Award.

Some of the activities undertaken by Anti-Slavery International include urging governments of countries with slavery to develop and implement measures to end it, lobbying governments and intergovernmental agencies to make slavery a priority issue, supporting research to assess the scale of slavery in order to fight it, and working with local organizations to raise public awareness.

Bureau for International Narcotics and Law Enforcement Affairs

U.S. Department of State
2201 C Street, NW
Washington, DC 20520

Tel: (202) 647-4000
Web site: http://www.state.gov/g/inl/

The Bureau for International Narcotics and Law Enforcement Affairs (INL) develops and coordinates U.S. international drug and crime policies and programs. To achieve its goal of disrupting international drug trafficking, the INL has developed diplomatic initiatives, bilateral programs, and multilateral programs that enhance countertrafficking efforts in over 150 countries. The INL also advises the president, secretary of state, and U.S. government agencies on initiatives to oppose international narcotics, human trafficking, human rights abuses, and crime.

Bureau of Alcohol, Tobacco, Firearms and Explosives
U.S. Department of Justice
Office of Public and Governmental Affairs
650 Massachusetts Avenue, NW
Room 8290
Washington, DC 20226
Tel: (202) 927-8500
Fax: (202) 927-1083
Web site: http://www.atf.gov/index.htm

The Bureau of Alcohol, Tobacco, Firearms and Explosives (ATF) is a preeminent federal law enforcement agency fighting violent crime in the United States. In terms of fighting trafficking in firearms on an international scale, ATF has an International Response Team (IRT) that participates with the Diplomatic Security Service of the U.S. Department of State to provide technical and investigative assistance at international explosives and fire incidents. There have been twenty-four IRT activations since 1991, including responses to Peru, Macedonia, Argentina, El Salvador, Ecuador, Pakistan, and Korea.

Coalition Against Trafficking in Women
P.O. Box 9338
North Amherst, MA 01059
Fax: (413) 367-9262
Web site: http://www.catwinternational.org

The Coalition Against Trafficking in Women (CATW) is an NGO that promotes women's rights by working internationally to combat sexual exploitation in all its forms. Founded in 1988, CATW was the first international NGO to focus on human trafficking, especially sex trafficking of women and girls. CATW is composed of regional networks and of affiliated individuals and groups. It serves as an umbrella that coordinates and takes direction from its regional organizations and networks in its work against sexual exploitation and in support of women's human rights.

Drug Enforcement Administration
2401 Jefferson Davis Highway
Alexandria, VA 22301
Tel: (202) 307-1000
Web site: http://www.dea.gov

The Drug Enforcement Administration (DEA) has worked against drug trafficking since its creation in 1973. Its primary responsibilities include investigation and preparation for the prosecution of major violators of controlled substance laws operating at interstate and international levels, investigation and preparation for prosecution of criminals and drug gangs, and management of a national drug intelligence program in cooperation with federal, state, local, and foreign officials to collect, analyze, and disseminate strategic and operational drug intelligence information. Regarding international drug control programs, the DEA is the U.S. liaison with the United Nations, Interpol, and other organizations that seek to end the trafficking of drugs.

Europol
P.O. Box 90850
NL-2509 LW The Hague
The Netherlands
Tel: +31-70-302-5000
Fax: +31-70-345-5896
E-mail: info@europol.eu.int
Web site: http://www.europol.eu.int

Established in 1992, but not fully operational until 1999, Europol is the EU's law enforcement organization. It serves as a support service for the law enforcement agencies of the EU member states. Europol focuses mainly on drug, vehicle, and human trafficking, together with forgery, money laundering, and terrorism. The agency is becoming the center for intelligence exchange, development, analysis, cooperation, and support in relation to the fight against international organized crime across the Continent. Europol supports member states by facilitating the exchange of information, in accordance with national law, between Europol liaison officers (ELOs) who represent their home countries, by providing operational analysis in support of member states' operations, by generating strategic reports (e.g., threat assessments) and crime analysis on the basis of information and intelligence supplied by member states, generated by Europol or gathered from other sources, and by providing expertise and technical support for investigations and operations carried out within the EU, under the supervision and the legal responsibility of the member states concerned.

Foundation Against Trafficking in Women
P.O. Box 1455
3500 BL Utrecht
The Netherlands
Tel: +31-30-716044
Fax: +31-30-716084
E-mail: fe@stv.vx.xs4all.nl
Web site: http://www.bayswan.org/FoundTraf.html

The Foundation Against Trafficking in Women (STV) was initiated in the early 1980s in response to the then highly publicized issue of prostitution tourism. Women's organizations, development nongovernment organizations, and various action groups, especially in regions where mass tourism was becoming the alternative for development, were awakening to the fact that not only the natural resources but also the human resources, namely, the young women, of their countries were being traded for foreign exchange. Officially set up in 1987, STV aimed its first campaigns at developing and refining national legislation and litigation for addressing trafficking in women. STV is active in advocacy and campaigning as well as conducting research and training. In 1994, STV participated in launching the Global Alliance Against Traffic in Women (GAATW).

Global Alliance Against Traffic in Women
P.O. Box 36
Bangkok Noi Post Office
Bangkok 10700
Thailand
Tel: +66-2-864-1427/8
Fax: +66-2-864-1637

E-mail: gaatw@gaatw.org
Web site: http://www.gaatw.org

The Global Alliance Against Traffic in Women (GAATW) is a nongovernmental human rights network comprising individuals and organizations worldwide. Since its formation in 1994 in Chiang Mai, Thailand, GAATW has coordinated, organized, and facilitated work on issues related to trafficking in women and women's labor migration in virtually every region of the world. GAATW advocates for the inclusion of legal protection of the human rights of trafficking victims in domestic laws and policies to provide direct support to those in need. One of the founding members of the GAATW was the Foundation Against Trafficking in Women (STV).

Human Rights Watch
350 Fifth Avenue
34th floor
New York, NY 10118-3299
Tel: (212) 290-4700
Fax: (212) 736-1300
E-mail: hrwnyc@hrw.org
Web site: http://www.hrw.org

Originating in 1978 as Helsinki Watch, a name that reflected its sole mission of monitoring compliance with the 1975 Helsinki Accords, Human Rights Watch has evolved into the largest human rights organization based in the United States. The main work of Human Rights Watch is researching and reporting human rights abuses including human trafficking. Human Rights Watch currently conducts investigations in more than seventy countries around the world.

International Narcotics Control Board
Vienna International Centre
Room E-1339
P.O. Box 500
A-1400 Vienna
Austria
Tel: +43-1-26060-0
Fax: +43-1-26060-5867
E-mail: secretariat@incb.org
Web site: http://www.incb.org

The Single Convention on Narcotic Drugs of 1961 established the International Narcotics Control Board (INCB), which did not become operational until 1968. Although it is financed by the United Nations and its members are elected by the United Nations Economic and Social Council (ECOSOC), the INCB is an independent organization. The primary work of the INCB is to implement and serve as a quasijudicial control body for the drug conventions of the UN. The INCB also helps correct weaknesses found in international drug trafficking control systems as well as assessing the chemicals used to produce trafficked drugs.

International Organization for Migration
17, Route des Morillons
CH-1211 Geneva 19
Switzerland
Tel: +41-22-717-9111
Fax: +41-22-798-6150
E-mail: info@iom.int
Web site: http://www.iom.int

Founded in 1951 as the Provisional Intergovernmental Committee for the Movement of Migrants from Europe (PICMME), the International Organization for Migration (IOM) has become the leading international organization for migration. The IOM assists governments and nongovernmental organizations through rapid humanitarian responses to sudden migration flows, postemergency return and reintegration programs, rendering help to migrants in distress, and training officials. In addition, the IOM pursues extensive research and informational campaigns as well as programs providing counseling and assistance to victims of trafficking. The IOM also aids governments looking to improve their countertrafficking capabilities. Currently, the IOM has over seventy active countertrafficking programs and projects throughout the world.

International Peace Research Institute, Oslo
Fuglehauggata 11
NO-0260 Oslo
Norway
Tel: +47-22-54-77-00
Tel: +47-22-54-77-10
Fax: +47-22-54-77-01
E-mail: info@prio.no
Web site: http://www.prio.no

The International Peace Research Institute (PRIO) was founded in 1959 and became a fully independent institute in 1966. It was one of the first centers of peace research in the world, and it is Norway's only peace research institute. Its founding and early influence were instrumental in projecting the idea of peace research. Scholarly research is at the core of all Institute activities. Research at PRIO concentrates on the driving forces behind violent conflict and on ways in which peace can be built, maintained, and spread. In addition to theoretical and empirical research, PRIO also conducts policy-oriented activities and engages in the search for solutions in cases of actual or potential violent conflict, including issues surrounding human trafficking and trafficking in weapons.

Interpol
General Secretariat
200, quai Charles de Gaulle
69006 Lyon
France
Drug trafficking e-mail: drugs@interpol.int
Human trafficking e-mail: children@interpol.int
Web site: http://www.interpol.int/

Since its inception in 1923 as the International Criminal Police Commission, Interpol has become the world's largest international police organization with 182 member states. Interpol provides three core services to member states: a unique global police communication system, a range of criminal databases and analytical services, and proactive support for police operations throughout the world. Participation in Interpol is facilitated through National Central Bureaus (NCBs), which are located in a law enforcement agency within each member state. Interpol priorities include providing information to law enforcement and conducting research in the areas of human trafficking, drug-related crime, terrorism, financial and high-tech crime, criminal organizations, fugitive investigations, and other activities that affect public safety.

La Strada—The Foundation Against Trafficking in Women
P.O. Box 5
PL. 00-956 Warsaw 10
Poland
Tel: (48-22) 628-3177

Fax: (48-22) 628-3177
Web site: http://free.ngo.pl/lastrada/page1.html

La Strada—The Foundation Against Trafficking in Women, was registered in September 1996. It grew out of a program, which began in September 1995, for preventing trafficking in women in Central and Eastern Europe. This program was itself founded on the initiative of the Dutch Foundation Against Trafficking in Women (STV). The objectives of La Strada are to distribute information on the crime of trafficking in women, in particular young girls, as well as to provide support in solving problems of the victims who return to Poland. La Strada works in Belarus, Hungary, Moldova, Romania, Bulgaria, Poland, Russian Federation, Czech Republic, Slovakia, and Ukraine.

National Institute of Justice
810 Seventh Street, NW
Washington, DC 20531
Tel: (202) 307-2942
Fax: (202) 307-6394
National Criminal Justice Reference Service:
(301) 519-5500, (800) 851-3420
Office of Justice Programs Online Research Information
Center: (202) 307-6742
Web site: http://www.ojp.usdoj.gov/nij/

The National Institute of Justice (NIJ) is the research, development, and evaluation agency of the U.S. Department of Justice and is dedicated to researching crime control and justice issues. NIJ provides independent, evidence-based knowledge and tools to meet the challenges of crime and justice, particularly at the state and local levels.

The NIJ director, appointed by the president and confirmed by the Senate, establishes the Institute's objectives, guided by the priorities of the Office of Justice Programs (OJP), the U.S. Department of Justice, and the needs of the field. The Institute actively solicits the views of criminal justice and other professionals and researchers to inform its search for the knowledge and tools to guide policy and practice. NIJ also sponsors the National Criminal Justice Reference Service (NCJRS), an international clearinghouse of criminal justice information.

In 1997, NIJ established the International Center in response to the rapid globalization of crime. The mission of the International

Center is fourfold: to stimulate, facilitate, evaluate, and disseminate both national and international criminal justice research and information. Areas of research of particular interest to the International Center are trafficking in humans and transnational organized crime. NIJ works closely with the U.S. State Department and the Criminal Division of the Department of Justice. NIJ and International Center staff also participate in United Nations committees, panels, and expert working groups on the subject, including the Convention Against Transnational Organized Crime.

Organization for Security and Co-operation in Europe
Headquarters
Karntner Ring 5-7
4th Floor
1010, Vienna
Austria
Tel: +43-1-514-36-0
Fax: +43-1-514-36-96
E-mail: info@osce.org
Web site: http://www.osce.org

OSCE's Office for Democratic Institutions and
Human Rights
Aleje Ujazdowskie 19
00-557 Warsaw
Poland
Tel: +48-22-520-06-00
Fax: +48-22-520-06-05
E-mail: trafficking@odihr.pl
Web site: http://www.osce.org/odihr

The Organization for Security and Co-operation in Europe (OSCE) is the largest regional security organization in the world with fifty-five participating states from Europe, Central Asia, and North America. It is active in early warning, conflict prevention, crisis management, and postconflict rehabilitation. The OSCE approach to security is comprehensive and cooperative: comprehensive in dealing with a wide range of security-related issues including arms control, preventive diplomacy, confidence- and security-building measures, human rights, democratization, election monitoring and economic and environmental security; cooperative in the sense that all OSCE participating states have equal status, and decisions are based on consensus.

The OSCE operates the Office for Democratic Institutions and Human Rights (ODIHR). Created in 1990, the ODIHR is the principal institution of the OSCE responsible for the security of the individual human being. To this end, the ODIHR runs numerous programs including an antitrafficking program that emphasizes victims' rights. The program also focuses on awareness-raising as well as legislative review and reform.

Organization of American States
17th Street and Constitution Avenue, NW
Washington, DC 20006
Tel: (202) 458-3000
Human trafficking e-mail: spcim@oas.org
Drug trafficking e-mail: oidcicad@oas.org
Web site: www.oas.org

The Organization of American States (OAS), chartered in 1948, consists of thirty-five independent countries of the Western Hemisphere. The OAS has two antitrafficking commissions. The Inter-American Commission of Women (CIM), which works against human trafficking, was established in 1928 and has become an OAS specialized organization. The Inter-American Drug Abuse Control Commission (CICAD), established in 1948, is an OAS agency committed to reducing the trafficking of illicit drugs and related firearms.

Through the OAS Inter-American Drug Abuse Control Commission (CICAD), the nations of the hemisphere are strengthening antidrug laws, enhancing prevention programs, and taking other steps to stem the trafficking of illegal narcotics, related chemicals, and firearms. The Multilateral Evaluation Mechanism (MEM), which monitors progress against drugs in each country and the region as a whole, has significantly increased cooperation on this issue. By sharing knowledge on accomplishments, obstacles, and strategies, the countries develop a clearer picture of needs and weaknesses and identify areas that warrant closer coordination, better legislation, more research, or additional resources.

Polaris Project
P.O. Box 77892
Washington, DC 20013
Tel: (202) 547-7909
Fax: (202) 547-6654

E-mail: info@PolarisProject.org
Web site: http://www.polarisproject.org

Polaris Project is a multicultural grassroots nonprofit agency combating sex trafficking and modern-day slavery. Based in the United States and Japan, Polaris Project works closely with survivors and community members to identify victims, provide services, conduct advocacy and technical training, and raise awareness. Polaris Project was founded in 2002 to address the vital need for direct intervention, grassroots advocacy, and survivor support to combat human trafficking. It is one of the largest grassroots antitrafficking organizations in the United States and Japan. The organization has approximately 3,000 members and supporters in the United States and around the world.

The Protection Project
Johns Hopkins University-SAIS
1717 Massachusetts Avenue, NW
Suite 515
Washington, DC 20036
Tel: (202) 663-5896
Fax: (202) 663-5899
E-mail: Protection_Project@jhu.edu
Web site: http://www.protectionproject.org

Located at the Johns Hopkins University School of Advanced International Studies, the Protection Project is a legal institute that conducts research on human trafficking. The Project documents and disseminates information about the scope of the problem of trafficking in persons, especially women and children, with a focus on national and international laws, case law, and implications of trafficking on U.S. and international foreign policy. The Project educates and advises the public and government officials through research, participation in conferences, publications, and raising awareness. Along with a comprehensive trafficking database, which includes a collection of trafficking laws from over 190 countries, the Protection Project provides an annual trafficking report, a law enforcement survey, and model countertrafficking legislation.

United Nations
United Nations Office on Drugs and Crime
Vienna International Centre

P.O. Box 500
A-1400 Vienna
Austria
Tel: +43-1-26060-0
Fax: +43-1-26060-5866
E-mail: unodc@unodc.org
Web site: http://www.unodc.org

The name "United Nations," coined by U.S. president Franklin D. Roosevelt, was first used in the "Declaration by United Nations" of January 1, 1942, during World War II, when representatives of twenty-six nations pledged their governments to continue fighting together against the Axis powers.

In 1945, representatives of fifty countries met in San Francisco at the United Nations Conference on International Organization to draw up the United Nations Charter. Those delegates deliberated on the basis of proposals worked out by the representatives of China, the Soviet Union, the United Kingdom, and the United States at Dumbarton Oaks in August–October 1944. The Charter was signed on June 26, 1945, by the representatives of the fifty countries. Poland, which was not represented at the Conference, signed it later and became one of the original fifty-one member states. The United Nations officially came into existence on October 24, 1945.

The United Nations Office on Drugs and Crime (UNODC), created in 1997, has become a global leader against international crime with 500 staff members located in its twenty-one field offices throughout the world. The UNODC has numerous counter-drug-trafficking operations, including the Illicit Crop Monitoring Programme (ICMP), the Alternative Development Programme, and the Global Programme Against Money Laundering (GPML). In its work against human trafficking, the UNODC created the Global Programme against Trafficking in Human Beings (GPAT).

Witness
353 Broadway
New York, NY 10013
Tel: (212) 274-1664
Fax: (212) 274-1262
E-mail: orders@witness.org
Web site: http://www.witness.org

Witness is a human rights program that encourages the pursuit of equality and fairness through the production of provocative video documentary material. Witness strengthens local activists by giving them video cameras and training in production and advocacy. The organization uses an arsenal of computers, imaging and editing software, satellite phones, and e-mail in the struggle for justice. Witness has worked with over 150 partner groups from fifty countries to use video to overcome political, economic, and physical barriers, and to expose human rights abuses to the world via television, grassroots advocacy, and Internet broadcasting.

7

Print and Nonprint Resources

Print Resources

Books and Articles

Setting the Stage: Trafficking Issues in a Global Context

Edwards, Adam, and Peter Gill (eds.). 2003. *Transnational Organised Crime: Perspectives on Global Security.* London: Routledge. 290 pages.

In the 1990s, transnational organized crime rose rapidly up the policy-making agenda, including becoming the subject of a special UN Conference convened in Naples in 1994. The initial sense was that transnational organized crime might most simply be explained by the demise of the USSR and the search by security agencies for a new threat by which to justify their existence. It has since been accepted that transnational crime was developing for decades in various parts of the world, particularly as pertains to narcotics trafficking. This volume argues that the various security threats must be examined in the context in which they occur and that policy measures must follow suit. Many of the collected materials concern themselves with enforcement measures. For example, one paper presents transnational organized crime as seen from a police perspective. Other chapters address controlling drug trafficking and sex trafficking in the European Union. Countering money laundering, including terrorist financing, is addressed, and a general discussion of the legal regulation of transnational organized crime is presented.

Farer, Tom (ed.). 1999. *Transnational Crime in the Americas.* New York: Routledge. 311 pages.

The first half of this volume of collected works provides a framework through which to consider criminal organizations and narcotics trafficking in Latin America. It begins with a broad overview of transnational organized crime in the global arena, outlining the threats of criminal organizations, the actors involved, and the preconditions that allowed for their rise. Other critical topics presented in the first five articles include money laundering's central role in fueling global crime, law enforcement concerns regarding countering a rapidly growing and diffuse threat, and the European perspective on transnational groups as national borders continue to fall with the expansion of the European Union. The second half of the volume concentrates on narcotics trafficking issues primarily in Mexico, Colombia, and Bolivia. The editor maintains that, with the exception of the former Soviet Union, nowhere has the salience of organized crime been as high as in the Americas and nowhere else has it so complicated interstate relations.

Friman, H. Richard, and Peter Andreas (eds.) 1999. *The Illicit Global Economy and State Power.* Lanham, MD: Rowman & Littlefield. 207 pages.

This volume puts transnational crime issues in a context of creating a challenge to state power. A critical question that any researcher will have to consider is: How does transnational crime erode the ability of nations to maintain effective governance? The illegal flow of goods and services across borders—trafficking of drugs, migrants, weapons, toxic waste, and dirty money—is increasingly fueling both conflict and cooperation among states and nonstate actors. The editors note that, in a sea of writing on transnational crime, relatively little remains to be said of turf wars, increasing firepower of criminals, attacks on state enforcement agencies, corruption of political officials, and so on, in the context of the illicit global economy. Whereas some contributors claim that the retreat of the state is selective and at times strategic (in control over tax evasion and capital flight versus money laundering), others believe that transnational crime groups have coopted or displaced the state to the extreme point of facilitating the emergence of a new form of nonstate authoritarianism. The last three of the seven chapters are detailed considerations of criminal activity and its impact on market dynamics in three countries: Mexico, Colombia, and Japan.

Godson, Roy (ed.). 2003. *Menace to Society: Political-Criminal Collaboration Around the World.* New Brunswick, NJ: Transaction Publishers. 301 pages.

Corruption is the fuel of organized crime and many of the trafficking activities engaged in, whether on the domestic or international scale. Trafficking of all types is made possible by the exchange of money and favors in return for turning a blind eye. Godson has gathered leading scholars in the study of transnational crime to comment on the state of crime and corruption in countries that are in many ways centers of trafficking activities. These countries include the United States, Colombia, Nigeria, Mexico, Russia, Ukraine, China (including Hong Kong), and Taiwan. The collaboration of the political establishment with the criminal underworld increasingly undermines the rule of law, human rights, and economic development in many parts of the world. Godson calls this the political-criminal nexus (PCN). As he notes, it is a problem in many parts of the world, in some countries a chronic problem, in other places more acute and violent, and it often dominates political, economic, and social life. In his introduction, Godson lays out the significance of the problem and explains why it has now become of major importance in regional and global trends. He goes on to diagnose contemporary factors or causes that facilitate and exacerbate the problem.

Liddick, Donald R. 2004. *The Global Underworld: Transnational Crime and the United States.* Westport, CT: Praeger. 159 pages.

In what is essentially a brief introduction to transnational crime issues, the author gives a bird's-eye view of the threat facing the United States and Canada. He starts with a brief discussion of transnational crime, providing a useful conceptualization of the problem. From there, various criminal organizations are considered, including Yakuza, Triads, outlaw motorcycle gangs,

Colombian and Mexican drug cartels, Italian-based groups, as well as groups that have emerged from the former Soviet Union. In Chapter Three, titled "Smuggling, Transnational Theft, and 'Eco-Crime,'" Liddick provides brief overviews of drug trafficking, arms trafficking, alien smuggling and trafficking in people, trafficking human organs, transnational theft, and environmental crimes. Money laundering, identified as the most critical element making transnational crime possible, is summarized in terms of actual cases and mechanisms for its control. The author concludes with a summary of legal tools and organizations in place to counter transnational crime.

Martin, John M., and Anne T. Romano. 1992. *Multinational Crime: Terrorism, Espionage, Drug and Arms Trafficking.* Thousand Oaks, CA: Sage Publications. 162 pages.

This book considers multinational systemic crime—crimes by various kinds of organizations that operate across national boundaries and in two or more countries simultaneously. This concept refers to a variety of criminal behavior systems including, but not limited to, the four crimes examined in this volume: terrorism, espionage, drug trafficking, and arms trafficking. These offenses carry strong connotations of evil, and yet outrage quickly becomes justification when, for example, espionage is carried out in the name of national security.

Reichel, Philip (ed.). 2005. *Handbook of Transnational Crime and Justice.* Thousand Oaks: Sage Publications. 512 pages.

Editor Philip Reichel, well respected for his work on comparative criminal justice and transnational crime issues, has brought together renowned scholars from around the world to offer various perspectives providing global coverage of the increasingly transnational nature of crime and the attempts to provide cooperative cross-national responses. This volume not only has a comprehensive introduction to the topic of transnational crime but also provides specific examples such as international terrorism, drug trafficking, and money laundering to illustrate this ever expanding phenomenon. The handbook also examines cross-national and international efforts by police, courts, international agencies, and correctional authorities to deal with transnational crime. Part IV concludes the book by addressing emerging issues in transnational crime and justice, with particular attention given to transnational organized crime in all regions of the world.

Seita, Alex Y. 1997. "The Role of Market Forces in Transnational Violence." *Albany Law Review*, 60: 635–651.

Seita analyzes how the market forces of supply and demand can lead to transnational violence. Globalization and the lowering of trade barriers have made it easier to move market commodities across national boundaries. However, this has also had a strong impact on the increase in transnational violence. Using the example of child sexual exploitation, he describes trafficking in persons as an example of a "violence commodity," concluding that the price and output for such trafficking are market driven.

Human Trafficking and Smuggling Issues

General

Bales, Kevin. 1999. *Disposable People: New Slavery in the Global Economy.* Berkeley: University of California Press. 298 pages.

The author, a lecturer at the University of Surrey in England, has traveled the world examining various conditions that enslave vast numbers of people in the twenty-first century. His journey took him to Thailand, Mauritania, Brazil, Pakistan, and India. Within the larger context of slavery, he considers trafficking in prostitutes and trafficking in slaves, as well as key issues that make trafficking possible such as false passports, extensive bribery of border guards, false work contracts, and fraudulent visas. Bales cites a 1993 Human Rights Watch report on trafficking, saying that the trafficking of Burmese women and girls into Thailand is appalling in its efficiency and ruthlessness. As HIV/AIDS becomes an even larger problem in the region, he says, traffickers search deeper into the country as virgins bring a higher price and pose less threat of exposure to sexually transmitted disease. He reaches the disturbing conclusion that national laws on trafficking are vague, punishments are slight, cooperation between countries is rare, and criminal gangs find it easier to transport women than drugs.

Campagna, Daniel I. S., and Donald L. Poffenberger. 1987. *The Sexual Trafficking in Children.* Westport, CT: Auburn House. 264 pages.

This text investigates the components of the child sex trade, victims, victimizers, and the business aspects, using information obtained from five years of field research. Case studies, interviews with pimps, child sex workers, and personnel from various agencies charged with stopping the child sex trade, as well as field observations of the sex trade at work are included to provide multiple perspectives. The division of the book allows for a detailed discussion of the various areas encompassed by the child sex trade, including pedophilia, sex tourism, indenturing, hustling, and child pornography. One unique aspect of this book is that it takes a multidisciplinary approach to the topic, combining psychological considerations, law enforcement concerns, victims' assistance concerns, and judicial concerns.

Demleitner, Nora V. 1994. "Forced Prostitution: Naming an International Offense."*Fordham International Law Journal* 18: 163–197.

According to Demleitner, the difficulty in prosecuting and punishing the traffickers of women and children derives from a "general unwillingness to recognize forced prostitution as an offence in its own right." In fact, the acts that comprise the crime of forced prostitution are labeled as individual offenses instead of being acknowledged as a composite crime. Demleitner suggests attaching the label "forced prostitution" to the whole range of abuses it encompasses and recognizing the procurer or financier as well as the customer as offenders. This will make it easier to prosecute the offense domestically, she argues.

Hotaling, Norma, and Leslie Levitas-Martin. 2002. "Increased Demand Resulting in the Flourishing Recruitment and Trafficking of Women and Girls: Related Child Sexual Abuse and Violence Against Women." *Hastings Women's Law Journal* 13: 117–125.

This article discusses the demand for women and children in the international sex trade and the prevalence of child sexual abuse in the commercial sex industry. Hotaling and Levitas-Martin specifically examine the decriminalization of trafficked women forced into prostitution, the consequences of criminalizing forced prostitution, aftercare needs for victims of trafficking, and the demand for the commercial sex industry.

Kyle, David, and Rey Koslowski. 2001. *Global Human Smuggling: Comparative Perspectives.* Baltimore, MD: Johns Hopkins University Press. 374 pages.

This volume explores the global dimensions of human smuggling in several forms and regions, examining its deep social, economic, and cultural roots and its broad political consequences. Part I discusses the sociohistorical context and the contemporary diversity of human smuggling of migrants, asylum seekers, and those who are tricked into slavery, including the conflicting role of states and corrupt state officials as contributing to the problem. In Part II, the authors present high-profile case studies that include U.S.-Mexican border smuggling, the international business of trafficking women from the former Soviet Union, and the origins and social organization of human smuggling as a global business from China and Southeast Asia. In Part III, contributors examine the politics of human smuggling, looking more closely at the legal construction of victimized women trafficked into slavery, the social construction of smuggled immigrants as threats to the social order, and the sanctioning of unauthorized employment of illegal immigrants.

Williams, Phil (ed.). 1999. *Illegal Immigration and Commercial Sex: The New Slave Trade.* London: Frank Cass. 241 pages.

During the 1990s illegal immigration became a global problem of immense proportions. South Africa, for example, is host to between 1 and 2 million illegal immigrants, while it is believed that over 100,000 Chinese citizens illegally enter the United States every year. With migration flows from the developing world to the developed, many countries have become both transshipment centers and unwilling hosts for migrants en route to their final destinations. During their travel, illegal immigrants are easily victimized, and, even when they arrive, many are forced into a life of hardship and crime. This volume studies the role of criminal organizations in human commodity trafficking, examining the problem from a global vantage point and from a variety of regional perspectives. It also assesses the adequacy of existing policy responses and identifies additional measures that need to be taken.

Historical

Cordasco, Francesco. 1981. *The White Slave Trade and the Immigrants.* Detroit: Blaine Ethridge Books. 118 pages.

On the afternoon of November 21, 1902, New York newspapers carried the story of large-scale vice raids in Philadelphia that had revealed the existence of an international ring trafficking in young girls. It was said that the ring had its headquarters in Germany, with branches in Philadelphia and New York, and that its business was to supply girls for public houses in those two cities, in Baltimore, Chicago, and elsewhere. As with the Janney book (described later), the reader is reminded that international trafficking in women is not a new phenomenon. Other sources have shown that the white slave trade was an integral part of America in the period of the great migrations of the nineteenth and early twentieth centuries. The white slave trade was, if anything, an indigenous enterprise; the immigrants and their women were only peripherally related to the criminal activity. There had been a federal law on the statute books since 1875 that prohibited the importation of women for purposes of prostitution and provided penalties for such importation. Cordasco presents all of the major areas of interest, including recruiting, methods of importation, the system of exploitation, and profits derived from trafficking activity. His introduction lays out the context including the reasons for the business and the extent of trafficking activity. The second half of the book presents a 1909 report prepared by the U.S. Senate's Immigration Commission on the Importation and Harboring of Women for Immoral Purposes.

Dunbar, Michelle O. P. 1999–2000. "The Past, Present, and Future of International Trafficking in Women for Prostitution." *Buffalo Women's Law Journal* 8: 103–128.

In addition to reviewing the history of trafficking in women for prostitution, Dunbar emphasizes that more effort must be exerted on the domestic level in order to put a dent in the thriving business of trafficking in women. International conventions must be evaluated in terms of the difference between international trafficking and forced prostitution, and enforced to a greater degree in order to change the global sex industry. Traffickers must be prosecuted and brought to justice by the proposed international criminal court.

Janney, O. Edward. 1911. *The White Slave Traffic in America.* Baltimore, MD: Lord Baltimore Press. 201 pages.

The initial attraction of this book is that it was written almost 100 years ago, reminding the reader that while the scope of human trafficking may be far greater today, the trade in human beings to the United States is not a new challenge by any means. The author was chairman of the National Vigilance Committee for the Suppression of the White Slave Traffic. Dr. Janney outlines the three major players in the traffic of humans—the procurer, the importer or exporter, and the so-called keeper of the house. Janney reports in detail the process by which the victim—most often women for the purposes of prostitution—were lured into a life of slavery, frequently attracted to the procurer by promises of high incomes and a better life, a common motive in human trafficking today. Janney also discusses the traffic in women on the Pacific Coast, particularly Japanese and Chinese women. The last part of the book is dedicated to a discussion of the suppression and prevention of the white slave traffic.

Regional

Altink, Sietske. 1996. *Stolen Lives: Trading Women into Sex and Slavery.* Binghamton, NY: Haworth Press. 180 pages.

Although human trafficking is a global issue, a regional divide is usually seen in the discussion of this topic. However, this book seems to touch on most of the trafficking hot spots including the Netherlands, Thailand, Colombia, Greece, Belgium, and the former Yugoslavia, to name a few. Altink peers into the gritty world of trafficking, looking at how young women in search of a better life are persuaded to leave their countries only to end up stranded and forced into prostitution and/or domestic slavery once they reach their destination. These girls are placed in a desperate situation: they are denied the better life they sought but are keenly aware that they are alone and illegal aliens in a foreign country with little or no recourse. Also addressed are smuggling routes and ways that human traffickers avoid the law.

Chin, Ko-lin. 1999. *Smuggled Chinese: Clandestine Immigration to the United States.* Philadelphia: Temple University Press. 221 pages.

Chin presents an extensive study of the smuggling process, conducting interviews at points of origin in China as well as destinations in the United States. The first three chapters that make up Part I lay the groundwork, explaining the push-pull factors influencing the decisions of those smuggled, as well as the characteristics of groups involved in the activity. Although, strictly speaking, smuggling and trafficking differ, it is important to include Chin's work in a discussion of transnational crime and the mechanisms by which the smuggling process is undertaken. Part II consists of three chapters that undertake a discussion of how people are actually moved from China to the United States, detailing air, sea, and land routes and the logistics involved. Finally, in Part III, the author looks at the last major stage of the process— at the destination point—including conditions of safe houses and the payment of smuggling debts. The last chapter presents policy issues and recommendations for stemming the tide of Chinese human smuggling.

Guinn, David E., and Elissa Steglich. 2003. *In Modern Bondage: Sex Trafficking in the Americas.* Ardsley, NY: Transnational Publishers. 460 pages.

Researched by staffers at the International Human Rights Law Institute at DePaul University College of Law in Chicago, this volume provides an overview of Central America, including the socioeconomic context of poverty and migration as well as a look at legislation and other response mechanisms to the problem of sex trafficking. Countries examined are Belize, Costa Rica, Dominican Republic, El Salvador, Guatemala, Honduras, Nicaragua, and Panama. National reports submitted by these countries detail the types of trafficking, means of recruiting, transferring, and harboring victims, and conditions they are kept under, and they also provide examples of cases. There is a section on the enforcement mechanisms currently in place as well as shortcomings in the governmental apparatus. An extensive appendix includes a list of the institutions and organizations in each country that were consulted for the project, including government and nongovernment organizations. An index of the 200 United Nations reports that were used in the study is provided.

Hauber, Laurie. 1998. "The Trafficking of Women for Prostitution: A Growing Problem within the European Union." *Boston College International and Comparative Law Review* 21: 183–199.

Hauber examines the problem of trafficking in women for the purpose of sexual exploitation within the European Union, noting that it is either directly or indirectly addressed in EU resolutions and by individual member states. The EU suggested formulating a common strategy for combating trafficking as early as 1989 and continues to address the problem within the community. Hauber concludes that the EU must develop a comprehensive response that includes both legal and nonlegal measures. She suggests that the necessary provisions in laws should include law enforcement cooperation, witness protection, victim assistance, and victim rehabilitation.

Human Rights Watch. 2000. *Owed Justice: Thai Women Trafficked into Debt Bondage in Japan.* New York: Human Rights Watch. 227 pages.

The trafficking of women from Thailand to Japan occurs within the context of large-scale regional migration in Asia, which has grown dramatically over the last two decades. The vast majority of this migration is illegal, as Japan accepts only a very limited number of legal migrants each year. In practice, the high demand for foreign workers in Japan has fostered the growth of large transnational networks able to bypass legal barriers and facilitate illegal migration into Japan. Three chapters deal with responses to trafficking in persons: one section on the response of the Japanese government, one on that of the Thai government, and one on the international response to the Thai-Japanese traffic problem. The book offers profiles of trafficking victims and details the recruitment and export process from Thailand to Japan and the conditions of servitude under which the women are held in Japan.

Human Rights Watch. 1995. *Rape for Profit: Trafficking of Nepali Girls and Women to India's Brothels.* New York: Human Rights Watch. 90 pages.

Human Rights Watch uses this book to describe the conditions of Nepali girls who are either deceived or simply kidnapped into a world of forced prostitution. The abuse these women suffer, including rape, physical abuse, emotional abuse, and exposure to the AIDS virus, are chronicled in the text. Aggravating the already desperate situation of these girls is the complicit role the Nepali and Indian governments play in the sex/slave trade. The volume concludes with policy suggestions aimed at both governments to try to curb their silent support of the trafficking of Nepalese girls into the sex trade, to help end the abuse these women face, and to enforce legal ramifications on those who perpetuate the cycle.

Malarek, Victor. 2004. *The Natashas: Inside the New Global Sex Trade.* New York: Arcade Publishing. 320 pages.

After the fall of the Soviet Union in 1991, human trafficking in young girls and women expanded as the social structure eroded and organized crime gained more power. The author looks at how young women, believing that they will be employed as waitresses, models, and nannies, are deceived into a life of forced prostitution where they are considered "expendable." Malarek often uses personal testimony from girls who have lived through this nightmare to further his explanation. He also discusses current efforts to curb the problem but is well aware that one of the reasons for the perpetuation of the problem is a high level of complicity and corruption found in various institutions.

Smith, Paul J. (ed.) 1997. *Human Smuggling: Chinese Migrant Trafficking and the Challenge to America's Immigration Tradition.* Washington, DC: Center for Strategic and International Studies. 207 pages.

Despite the amount of press that has exposed the smuggling of Chinese migrants into the United States, the situation persists. This text examines how this problem continues, utilizing a complex and intricate network of smugglers that spans across more than thirty countries and generates hundreds of millions of dollars annually. Also discussed are influencing factors, such as unemployment rates and the overwhelming pressures that exist in the most populous country in the world.

Stoecker, Sally, and Louise I. Shelley (eds.) 2004. *Human Traffic and Transnational Crime: Eurasian and American Perspectives.* Lanham, MD: Rowman & Littlefield. 161 pages.

A conservative estimate of the extent of human trafficking places the number of annual global victims somewhere around 2 million people. Trafficking in people is believed to be the third largest trafficking concern, after drugs and arms. The present volume focuses on the trafficking hot spots of Russia and Ukraine. Seeking to further understand the motivations as well as how the problem is commonly understood and conceptualized, the editors compiled a collection that not only discusses trafficking as a crime in general, but identifies its elements, examines trends, compares smuggling between regions, and attempts to decipher the fact and fiction of human trafficking in this region. Policy implications and legislative attempts to curb human trafficking are also addressed.

Narcotics Trafficking

Bagley, Bruce Michael. 1997. *Drug Trafficking Research in the Americas: An Annotated Bibliography.* Miami, FL: North-South Center Press. 455 pages.

This volume provides a guide to the ever-expanding drug-related literature, concentrating on the most important, relevant sources chosen by a collection of scholars, analysts, and practitioners from a variety of disciplines. This multidisciplinary, multinational approach critically assesses the current social science literature on a complex and highly contentious issue in U.S.–Latin American relations. It is the second in a series of three volumes resulting from the North-South Center Drug Trafficking Task Force, cosponsored by the North-South Center and the Graduate School of International Studies, University of Miami, and the Centro de Estudios Internacionales, Universidad de los Andes, Bogotá.

Clawson, Patrick, and Rensselaer W. Lee, III. 1998. *The Andean Cocaine Industry.* New York: Palgrave Macmillan. 292 pages.

Basing their findings largely on field research, economist Clawson and political analyst Lee offer a thorough overview and analysis of the cocaine industry in Colombia, Peru, and Bolivia. Convinced that the United States cannot stop the Andean cocaine trade and that what ultimately happens will depend more on local politics than on U.S. intervention, they examine cocaine use; cocaine trafficking; the effects of the industry on Andean societies, economies, and politics; and realistic policy options for shrinking the industry. Among some of their interesting findings: cocaine revenues in Peru and Bolivia are less than 6 percent of gross national product; for every $100 of drugs sold in the United States, the federal government spends $60 trying to control distribution.

Fazey, C. S. J. 2003. "The Commission on Narcotic Drugs and the United Nations International Drug Control Programme: Politics, Policies and Prospect for Change." *International Journal of Drug Policy* 14 (2):155–169.

The author, a former senior officer of the United Nations International Drug Control Programme (UNDCP), shows how Commission on Narcotic Drugs (CND) meetings are manipulated in the interests of seventeen developed countries that largely fund the UNDCP. However, these major donors are not united on policy or on how to apply the UN drug Conventions, so CND decisions reflect the lowest level of disagreement, with major splits on policy ignored. The paper shows how inherent conflict between specialists and generalists plus an eclectic mixture of nationalities and abilities have compounded problems of leadership and management.

Fowler, Thomas B. 1996, June. "The International Narcotics Trade: Can It Be Stopped by Interdiction?" *Journal of Policy Modeling* 18 (3): 233–270.

A dynamic model of the illegal drug business indicates that feedback mechanisms exist that will thwart interdiction efforts by stabilizing price and street supply. The model suggests that efforts to control drug traffic and disrupt international drug cartel operations should concentrate on money flows and reduction of demand. It also suggests ways to maximize the effect of interdiction, should that still be used as a strategy.

Green, Penny. 1998. *Drugs, Trafficking and Criminal Policy: The Scapegoat Strategy.* Winchester, UK: Waterside Press. 208 pages.

Green explores the context of drug trafficking and its crucial place within international trade and the global economy. Demonizing couriers, often desperate and tragic people from the poorest regions of the world, gets in the way of rational analysis, and Dr. Green insists that it is underlying geopolitical issues that ultimately must be addressed. She draws on a large sample of people imprisoned for trafficking and on the interviews she conducted within prisons in England and Wales. Dr. Green's analysis leads her to conclude that contemporary policy must be freed from the "scapegoat strategy" of blaming the small-fry dealers; complex issues such as developmental politics and Third World debt need to be at the forefront of the debate, Green asserts.

Jamieson, Alison (ed.). 1994. *Terrorism and Drug Trafficking in the 1990s.* Aldershot, UK: Dartmouth Publishing Company. 285 pages.

Jamieson's work is an important reminder that illicit trafficking activities serve not only to fulfill the goals of organized crime groups; they are undertaken by terrorist organizations needing to fund their own activities. Indeed, the connection between organized criminal activities and terrorist financing has in recent years become increasingly important. This volume, compiled by a leading researcher in the field, brings under one cover a collection of articles published by the Research Institute for the Study of Conflict and Terrorism. The discussion moves from a review of the development of the modern Mafia and its significant involvement in drug trafficking in the late 1970s to a detailed overview of the development of narcotics trafficking as an industry. Chapters 3 and 4 are most useful overviews of the development, scope, and characteristics of global drug trafficking from the 1970s up to 1994.

Krajewski, K. 2003. "Drugs, Markets and Criminal Justice in Poland." *Crime, Law & Social Change* 40 (2/3): 273–293.

Since 1989, the drug situation in Poland has changed considerably. First, Poland has become a major European producer of synthetic drugs. Second, it has become a major transit country for smuggling drugs. Third, while its drug markets are not yet fully developed, they now offer a much broader selection of drugs than the pre-1989 staple drug, the home-made "Polish heroin." Despite some alarm about a growing drug problem, Polish drug policies for many years remained primarily public health oriented. The recent drug law reform, however, may signify a shift toward a more punitive approach. This paper explores the conditions surrounding the emergence of both new markets and new control strategies.

Stares, Paul. 1996. *Global Habit: The Drug Problem in a Borderless World.* Washington, DC: Brookings Institution. 171 pages.

Stares traces the rise of the global drug market since 1900, demonstrating that it is no longer a marginal area of criminal activity. From the 1970s to the mid-1990s it developed into a major global enterprise, which, Stares contends, means that a fundamental reorientation of current international drug control policies is necessary so that they may better meet the challenge ahead. The author calls for better, broader information about the characteristics and dynamics of global narcotics trafficking, saying that previous studies are too narrow in their focus. He says that the primary emphasis of international drug control should be on positive rather than negative controls: development of international law enforcement programs to combat drug trafficking needs to be continued, organized crime groups must be targeted to prevent the accumulation of threatening levels of wealth and power, and, generally, nations' attitudes toward sovereignty in a borderless world (for the criminal) must be reoriented. Success, he says, will ultimately depend on the international community's willingness to address the larger concerns that drug abuse is attached to: overpopulation, environmental degradation, poverty, illiteracy, ethnic strife, and disease.

Tullis, LaMond. 1991. *Handbook of Research on the Illicit Drug Traffic: Socioeconomic and Political Consequences.* Westport, CT: Greenwood Press. 672 pages.

Tullis provides a survey of the social and economic consequences of the production and consumption of narcotic drugs. The volume is divided into two parts. The first half provides an overview of the subject, consisting of three sections that survey the published literature on the production and consumption of illicit drugs. Chapters are devoted to the global patterns of production and consumption of cocaine, heroin, and cannabis, consequences of drug consumption and production, and policy measures that have been adopted in both consuming and producing countries. The second half provides an annotated bibliography of over 2,000 entries. This reference book is an extremely useful resource for researchers as well as general readers. The book is organized so that the main text raises relevant issues, which are then referenced to the literature and discussed in further detail in the endnotes. The period examined—the 1970s and 1980s—is the critical period in the growth of drug trafficking, dramatically expanding from cottage export production to highly organized, international economic exchanges employing hundreds of thousands of people and earning billions of dollars.

Willoughby, R. 2003. "Crouching Fox, Hidden Eagle: Drug Trafficking and Transnational Security: A Perspective from the Tijuana-San Diego Border." *Crime, Law & Social Change* 40 (1): 113–142.

The combination of mobilizing for homeland protection and conducting a major military campaign in Afghanistan underscores the profound security implications of drug trafficking. In the case of Mexico, drug smuggling has evolved under the influence of several dynamics and has become particularly threatening to the state and society in the last ten to twenty years with the cocaine boom. The historic ability of the Mexican political system to manage corruption has diminished, if not collapsed, as cartels have largely moved from a relationship of symbiosis with and subordination to the authorities to one of dominance and intimidation of them.

Zabludoff, Sidney Jay. 1998, Summer. "Colombian Narcotics Organizations as Business Enterprises." *Transnational Organized Crime* 3 (2): 20–49.

Zabludoff examines how the narcotics industry as a whole and Colombian drug trafficking enterprises in particular function as a business. Much of the study is based on discussions with law enforcement officers who have acquired insights into the operations of Colombian traffickers. The discussion notes that narcotics trafficking organizations clearly are businesses and that the structure of the cocaine, heroin, and marijuana industries closely resembles that of agribusiness. The Colombian cocaine industry has a triangular structure. The dominating firms at the top of the pyramid directly employ a relatively small number of people. The numbers increase through several layers of support entities.

Trafficking in Small Arms

Alves, Pericles G., and Diana B. Cipollone (eds.). 1998, March. *Curbing Illicit Trafficking in Small Arms and Sensitive Technologies: An Action-Oriented Agenda,* United Nations Institute for Disarmament Research (UNIDIR), Geneva, Brief No. 2/1998.

The contributors make a link between crime, small-arms trafficking, and sensitive technologies on the premise that illicit trafficking in drugs and small arms can lead to trafficking in sensitive technologies, creating ever-greater problems of national and international proportions. The authors examine the role of terrorism in illicit trafficking, posing the question: "How and when did drug cartels start supporting terrorist groups?" The report emphasizes that any agreement(s) will become mere paper tigers if those whose job it is to actually counter trafficking (customs, police, and intelligence) do not receive adequate means to enforce the law.

Dyer, Susannah, and Geraldine O'Callaghan. 1998, January. "Combating Illicit Light Weapons Trafficking: Developments and Opportunities." *British American Security Information Council.* 36 pages.

This report provides a comparative analysis of the efforts to control illicit light weapons trafficking being pursued by the OAS, the EU, the UN, and the G8. Recommendations include improving national enforcement of existing laws; adopting codes of conduct to establish stricter criteria for weapons transfers; improving domestic legislation in postconflict societies, and strengthening overall domestic gun control; registering and marking weapons; improving recordkeeping; developing a "security first" approach; supporting capacity building; involving NATO in controlling illicit weapons trafficking, and developing international legal mechanisms.

Graduate Institute of International Studies. 2003. *Small Arms Survey 2003: Development Denied.* New York: Oxford University Press. 336 pages.

This is the third annual report on the global production, use, and control of small arms. This edition documents evidence that small-arms availability and misuse can undermine development. It features chapters on production, stockpiles, transfers, and weapons collection, providing comparative data for a range of regions and countries. One chapter considers the emergence of new international norms in efforts to control small arms specifically against the backdrop of the United Nations Programme of Action. The final chapter provides a comparative analysis of peace negotiations to argue that disarmament and weapons disposal should be spelled out in agreements to cease hostilities.

ICPO-Interpol. 2001. "International Criminal Police Review. Special Issue: Combating the Traffic in Human Beings." *Interpol* No. 487–488. 64 pages.

This special issue of Interpol's publication presents a number of articles on smuggling and trafficking issues around the world.

Countries explored include Australia, Canada, China, Italy, Spain, Nigeria, and the Russian Federation. The second half of the publication features the point of view of international organizations including Europol, the Council of Europe, and the United Nations High Commissioner for Refugees.

Jaramillo, Daniel Garcia-Pefia. 1998, November 18–20. "Linkages between Drug and Illicit Arms Trafficking: Issues of Current Concern to Colombia." *United Nations Department for Disarmament Affairs.*

The author of this conference paper, using Colombia as a point of reference, analyzes the links between drugs and guns, asserting that they are so interrelated it is practically impossible to deal with either in an isolated manner. The author claims that most of the weaponry demanded by those directly involved in the drug business is bought in the United States. That said, the author suggests supply patterns may change as drug cartels extend their reach to Europe.

Lumpe, Lora. 2000. *Running Guns: The Global Black Market in Small Arms.* London: Zed Books. 256 pages.

This collection of nine papers examines aspects of illegal trafficking of small arms beginning with the definition of "legal" and "illegal" in the context of international humanitarian law. The book examines the movement of weapons from governments to guerrilla or insurgent forces during the Cold War and the shape of several major weapons "pipelines." Lumpe looks at military small-arms production trends as well as the links between domestic firearms markets and international illicit markets. The book examines the mechanics of illicit trafficking in considerable detail, including the role of brokers and shippers, which are often outside of the scope of existing regulations and the financing of the illicit trade. Finally, it reviews a number of proposals to address aspects of the illicit trade.

McShane, James P. 1999. "Light Weapons and International Law Enforcement." In Jeffrey Boutwell and Michael T. Klare, (eds.), *Light Weapons and Civil Conflict*, pp. 173–182. New York: Carnegie Commission on Preventing Deadly Conflict.

A former U.S. Customs criminal investigator stationed in the United States and Europe, McShane writes from the perspective of an expert with thirty years of first-hand experience in combating the illicit movement of firearms. He stresses the importance of having both international agreements and effective law-enforcement activities, and argues that these two measures must work in concert. He also raises concerns about the recent proliferation of international agreements on the illicit movement of firearms and the danger that these initiatives are not sufficiently coordinated in their goals and are sometimes working at cross-purposes.

Organization of American States Permanent Council. 1997, November 13. "Inter-American Convention Against the Illicit Manufacturing of and Trafficking in Firearms, Ammunition, Explosives, and Other Related Materials." *OAS General Assembly AG/RES.1 (XXIV-E/97).*

The stated purpose of this comprehensive document containing thirty sections is "to prevent, combat, and eradicate the illicit manufacturing of and trafficking in firearms, ammunition, explosives, and other related materials" and "to promote and facilitate cooperation and exchange of information and experience among States Parties to prevent, combat, and eradicate the illicit manufacturing of and trafficking in firearms, ammunition, explosives, and other related materials."

Rahman, Reaz. 1997. "The Illicit Flow of Small Arms in South Asia." *Disarmament: A Periodical by the United Nations* 10 (2 and 3): 79–102.

Rahman argues that, since the end of the Cold War, most of the conflict in South Asia has been cross-border in nature and that small arms are the preferred weapons. The author reviews recent developments in the small-arms trade and examines the routes through which weapons arrive in South Asia. Particular focus is placed on Bangladesh and northeast India. Rahman is not optimistic that the illicit small-arms trade will be addressed in this region, owing largely to a lack of governmental will. He concludes by offering a number of suggestions the international community should pursue in tackling the problem.

Revilla, Antonio Garcia. 1998. "Interrelationship Between Small Arms Trafficking, Drug Trafficking and Terrorism." In Pericles Gasparini Alves and Diana Belinda Cipollone (eds.), *Curbing Illicit Trafficking in Small Arms and Sensitive Technologies: An*

Action-Oriented Agenda, pp. 85–92. UNIDIR/98/16. New York: United Nations.

According to the author, the relationship between the firearms trade and the drug trade is complicated by the vast increase in the number of small arms available since the end of the Cold War. Tackling the scourge of the illicit small-arms trade will require governmental will, increased information sharing among member states of the United Nations, and creation of complementary internal legislation.

Williams, Phil. 1999, January–February. "Drugs and Guns." *Bulletin of the Atomic Scientists* 55 (1): 46–48.

According to Williams, the black market in arms involves participants who do not think of themselves as criminals, including governments and intelligence agencies. This article uses case studies to illustrate the drugs/firearms link. For example, an Italian magistrate described how much of the profit in drug trafficking was used by the Mafia to purchase arms, most of which were subsequently exported through a Syrian connection to various Arab countries; Tamil Tigers trafficked in drugs to fund their separatist struggle in Sri Lanka; and there were frequent reports of drugs-for-arms swaps in the conflicts in the Balkans.

Trafficking in Nuclear Materials

Allison, Graham. 2004. *Nuclear Terrorism: The Ultimate Preventable Catastrophe.* New York: Henry Holt and Company. 263 pages.

Allison's book is a natural extension of Rensselaer Lee's work (see below) outlining the consequences of trafficking in nuclear material and weapons components. Allison focuses on the use of nuclear weapons by terrorists, addressing key questions such as: Who could be planning a nuclear terrorist attack? What nuclear weapons could terrorists use? Where could terrorists acquire a nuclear bomb? When could terrorists launch the first nuclear attack? And how could terrorists deliver a nuclear weapon to its target? The answers to these questions constitute the first five chapters of the book. The ultimate danger of trafficking is illustrated by an incident Allison relates in the opening pages of the book. On October 11, 2001, one month to the day of the 9/11 attacks, the director of the CIA told President Bush that one of his agents reported that al-Qaeda terrorists had a 10-kiloton nuclear bomb which was stolen from the Russian arsenal and that the bomb was now located in New York City. Allison concludes that a nuclear terrorist attack on the United States by 2014 is more likely than not. However, he holds that nuclear terrorism is preventable, largely through generating the will to monitor and control trafficking efforts.

Lee, Rensselaer W. III. 1998. *Smuggling Armageddon: The Nuclear Black Market in the Former Soviet Union and Europe.* New York: St. Martin's Press. 200 pages.

In this slim volume, Lee addresses a crucial international concern—the illegal trade in nuclear materials that grew in the former Soviet Union and Europe after the collapse of the USSR. He raises the central issue of whether such traffic poses a threat of consequence to international security and stability. Lee notes that the subject matter itself is surrounded by considerable ambiguity and that quantifying the significance of illegal trafficking in nuclear materials is all but impossible. The first two chapters outline in general terms the scope, setting, and principal characteristics of the illegal nuclear trade. Chapter 3 identifies and analyzes the principal economic and environmental factors that facilitate the theft of nuclear materials. Chapter 4 describes the overall criminal environment in Russia and its possible influence on nuclear smuggling dynamics. Chapters 5 and 6 detail reported theft and smuggling cases in Central Europe and the former Soviet Union. The final chapter assesses the implications of these findings for U.S. policy and offers insights on the future of the nuclear smuggling business in the former Soviet Union.

Zaitseva, Lyudmila, and Kevin Hand. 2003, February. "Nuclear Smuggling Chains: Suppliers, Intermediaries, and End-Users." *American Behavioral Scientist* 46 (6): 822–844.

This article analyzes the supply and demand sides in nuclear smuggling, as well as intermediaries between them, based on the 700 illicit trafficking incidents collected by the Stanford Database on Nuclear Smuggling, Theft and Orphan Radiation Sources (DSTO) for the period 1991 to 2002. The supply side consists of people with access to nuclear and other radioactive material. It is subdivided into civilian employees at source facilities, ranging from technicians to top managers; military personnel; and security guards. Intermediaries—traffickers and middlemen—are usually amateurs, opportunist businessmen and firms, and organized crime groups. The demand side is represented by proliferating nation-states, terrorist organizations, religious sects, separatist movements, and criminal groups or individuals interested in using nuclear and other radioactive material for malevolent purposes, such as murder, deliberate exposure, blackmail, and extortion.

Combating Illicit Trafficking Activity

Berkman, Eric Thomas. 1996. "Responses to the International Child Sex Tourism Trade." *Boston College International and Comparative Law Review* 19: 397–422.

Berkman's article examines the parties involved in the child sex industry and measures taken against their activities in those countries where it thrives. He also describes the actions that consumer countries have taken or could take to stop child sex tourism. He concludes that, although countries that host child sex industries have passed laws forbidding such activities, without the cooperation and involvement of industrialized consumer countries those industries will continue to thrive.

Corrigan, Katrin. 2001. "Putting the Brakes on the Global Trafficking of Women for the Sex Trade: An Analysis of Existing Regulatory Schemes to Stop the Flow of Traffic." *Fordham International Law Journal* 25: 151–214.

Corrigan provides a general overview of trafficking in women and its patterns, describes and analyzes existing laws and their shortcomings, and details what remains unaccomplished in order to combat trafficking worldwide. She focuses on the existing laws of the United States and the European Union, as well as on relevant international treaties. She concludes with several suggestions for combating trafficking.

Hyland, Kelly E. 2001. "Protecting Human Victims of Trafficking: An American Framework." *Berkeley Women's Law Journal* 16: 29–71.

Hyland explores the adequacy of U.S. legislation in protecting and assisting trafficking victims. After discussing the nature of trafficking and the experiences of its victims, she addresses the needs of victims and suggests possible U.S. responses to such needs through legislation and provision of services to meet individual needs. She analyzes the Trafficking Victims Protection Act of 2000, concluding that its worldwide impact cannot be assessed until it is properly implemented.

Jensen, Troy R. 2000. "Organ Procurement: Various Legal Systems and Their Effectiveness." *Houston Journal of International Law* 22: 555–584.

Jensen begins by stating that the disparity between the supply and demand for human organs available for transplantation often leads to illegal methods of procuring needed organs. Consequently, governments throughout the world are now adopting laws to protect the exploited organ donors. Similarly, international organizations, including the World Health Organization and the United Nations, have condemned trafficking in human organs. Jensen then explores the advantages and disadvantages of the Brazilian law on organ donation, as well as approaches adopted by other countries for regulating organ donation and curbing the illegal trade in human organs.

Kennard, Holly C. 1994. "Curtailing the Sale and Trafficking of Children: A Discussion of the Hague Conference Convention in Respect of Inter-country Adoptions." *University of Pennsylvania Journal of International Economic Law* 14: 623–649.

Kennard begins by discussing the growth of black markets alongside the practice of intercountry adoptions, noting that before 1993 there was no applicable international convention, just national laws that banned this practice. In 1993, the Convention on Protection of Children and Cooperation in Respect of Inter-Country Adoption was adopted for this purpose. Kennard critically analyzes the convention and offers proposals for federal implementing legislation that would ensure that gray markets or independent agencies would not illegally profit from these adoptions.

McDonald, William F. (ed.) 1997. *Crime and Law Enforcement in the Global Village.* Cincinnati, OH: Anderson Publishing. 245 pages.

Much has been written about the rapid rise of transnational crime and trafficking issues in the 1990s, but comparatively little material has been presented on the internationalization of policing or how it might be pursued. McDonald's volume of collected articles is a welcome addition to the discussion. Stated most simply, this book argues that the emergence and significance of crime and justice issues that span national boundaries require global responses. The first four chapters provide an overview of the transnational crime problem. The five chapters comprising the second section undertake a discussion of law enforcement responses to transnational crime. International police cooperation is discussed from a number of perspectives including Interpol, the development of a system of police cooperation in the European Union, the approach to transnational crime taken by the United States and the spread of those tactics around the globe, and fighting the Mafia and organized crime in Italy and Europe. This volume is rounded out by a discussion of the political and ethical dimensions of fighting transnational crime, a particularly difficult area to confront given issues of sovereignty, considerations of national interest, and questions about the extraterritorial reach of the U.S. Constitution.

Nadelmann, Ethan A. 1993. *Cops Across Borders: The Internationalization of U.S. Criminal Law Enforcement.* University Park: Pennsylvania State University. 524 pages.

Nadelmann discusses the challenges facing international law enforcement. A major theme is the impact that U.S. pursuit of enforcement goals has had on internationalizing policing. The U.S. influence has occurred in large part as a result of drug policy and the rapid globalization of narcotics trafficking. The author notes that the complexity and scale of contemporary international criminal investigation have increased and are becoming ever more intertwined with foreign policy considerations. Traditional concerns of statehood such as maintaining sovereignty, controlling the nation's borders, and suppressing smuggling are discussed in the context of law enforcement efforts. Nadelmann, an expert on the Drug Enforcement Administration and narcotics issues, presents an analysis of the DEA and the challenges it faces in investigating drug cases overseas.

Occhipinti, John. 2003. *The Politics of EU Police Cooperation: Toward a European FBI?* Boulder, CO: Lynne Rienner. 286 pages.

Understanding law enforcement agencies, their mandates, structures, and jurisdictions is critical in analyzing the means and methods to be employed in countering trafficking activities in an increasingly global world. Occhipinti draws from competing theories of European integration to explain the development of supranationalism in European police cooperation. Considering forces stemming from both within and outside of the European Union and reflecting concerns over international terrorism and transnational organized crime, he explores the roles played by key actors and events at every stage of Europol's development, from the initial creation of the Trevi Group in 1975 to mid-2002.

Raviv, Tal. 2003. "International Trafficking in Persons: A Focus on Women and Children—The Current Situation and the Recent International Legal Response." *Cardozo Women's Law Journal* 9: 659–868.

Raviv notes that trafficking in persons as a grave violation of human rights has drawn the renewed attention of the international community in recent years. A number of international laws to combat trafficking have been in place since the early twentieth century, but their lack of effective enforcement mechanisms has made them essentially useless. A modern comprehensive international tool to combat trafficking did not exist until 2000, when the United Nations Protocol to Prevent and Punish Trafficking in Persons, Especially Women and Children was adopted. Raviv analyzes the UN Protocol in greater detail, focusing particularly on its victim protection provisions, and points out that a state, by assenting to a human rights convention, undertakes a dual obligation: not to act in a way that results in a human rights violation and to prevent private actors present in its territory from acting in such a way.

Report of the Expert Group on Strategies for Combating the Trafficking of Women and Children. 2003. London: Commonwealth Secretariat. 55 pages.

This 2003 report, published in book form by the Commonwealth Secretariat, claims that trafficking in persons is the third largest source of profits for organized crime, behind drugs and guns, generating billions of dollars annually. As in most other criminal enterprises, profits are reinvested in illicit activity, frequently being pumped into the trade in drugs and guns. Groups involved in trafficking take advantage of the freer flow of people,

increasingly weaker borders, the enormous profits to be reinvested, and the weakening of domestic economies, thus providing an endless reserve of potential victims. The report notes that
trafficking in human beings is not a new problem but is marked
by its growing scale and magnitude, newer source and destination sites, and diverse and sophisticated mechanisms. The prevention strategies cited include economic empowerment, education, legal intervention, advocacy and awareness raising,
reduction in demand in destination countries, and the creation of
systems of victim assistance.

Rijken, Conny. 2003. *Trafficking in Persons: Prosecution from a
European Perspective.* Cambridge: Cambridge University Press.
345 pages.

One of the most important barriers to effective legislation and
policy formation against human trafficking is the global nature of
the problem. This text examines the impact of sovereignty on
prosecuting trafficking offenses. Emerging primarily from a
study conducted in the Netherlands, the book emphasizes the notion that the nature of trafficking, as a transnational crime often
involving multiple jurisdictions, can hinder prosecution. The author suggests that this crime needs to be approached on an international level, through a body such as the European Union. Until
a truly international approach is developed, the author suggests
maintaining a dual system, considering the jurisdiction of independent sovereignties and that of the EU.

Smith, Linda, and Mohamed Mattar. 2004. "Creating International Consensus on Combating Trafficking in Persons: U.S. Policy, the Role of the UN, and Global Responses and Challenges."
Fletcher Forum of World Affairs 28: 155–178.

Smith and Mattar address the seriousness of the United States' efforts in combating international trafficking in persons. They
argue that the United States Trafficking Victims Protection Act of
2000 (TVPA) has had a significant impact on how the government
perceives and fights the practice of trafficking in persons. Establishing the Interagency Task Force to Monitor and Combat Trafficking in Persons, providing financial and economic support to
countries that reform their actions in order to curb trafficking,
and recognizing the link between HIV/AIDS and trafficking have

made the TVPA an important legal mechanism to monitor the status of the trafficking in persons. The authors suggest, however, that only through diligence and international cooperation will trafficking be eliminated.

Williams, Phil, and Ernesto U. Savona (eds.). 1996. *The United Nations and Transnational Organized Crime.* London: Frank Cass. 194 pages.

This volume is compiled from papers presented at the World Ministerial Conference on Transnational Organized Crime held in Naples from November 21 to 23, 1994, convened by the United Nations to discuss the dangers posed by transnational organized crime and to identify various forms of international cooperation for its prevention and control. Ministers of justice and ministers of interior from 142 countries attended the meetings. The book begins with an overview of the challenge posed by transnational organized crime in terms of information collection, intelligence analysis, penetrating groups, and measures to be taken to create greater transparency in the banking and financial sectors. The Political Declaration and Action Plan adopted at the conference emphasizes the need for efforts to achieve a more reliable knowledge base about transnational criminal organizations and methods most effective in combating them.

Periodicals and Publications

Crime and Justice International
Office of International Criminal Justice
Sam Houston State University
College of Criminal Justice
Box 2296
Huntsville, TX 77341-2296
Tel: (936) 294-1688
Fax: (936) 294-1638
E-mail: *subscriber@oicj.org*
Web site: *www.oicj.org*

Published six times a year by the Office of International Criminal Justice at Sam Houston State University, *Crime and Justice International* reaches an audience of academics and practitioners in criminal justice and law enforcement in more than twenty-five countries. Articles address a wide variety of issues, including transnational crime, trafficking issues, and terrorism. Subscription fee for United States: $59.00; International: $89.00.

Antonopoulos, Georgios A. 2003, November–December. "Albanian Organized Crime: A View from Greece." 19 (77): 5–9.

———. 2004, November–December. "The Financial Exploitation of the Sexuality of Migrant Children in Greece." 20 (83): 19–22.

Klychnikov, Daniil, Vladyslav Smelik, and Volodymyr Smelik. 2004, May–June. "Combating Transnational Crime: The View from Ukraine." 20 (80): 9–13.

Mabrey, Daniel. 2003, March. "Human Smuggling from China." 19 (71): 5–11.

Crime, Law and Social Change
Kluwer Academic Publishers
P.O. Box 358
Accord Station
Hingham, MA 02018-0358
Web site: *www.kluweronline.com*

Crime, Law and Social Change is a peer-reviewed journal that publishes essays and reviews dealing with the political economy of organized crime whether at the transnational, national, regional, or local levels anywhere in the world. In addition, the journal publishes work on financial crime, political corruption, environmental crime, and the expropriation of resources from developing nations. Subscription fee for United States: institutional $679.00, individuals $291.00; for Europe: institutional EUR678.00, individuals EUR291.00.

Mameli, P. A. 2002. "Stopping the Illegal Trafficking in Human Beings." 38: 67–80.

Morrison, Shana. 1997. "The Dynamics of Illicit Drugs Production: Future Sources and Threats." 27: 21–138.

Shelley, Louise. 2003. "The Trade in People in and from the Former Soviet Union." 40: 231–249.

Zhang, S. X., and M. S. Gaylord. 1996. "Bound for the Golden Mountain: The Social Organization of Chinese Alien Smuggling." 25 (1): 1–16.

International Journal of the Sociology of Law
Elsevier
6277 Sea Harbor Drive
Orlando, FL 32887-4800
Tel: (877) 839-7126
Fax: (407) 363-1354
E-mail: *usjcs@elsevier.com*

The International Journal of the Sociology of Law, produced by the Institute of Criminal Justice Studies at the University of Portsmouth (UK), provides a forum for high-quality research and debate on the social context and social implications of law, law enforcement, and the legal process. The refereed journal accepts contributions from all areas of sociolegal study, particularly those that address comparative issues and questions of development, change, and reform in sociolegal processes. In addition to academic research papers, the journal invites contributions from practitioners and those concerned with policy formation and implementation in the fields of legal process and law enforcement. Subscription fee for United States: institutional $323.00, individual $83.00; for Europe: institutional EUR 363.00, individual EUR 94.00.

Ruggiero, Vincent. 1997. "Trafficking in Human Beings: Slaves in Contemporary Europe." 25 (3): 231–244.

———. 2000. "Transnational Crime: Official and Alternative Fears." 28 (3): 187–199.

Schloenhardt, Andreas. "Trafficking in Migrants: Illegal Migration and Organized Crime in Australia and the Asia Pacific Region." 29 (4): 331–378.

Transnational Organized Crime/Global Crime
Taylor & Francis Group/Routledge
325 Chestnut Street
Suite 800
Philadelphia, PA 19106
Tel: (800) 354-1420
Fax: (215) 625-8914
Web site: *http://www.routledge.com*

With a new name, focus, and editorial team, *Global Crime* builds upon the foundations laid by *Transnational Organized Crime* to consider serious and organized crime, from its origins to the present, as well as a wide range of other transnational crime issues. Its focus is deliberately broad and multidisciplinary, aiming to make the best scholarship on organized, serious, and transnational crime available to specialists and nonspecialists alike. It endorses no particular orthodoxy and draws on authors from a variety of disciplines, including history, sociology, economics, political science, anthropology, and area studies. Published four times a year, *Global Crime* is a peer-reviewed journal. Subscription fee for United States: institutional $364.00, individual $78.00; for Europe: institutional £224, individual £49.

Albanese, Jay S. "North American Organized Crime." 6 (1): 8–18.

Galeotti, Mark. "The Russian 'Mafiya': Consolidation and Globalisation." 6 (1): 54–69.

Perl, Raphael F. "State Crime: The North Korean Drug Trade." 6 (1): 117–128.

Zabludoff, Sidney Jay. 1998, Summer. "Colombian Narcotics Organizations as Business Enterprises." 3 (2): 20–49.

Trends in Organized Crime
Transaction Periodicals Consortium
Rutgers University
35 Berrue Circle
Piscataway, NJ 08854-8042
Tel: 732-445–2280
Web site: *http://www.transactionpub.com*

Trends in Organized Crime (TOC) provides information and analysis about organized crime that is sometimes difficult to access. Focusing on crime's linkage to organized agencies of the state and its affiliated agencies, *TOC* draws on research from international organizations, public policy institutes, law enforcement organizations, intelligence agencies, and independent scholars. *TOC* reports on international efforts to anticipate the development of organized criminal activities and to devise strategies to counter them. *Trends in Organized Crime* is the official journal of the International Association for the Study of Organized Crime (IASOC). Subscription fee for United States: institutions $260.00, individuals $80.00.

Denisova, Tatyana. 2001. "Trafficking in Women and Children for Purposes of Sexual Exploitation: The Criminological Aspect." 6 (3–4): 30–36.

Layne, Mary, Scott Decker, Meg Townsend, et al. 2001. "Measuring the Deterrent Effect of Enforcement Operations on Drug Smuggling, 1991–1999." 7 (3): 66–87.

Layne, Mary, Mykola S. Khruppa, and Anatoly A. Muzyka. 2001. "The Growing Importance of Ukraine as Transit Country for Heroin Trafficking: U.S.-Ukraine Research Partnerships." 6 (3–4): 77–93.

Office to Monitor and Combat Trafficking in Persons. 2004. "Trafficking in Persons Report." 8 (1): 38–66.

Bibliographies

There are numerous extensive bibliographies online regarding trafficking issues that will prove invaluable to the researcher. Listed here are several collections that address various aspects of trafficking.

An Annotated Bibliography: How Narcotics Trafficking Organizations Operate as Businesses. 2002, September. Compiled by John N. Gibbs. Library of Congress.

http://www.loc.gov/rr/frd/pdf-files/Bibliography-Narcotics.pdf

Bibliography of Trafficking. 2004, August. Compiled by Yukiko Nakajima, Violence Against Women—Online Resources.

http://www.vaw.umn.edu/documents/traffickbib/traffickbib.html

Bibliography on Narco-terrorism. 2003, July. Compiled by Ron Fuller, Air University Library, Maxwell Air Force Base.

http://www.au.af.mil/au/aul/bibs/narco/narco.htm

Bibliography on the Effects of Organized Crime on Women and Children. 1995, April. The International Centre for Criminal Law Reform and Criminal Justice Policy.

http://www.icclr.law.ubc.ca/Publications/Reports/Bibilio.PDF

Coalition Against Trafficking in Women (CATW) Resource Library. 2004.

http://www.catwinternational.org/resources.php

Cork Bibliography: Drug Trade and Trafficking.

http://www.projectcork.org/bibliographies/data/Bibliography_Drug_Trade_and_Trafficking.html

Detection of Illicit Trafficking in Nuclear and Other Radioactive Materials. International Atomic Energy Agency.

http://www-ns.iaea.org/security/detection.htm

Human Trafficking: A Bibliographical Search of the NCJRS Abstracts Database. Office for Victims of Crime Resource Center, Office of Justice Programs, U.S. Department of Justice.

http://www.ojp.usdoj.gov/ovc/ovcres/human_trafficking_abstracts.pdf

Organized Crime in North America and the World: A Bibliography. 2003, December. Compiled by Stephen Schneider, Nathanson Centre for the Study of Organized Crime and Corruption.

http://www.yorku.ca/nathanson/bibliography/contents.htm

Resources and Contacts on Human Trafficking. 2002. Compiled by The Initiative against Trafficking in Persons, The International Human Rights Law Group.

http://usmex.ucsd.edu/justice/documents/richard_trafficking_biblio.pdf

SAFER-Net Annotated Bibliography on Small Arms. 2000, December.

http://www.research.ryerson.ca/SAFER-Net/resources/ABibJE03.html

Trafficking in Human Beings and Organized Crime: A Literature Review. 2002, June. Compiled by Christine Bruckert and Colette Parent.

http://www.rcmp-grc.gc.ca/pdfs/traffick_e.pdf

Trafficking in Persons: An Annotated Legal Bibliography. 2004. Compiled by Mohamed Y. Mattar. Johns Hopkins University School of Advanced International Studies.

http://www.aallnet.org/products/2004–47.pdf

UNESCO Trafficking Project Bibliography. 2003.

http://www.unescobkk.org/culture/trafficking/publication.htm

United Nations Institute for Disarmament Research (UNIDIR) Light Weapons Bibliography and Resource List. 2000. Compiled by Joshua Margolin.

http://www.unidir.ch/pdf/articles/pdf-art157.pdf

United Nations Institute for Disarmament Research (UNIDIR) Selection of Publications Focusing on Small Arms. 2004.

http://www.unidir.ch/bdd/focus-search.php?onglet=5

Nonprint Resources

Videos

Armed to the Teeth: The Worldwide Plague of Small Arms
    Length: 56 minutes
    Date: 2000
    Cost: $149.95
    Source: Films for the Humanities and Sciences
    P.O. Box 2053
    Princeton, NJ 08543–2053
    Tel: (800) 257-5126
    Fax: (609) 671-0266
    E-mail: *custserve@films.com*
    Web site: *http://www.films.com*

With one gun for every ten people, the United Nations considers the small-arms crisis one of the gravest challenges facing the world. As well as investigating the proliferation of firearms and the economic, political, and cultural reasons why people carry them, this award-winning program shows what is being done to curb a human-made pestilence. Both devastation and successful disarmament are seen in case studies from Albania, Mozambique, South Africa, Colombia, El Salvador, and the world's largest small-arms manufacturer, the United States. Discussing these issues are Kofi Annan, secretary general of the United Nations; Jayantha Dhanapala, under secretary general for disarmament;

Carol Bellamy, executive director of UNICEF; and Robert Wall of the Firearms and Explosives Unit at Interpol. This program was produced by the United Nations.

Bought & Sold: An Investigative Documentary about the International Trade in Women
    Length: 42 minutes
    Date: 1997
    Cost: $50.00 domestic; $60.00 international; $150.00 institutional
    Source: Witness
    353 Broadway
    New York, NY 10013
    Tel: (212) 274-1664
    Fax: (212) 274-1262
    E-mail: *orders@witness.org*
    Web site: *www.witness.org*

This documentary was produced and directed by the current director of Witness, Gillian Caldwell, while she was codirector of the Global Survival Network (GSN). It is based on a two-year undercover investigation conducted by GSN into the illegal trafficking in women from the former Soviet Union, and it features interviews with traffickers, Russian mafia, trafficked women, and groups working to provide services to trafficked women. *Bought & Sold* is available in English and in Russian, and it comes with two complementary reports: "Crime & Servitude: An Expose on the Trafficking of Russian Women" which is also available in Russian and English, and "Trapped," a report on trafficking and forced labor in the Marianas Island.

Child Sex Trade
    Length: 50 minutes
    Date: 2000
    Cost: $24.95
    Source: A&E Investigative Reports
    Tel: (800) 423-1212
    Web site: *http://store.aetv.com*

Child Sex Trade reports that each year more than 300,000 children are bought, sold, exploited, and enslaved by child sex rings from California to New York, from Canada to the Midwest. On the street, a thirteen-year-old girl can earn up to $200,000 a year for her pimp. Worldwide last year these child prostitutes earned more than a billion dollars. Fifty-one percent of the teenagers working the streets are boys. Their greatest danger comes from their customers, who pay them money for sex and then introduce them to a lifestyle of degradation and pederasty. *Child Sex Trade* focuses on how pimp organizations operate and why they are able to reach into middle-class America for their victims. The video traces the largest pipelines for the child sex trade, from Kansas and Minnesota to the Las Vegas strip.

Human Traffic
> Length: 11 minutes
> Date: 2002
> Cost: £10
> Source: Anti-Slavery International
> Thomas Clarkson House
> The Stableyard
> Broomgrove Road
> London SW9 9TL
> Tel: 44-(0)20-7501-8920
> Fax: 44 (0)20-7738-4110
> E-mail: *info@antislavery.org*
> Web site: *www.antislavery.org/index.htm*

This campaign video exposes the booming trade in women, children, and men, from the prostitution rackets in Europe to child trafficking in West Africa. It contains footage from Ghana, Nigeria, Italy, and England with interviews from those trafficked, activists, social workers, and the police.

NARCs
> Length: 50 minutes
> Cost: $29.95
> Source: American Justice
> Web site: *http://store.aetv.com*

From the small-time user to the large-scale producer, the DEA is charged with eliminating illegal drugs in America. It is an uphill battle against powerful criminal cabals, the temptation of corruption, and America's seemingly insatiable appetite for drugs. From the origins of the Federal Bureau of Dangerous Drugs to the modern-day DEA, this documentary provides a look at the "war on drugs" and the men at the heart of the battle. Travel deep into South American jungles, where the DEA is taking the fight to the source, literally attacking the cocaine epidemic at the root. DEA operatives offer an up-close look at the tactics they employ and the dangers they face.

Nuclear Materials: Russia's New Export
    Length: 27 minutes
    Date: 1995
    Cost: $129.95
    Source: Films for the Humanities and Sciences
    P.O. Box 2053
    Princeton, NJ 08543–2053
    Tel: (800) 257-5126
    Fax: (609) 671-0266
    E-mail: *custserve@films.com*
    Web site: *http://www.films.com*

This program explores how the breakdown of the Soviet Union resulted in the emergence of a new and dangerous practice: the sale of plutonium and uranium from Russia's nuclear factories on the international market. At Moscow's Stock Exchange, every-thing, including nuclear material, can be bought "over the counter." Middle-management workers at nuclear factories discuss the economic changes wrought by the dissolution of the So-viet Union that are fueling the temptation to profit from the sale of these dangerous materials.

Out of Sight, Out of Mind
    Length: 15 minutes
    Date: 1999
    Cost: £10
    Source: Anti-Slavery International
    Thomas Clarkson House
    The Stableyard
    Broomgrove Road
    London SW9 9TL
    Tel: 44 (0)20-7501-8920
    Fax: 44 (0)20-7738-4110
    E-mail: *info@antislavery.org*
    Web site: *www.antislavery.org/index.htm*

This video was produced by Anti-Slavery as part of their campaign on child domestic workers in the Philippines. Made with a local Philippine nongovernmental organization, Visayan Forum, this video was shown on television and in Congress in the Philippines. This has led to the drafting of a new law that will protect child domestic workers.

Pizza Connection
> Length: 50 minutes
> Cost: $29.95
> Source: American Justice
> Web site: *http://store.aetv.com*

On July 12, 1979, Carmine Galante, notorious boss of the Bonanno crime family, was ambushed and killed in a Brooklyn restaurant. Federal officers investigating the hit soon found a link to a previously unknown, billion-dollar drug pipeline. *Pizza Connection* shows how the case soon expanded to include the Italian government and federal agents all across America. This documentary traces the network of crime that converted tons of Sicilian-made heroin to billions of dollars in cash using small businesses throughout America, from New York pizzerias to Midwest strip mall stores.

R & R in Southeast Asia
> Length: 15 minutes
> Date: 1996
> Cost: $29.95
> Source: *60 Minutes*
> 524 West 57th Street
> New York, NY 10019
> Tel: (800) 848-3256
> E-mail: *60m@cbsnews.com*
> Web site: *http://www.cbsnews.com/stories/1998/07/08 /60minutes/ main13504.shtml*

In this short segment, the interviewer confronts an individual who advertises sex tours to Southeast Asia. *60 Minutes* sent a reporter to follow up on what such tours entail; it includes footage of meetings with a "tour guide" and a very young prostitute and her pimp. It is a clear indictment of the practice of sex tourism. The confrontation with the American organizer is interesting; he comes across as nervous, deceitful, and immoral.

Sacrifice: The Story of Child Prostitutes from Burma
Length: 50 minutes
Date: 1998
Cost: $45.00 rental; $150.00 purchase (discount for nonprofit organizations)
Source: Ellen Bruno Film Library
P.O. Box 1084
190 Route 17M
Harriman, NY 10926
Tel: (800) 343-5540
Fax: (845) 774-2945
E-mail: *ellen@brunofilms.com*
Web site: *www.brunofilms.com*

The trafficking of Burmese girls has soared in recent years as a direct result of political repression in Burma. Human rights abuses, war, and ethnic discrimination have displaced hundreds of thousands of families, leaving families with no means of livelihood. An offer of employment in Thailand is a rare chance for many families to escape extreme poverty. *Sacrifice* examines the social, cultural, and economic forces at work in the trafficking of Burmese girls into prostitution. It is the story of the valuation and sale of human beings, and the efforts of teenage girls to survive a crisis born of economic and political repression. This documentary chronicles the horrors faced by young girls trafficked from Burma to work in the Thai sex industry.

Secret Passages
Length: 50 minutes
Cost: $24.95
Source: History Channel
Web site: *http://store.aetv.com*

The twin border towns of Nogales in Arizona and Mexico share an elaborate system of storm runoff drains that drug lords appropriated in the 1990s to great effect. Adding hand-dug tunnels to the existing network, they smuggled thousands of pounds of narcotics into America. But not every delivery went as planned, as footage of a customs raid shows. On the Mexican border in

Douglas, Arizona, DEA agents discovered the most sophisticated smuggling tunnel to date, complete with hatches, elevators, rail carts and more. In one bust alone, 2,300 pounds of cocaine were seized there.

The Agony of Ecstasy
> Length: 50 minutes
> Cost: $24.95
> Source: A&E Investigative Reports
> Tel: (800) 423-1212
> Web site: *http://store.aetv.com*

The latest "in" drug is not really that new—it has been around since the 1980s. But ecstasy did not really start to attract attention until the late 1990s when it became the drug of choice at the all-night dance parties known as raves. Before long it broke out of the club scene. This video ventures from clandestine manufacturing labs in the Netherlands to the floors of New York City's nightclubs, meeting with users, law enforcement professionals, and doctors to explore every aspect of the drug. Find out why the international distribution of ecstasy is dominated by Israeli organized crime and hear from users why they are drawn to the drug. Footage from a U.S. Customs investigation highlights the effort to halt its spread, while medical experts detail the long-term risks for users.

The Day My God Died
> Length: Feature-length film
> Date: 2002
> Cost: n/a
> Source: Andrew Levine Productions
> Tel: (435) 655-8319
> E-mail: *Levine@xmission.com*
> Web site: *http://www.thedaymygoddied.com/contact.html*

The Day My God Died is a feature-length documentary that presents the stories of young girls whose lives have been shattered by the child sex trade. They describe the day they were abducted from their village and sold into sexual servitude as "The Day My God Died." The film provides actual footage from the brothels of Bombay, known even to tourists as "The Cages," captured with spy camera technology. It weaves the stories of girls and their stolen hopes and dreams into an unforgettable examination of the growing plague of child sex slavery.

The Global Arms Market: Mayhem for Sale

 Length: 20 minutes
 Date: 2003
 Cost: $69.95
 Source: Films for the Humanities and Sciences
 P.O. Box 2053
 Princeton, NJ 08543–2053
 Tel: (800) 257-5126
 Fax: (609) 671-0266
 E-mail: *custserve@films.com*
 Web site: *http://www.films.com*

Assault rifles, heavy machine guns, artillery, tanks, planes, missiles—with money and the right connections, practically any military weapon can be bought in the global arms market. Where do all those weapons come from? Who is selling them? And how should the United States go about defending itself from trigger-happy "customers" looking for American targets? These and other questions are on the table as this timely ABC News program considers the booming business of weapon trafficking.

The War on Drugs: Winners and Losers

 Length: 93 minutes
 Date: 1999
 Cost: $129.95
 Source: Films for the Humanities and Sciences
 P.O. Box 2053
 Princeton, NJ 08543–2053
 Tel: (800) 257-5126
 Fax: (609) 671-0266
 E-mail: *custserve@films.com*
 Web site: *http://www.films.com*

Is the war on drugs in the United States causing greater societal harm than the problem of drug abuse itself? This provocative program features interviews with Bruce Benson and David Rasmussen, coauthors of *Illicit Drugs and Crime*; Eric Sterling, former counsel to the House Judiciary Committee; Joanne Page, director of the Fortune Society; and others. Together they indict flawed initiatives that have made criminal forfeitures into a cash cow, private corrections into a highly profitable industry, social workers and doctors into informants, and children of convicted mothers into wards of the state.

Trading Women
> Length: 60 minutes
> Date: 2003
> Cost: $29.95
> Source: Documentary Educational Resources
> 101 Morse Street
> Watertown, MA 02472
> Tel: (800) 569-6621 or (617) 926-0491
> Fax: (617) 926-9519
> E-mail: *docued@der.org*
> Web site: *www.der.org*

The culmination of five years of field research, *Trading Women* is the first film to demonstrate to viewers the relationship of the trade in drugs to the trade of women. The film dispels common beliefs about the sex trade, such as: "The problem is the parents—it's part of their culture to sell their daughters"; "the sex trade exists because of Western sex tours"; and "they sell their girls for TVs." Directed and written by David A. Feingold and narrated by Angelina Jolie.

Warlord
> Length: 50 minutes
> Cost: $24.95
> Source: A&E Investigative Reports
> Tel: (800) 423-1212
> Web site: *http://store.aetv.com*

The Golden Triangle at the border of Burma, China, and Thailand has long been a world center of opium production. This video is a rare inside look at one of the world's drug hot spots, though locals claim that they are systematically destroying the opium crops with alternative plantings over a five-year period. Whether or not this is actually happening, the U.S. DEA claims that 20 percent of the world's supply of opium currently originates in Myanmar. From its source in a remote Southeast Asian outpost, the video follows the trail of drugs to its end in America.

8

Summary

Illicit Trafficking—Trends and Issue

This book is, in an important sense, about unintend
quences. Nations diligently work to build markets and
their people; they seek to create an infrastructure of poli
economic institutions, as well as technological organizat
make the global marketplace possible. The expectation i
seeking technology and encouraging foreign investme
their societies, a nation's economic development and pr
will increase. Similarly, developed states (especially in th
promote openness in order to expand investment and tr
portunities. The belief is that democratic states are more
trade and investment partners and are less likely to go to
to experience chronic internal unrest.

States cannot be blamed, however, for creating an
structure in which transnational problems occur. What w
and indeed could not, be anticipated was that the dynam
in motion by the frenzy of change after 1991 when *Pere*:
and *Glasnost* dissolved the communist states in Eastern E
might deprive nations of their freedom of action. The r
emancipated nations rising out of the ashes of totalitaria
lice states produced new actors whose prosperity and p
did not depend or derive legitimacy and authority solely
territory. These new economies are technologically soph
cated; markets are broader and more expansive, operate in
berspace, and are not easily constrained by territorial bou
aries, borders, and laws. Thus, many of the new econo

233

entrepreneurs are not beholden to nations. Managing these new economic possibilities and realities requires new law enforcement approaches that transcend the historic parameters of nation-state structures.

It is becoming increasingly clear that the war on drugs is going badly because the control and eradication policies rest almost entirely on the coercive institutions and organizations of the state. Most of the world's illicit drug supply is cultivated within weak or failing states that lack effective enforcement capacities. However, even in strong states the drug trade operates in a legal context where government is least able to directly intercede. Police cannot infringe on a people's civil liberties and randomly break into homes to seize drugs and arrest users.

Given these limitations on drug control and efforts to discourage consumption, the trade flourishes. Perhaps nonstate groups—NGOs—are best situated and positioned to combat the demand and supply of illicit drugs. Unfortunately, the strong, developed states (in particular the United States) have been cutting resources to treatment facilities, clinics, hospitals, and centers for rehabilitation, and have increased resources for enforcement and interdiction of supply. In underdeveloped states, the root causes of the burgeoning drug trade are mainly economic. Consequently, a drug control policy in states where drugs are cash crops should incorporate attractive alternative economic development programs that promote nondrug agricultural plans. Some observers believe that regional drug crime task forces could facilitate the implementation of a comprehensive response in which economic investments could be spurred to deter drug crop cultivation and smuggling (Kelly 2001).

In contrast, responses to nuclear weapons trafficking need to be state controlled. IGOs and NGOs are limited in what they can bring to bear on these issues. An unintended consequence of private sector (NGOs) involvement in nuclear nonproliferation could actually promote proliferation by allowing nonnuclear powers in NGOs and IGOs access to nuclear information they otherwise would not have. Thus, bilateral efforts by existing nuclear powers may be the more efficient process to be used to stem the threat from weapons growth. Indeed, the problem of trafficking in nuclear weapons and materials reached a danger point when the Soviet Union collapsed. Clearly, Russian law enforcement and security need to be strengthened and stabilized if its weapons (now spread out among armed forces that are inopera-

tive and destitute) are not to become part of a supermarket of weapons auctions.

There is another dire problem associated with nuclear weapons and trafficking. While India and Pakistan have made public their status as nuclear states, Iran and North Korea are moving toward advanced development of nuclear weapons. More importantly, nonstate actors, terrorist groups such as al-Qaeda, Aum Shinrikyo, and the Chechens have been seeking nuclear weapons

Like drug traffickers, nuclear smugglers, and international crime cartels, terrorist groups exploit open societies. People, money, and goods move easily across borders that are comparatively open and unguarded; modern telecommunications enables such groups to publicize their actions and events that spread fear and inspire hate. For example, when Peru's Revolutionary Tupac Amaru Movement took over the Japanese ambassador's residence in Lima in 1996 and held 500 hostages at gunpoint for a month, the terrorist group communicated via CNN and the Internet. This dramatically expanded their reach and added to their notorious celebrity. A good base of operations for a terrorist group is a weak state (such as Afghanistan, Peru, or the Philippines) from which to strike Western targets. Al-Qaeda, initially based in Afghanistan and Pakistan, has also operated in Nairobi, Kenya; Yemen; and Dar es Salaam, Tanzania. With terrorists making full use of the structures of the international system of markets, technologies, and open societies, much like international businesspeople do, individual states cannot effectively combat terrorism alone. Clearly, multilateral approaches to the problem are essential if the violence is to be contained.

A distinctive feature of organized crime is that it lacks a political ideology (Sullivan 1996). Organized crime groups have a structured hierarchy of statuses, accompanied by ranks with specific roles and levels of authority. Organized crime groups are also defined by their continuity over time; their capacity and willingness to threaten or to use force; their restrictive membership; their profit making through racketeering, extortion, and other types of criminal activity; their provision of illegal goods and services to the general population; and their activities that through corruption and intimidation neutralize and nullify the anticrime efforts of public officials and politicians (Kelly et al. 1994).

The power of international criminal organizations has been increased and broadened by the rise in global drug trafficking, smuggling persons, weapons, and virtually anything of commercial value and utility—in short, by the rise and expansion of illicit trafficking. Globalization, with its open markets, advanced technologies, and borderless societies, has facilitated the business of legal multinational corporations and has also expanded opportunities and activities of international criminal organizations (Kelly et al. 2003).

Post-Perestroika and Rise of the Oligarchs: Examples of State Decay and Illicit Trafficking Opportunities

Between 1991 and 1999, new elites emerged from the old communist *nomenklatura* and the Mafia-ridden world of post-Soviet capitalism and seized precious national assets, including the country's gas and oil. They compromised the banks, press, and electronic media, and even threatened the primacy of the state itself as happened in Colombia when the cocaine cartels were at the peak of their power (Conquest 2003).

The nature of the political system that developed following the collapse of communism and the Soviet Union involved powerful and corrupt business managers, along with senior politicians who worked together to secure their mutual interests. Huge cash funds and support from the media were provided for President Boris Yeltsin's post-Soviet government in exchange for tax exemptions. For example, a powerful entrepreneur used his position in the old Soviet gas authority to set up a private company, Gazprom, the largest gas supplier in the world, to which Yeltsin then gave tax exemptions when he moved on to become the prime minister.

Between 1992 and 1998, the rise of the *oligarchs*—business tycoons with vast conglomerates in banking, gas and oil, precious metals, and the media—represented the most serious threat to Russia's fledgling democracy. A real danger arose that the entire state sphere would become corrupted and criminalized, as a small handful of magnates (and the Mafia gangs who protected their interests) moved into the seat of government. Within a short span of time, these economic "godfathers" gave a convincing impression that they were dictating policy. With the help of privileged, corrupted, criminally linked political and economic bosses, the new Russia may continue to squander its resources.

Russia has enormous social problems, notably, a huge gap between rich and poor, corruption and criminality, a crumbling housing stock, a rundown health system, alcoholism, and the highest rates of HIV outside of Africa. It is critical that the political establishment shake off its greed and mandate a larger social role for the state rather than merely servicing the wealthy. Through legislation that will ensure the transparency of the political process, accountability can emerge; police and members of the judiciary must stop taking bribes; and more taxes must be collected from the rich and powerful. Successful implementation of internal reforms designed to build the foundation of a stable new society will take decades (Figes 2000).

Another urgent consideration is the accelerated pace of movement of peoples across borders created by globalization. Adding to the dramatic increases in refugee numbers has been the collapse of states through internal violence and chronic political conflicts. Refugees can overwhelm and drain the energies and resources of already fragile institutions and infrastructures of states, whether the hosts are willing or unwilling, by increasing competition for scarce economic resources and jobs (as became evident in the United States, when opposition was raised to admission of refugees from Haiti and Cuba). Moreover, refugees can destabilize delicate ethnic or political balances (as Palestinian refugees did in Jordan and Lebanon and as Rwandan refugees did in Burundi). For these reasons among others, the United Nations High Commissioner on Refugees (UNHCR) in the post–Cold War period has not only worked to aid displaced persons but also to contain the movement of refugees that can inundate an unwitting host state and engender a political crisis.

As a further consequence of refugee and alien smuggling, state militaries have been used to directly contain the flow of refugees, as when the Italian military contained the flow of Albanian refugees into Italy in 1995–1996, or when the U.S. military interdicted Haitians and Cubans at sea and settled them at Guantánamo naval base in Cuba in 1994–1995. Strategic, more than humanitarian, concerns drive these activities.

The pressures of world politics, the ebb and flow of livelihoods, the adequacy or poverty of resources at hand, and the wars and conflicts that result constitute some of the driving forces of demographic change that set people in motion. The movement of people has become an unexceptional activity, but the process has also been affected by criminal organizations that have organized refugees seeking new opportunities in a rapidly changing world.

Perhaps the most notorious trafficking organization in recent history was "Odessa,"an efficient smuggling machine capable of extreme violence that now serves as a prototype for trafficking groups that handle people. In the immediate aftermath of World War II, the Nazis put together this smuggling organization in order to enable thousands of war criminals to escape to South America, the Middle East, and elsewhere. Monies and documents, transit locales, transport, housing, and new identities were provided former SS members. When the organization was exposed by Israeli intelligence services and the work of NGOs such as Simon Wiesenthal's Vienna-based anti-Nazi organization, Adolph Eichmann, a former SS officer who organized transportation for the millions of Holocaust victims to the death camps, was captured by the Israelis, tried, convicted, and executed in Israel. Similarly, Klaus Barbie, an SS chief in Lyons, France, was uncovered in Venezuela. He was extradited and tried in France for war crimes. Certain economic conditions, coupled with demographic and social trends, have contributed to the rise of illegal immigration and trafficking. International economic activity through interstate policy mechanisms such as NAFTA has generated competitive environments that depress wage levels. In certain service sectors, low pay and the growth of temporary work appear to make indigenous labor forces reluctant to accept such work and to rely instead on unemployment benefits. These sorts of economic and occupational situations create a demand for cheap foreign labor. For those without work in impoverished communities in developing states or transit countries, the possibilities of earnings even in the low-pay sectors of the Western economies are comparably attractive. Thus, many workers in the poorer states respond to the call of the employment markets in the more developed Western nations through either legal or illegal channels.

As women tend to be overrepresented in low-wage sectors where migrants are increasingly needed, this factor also favors the "feminization" of illegal migration. Women are preferred in the sex trade sector, which, in the past several years, has expanded in Southeast Asia, the Balkans, the Nordic states, and

Latin America. And with the expanded marketing of sexual and entertainment services, a reciprocal increase has taken place in criminal enterprises operating directly in the industry and in the ancillary services that accompany the sex services, including pornography and child prostitution.

After the dissolution of communism in East Central Europe, the region became as much a corridor for undocumented flows of migrants as an area of emigration targeting Western Europe and elsewhere. The territories through which the corridor zone exists include Russia, Ukraine, Belarus, Poland, Hungary, the Balkans, and the countries comprising the Transcaucasus region. The Baltic States are situated in the northwestern borders of the corridor zone (Askola et al. 2001).

A common obstacle in combating trafficking in persons, products, and services (licit or illicit) is the lack of adequate resources for police and law enforcement services in the countries that experience the drain of migrants and those that become transit and staging areas for people on the move. Migration management is not only a law enforcement problem: the issues require the implementation of a broad array of facilities, institution knowledge bases, and policy development to cope with the phenomenon of trafficking. This entails aid and assistance from the Euro-Atlantic states, the European Union, the Asian/Pacific Council of States, and the Organization of American States in the Western Hemisphere. Fortunately, trafficking in persons and illicit trafficking in general are being widely acknowledged and discussed. Every country in Central America and many other countries worldwide have passed laws against the smuggling of persons and proscribed commodities.

Finally, it is important to recognize the key differences between "smuggling" and "trafficking." In smuggling persons, for example, people usually come to, and illegally cross, a border and then are released by the smugglers. They pay for the privilege of clandestine travel and perhaps use false documents to facilitate their passage to their destinations. Trafficked migrants, on the other hand, typically find themselves unable to escape the control of the people who brought them into a country illegally. For example, traffickers promising their clients jobs as dancers, hairdressers, or factory workers frequently lure Eastern European and Asian women to the United States where, tragically, the women find themselves coerced into the sex industries.

Trafficking constitutes a challenge to nation-state institutions in profound ways. The Cold War shaped the United Nations, the Organization of American States, the North Atlantic Treaty Organization, the World Bank, and the International Monetary Fund—and even governmental bureaucracies such as the U.S. Department of Defense and the Central Intelligence Agency. Although many of these organizations implicitly promoted globalization, the architects could not have imagined a world in which communism was dead and in which Russia was open and an ally of sorts, crippled by a chaotic society riddled with crime and corruption. The question is: What new institutions must emerge to meet the challenges of the future? The world is increasingly open, and the trafficking problems appear to be beyond the scope of existing institutions and organizations. The obsolescence and threats to the capacities of world-level organizations created decades ago render them ineffective in protecting peoples and resources from the clutches of international crime in the form of illicit trafficking.

Though still unclear, solutions to illicit trafficking may necessitate the formation of networks of nation-state coordination and communication. In addition, although the creation of new state regional agencies is being debated and is designed to cope with illicit trafficking, existing institutions may continue to develop new integrative mechanisms that cross public/private sector boundaries. The tsunami crisis of December 2004 in Asia is a good example of regional cooperation and public/private sector aid coordination. The threat of trafficking in women and children in the disaster zones was immediately recognized.

By systematizing interagency and public/private sector contacts, trafficking problems may be deterred. Differences in culture, communication capacities, assets, and social organizations make interstate, public/private sector networking difficult but not impossible.

References

Askola, Heli, Marels Olsolski, Jujri Saar, and Andis Alven. 2001. *Trafficking in Women and Prostitution in the Baltic States: Social and Legal Aspects.* Helsinki: International Office of Migration.

Conquest, Robert. 2003. *Russia: Experiment with a People.* Cambridge, MA: Harvard University Press.

Figes, Orlando. 2000. *Natasha's Dance: A Cultural History of Russia.* Cambridge, MA: Harvard University Press.

Kelly, Robert J. 2001. "Twelve Years After: The Berlin Wall as Will and Idea." *Journal of Social Distress 10* (3). 217-233.

Kelly, Robert J., and Robert Rieber. 2003. *Terrorism, Organized Crime and Social Distress: The New World Order.* New York: Psyche-Logo Press.

Kelly, Robert J., Rufus Schatzberg, and Ko-lin Chin (eds.). 1994. *A Handbook of Organized Crime* Westport, CT: Greenwood Publishing.

Sullivan, Brian. 1996. "International Organized Crime: A Growing Security Threat," in *Strategic Forum.* Washington, DC: Institute for National Strategic Studies, National Defense University.

Index

About the Authors

Robert J. Kelly is Broeklundian Professor Emeritus at Brooklyn College and the Graduate School of The City University of New York. He served on the Manhattan Terrorism Task Force after 9/11 and consulted with the Department of Homeland Security (Northeast Region) and the National Institute of Justice on Terrorism and Organized Crime; he also teaches a seminar at the United Nations in the Permanent Delegate Seminar on Nationalism. Kelly has published numerous articles and books on terrorism, organized crime, and social distress.

Jess Maghan, Professor and Director of the Forum for Comparative Correction, is a specialist in justice operations and organizational development with a specific focus on incarcerated radicals and intelligence-led penology. He has an extensive background in corrections and police operations internationally. Maghan is a recipient of the Peter P. Lejins Research Award of the American Correctional Association and a recipient of the Elmer and Carol Johnson Criminology Award. Along with Robert J. Kelly, Dr. Maghan is co-editor of *Hate Crime: The Global Politics of Polarization*, published by Southern Illinois University Press (1998). Dr. Maghan served as the first Director of Training for the New York City Police Department and Commissioner for Training, New York City Department of Correction.

Joseph D. Serio was the only American to work in the Organized Crime Control Department of the Ministry of Internal Affairs of the USSR (1990–1991). Spending a total of seven years in the former Soviet Union, he was a consultant to the international corporate investigative and business intelligence firm, Kroll Associates. He became the director of its Moscow office in 1997. While in Russia, he served as consultant to CNN, *The New York*

259

Times, The Washington Post, and other media outlets. In addition to his experience in the former Soviet Union, he has studied criminal justice issues at police academies in China, Poland, Spain, and England. He is currently Editor-in-Chief of *Crime and Justice International,* published by the Office of International Criminal Justice, and co-coordinator of the U.S. Department of State's International Law Enforcement Academy (ILEA) in Roswell, New Mexico. Mr. Serio is a third-year doctoral student at Sam Houston State University in Huntsville, Texas.